ACT for Sport and Performance

ACT for Sport and Performance examines how to apply Acceptance and Commitment Therapy (ACT) to various scenarios in sport and performance psychology. By capturing the theoretical underpinnings and the practical applications of ACT in sport, this book highlights how ACT encourages a switch in attention from an internal state to the relevant task so the athlete can behave like the athlete they want to be.

This cutting-edge textbook details how ACT can be used across various presenting problems in sport psychology, such as confidence, motivation, team cohesion, and injury rehabilitation. It brings together and presents the work of key senior sport psychologists using ACT in their practice who share their working methods, exercises, and cases to inspire the reader to use ACT in their work. Chapters provide an overview of the theoretical underpinning of ACT, as well as case study examples demonstrating the application of ACT to common and uncommon performance scenarios.

Aimed at students, academics, practitioners, and coaches of sport psychology, *ACT for Sport and Performance* is key reading for all those interested in applied and performance sport psychology and related disciplines.

Samuel Wood, PhD, is a Lecturer in Sport Psychology at Manchester Metropolitan University. He is a Chartered Sport and Exercise Psychologist with the British Psychological Society (BPS) and a registered practitioner psychologist with the Health and Care Professions Council (HCPC) with nine years of applied experience across developmental and high-performance sport. He has worked with national and world governing bodies of sport to enhance psychological flexibility among athletes, coaches, and support staff. Sam also supervises trainee sport and exercise psychologists on the BPS and CASES training pathways. As a researcher, his work centres on the application of ACT within sport, and assessing, identifying, and supporting neurodivergent individuals in sporting environments.

Martin J. Turner, PhD, is a Reader in Psychology at Manchester Metropolitan University. He is a researcher, author, teacher, and Chartered Sport and Exercise Psychologist (BPS, HCPC Reg., CSci), specialising in well-being and performance under pressure and adversity. He is most known for his work examining the use of Rational Emotive Behaviour Therapy within performance settings. Martin works within elite sport and private and public sector organisations.

ACT for Sport and Performance

Edited by Samuel Wood and Martin J. Turner

Routledge
Taylor & Francis Group
NEW YORK AND LONDON

Designed cover image: Getty Images

First published 2027
by Routledge
605 Third Avenue, New York, NY 10158

and by Routledge
4 Park Square, Milton Park, Abingdon, Oxon, OX14 4RN

Routledge is an imprint of the Taylor & Francis Group, an informa business

ISBN: 978-1-032-84829-7 (hbk)
ISBN: 978-1-032-84837-2 (pbk)
ISBN: 978-1-003-51520-3 (ebk)

DOI: 10.4324/9781003515203

Typeset in Times New Roman
by Apex CoVantage, LLC

Contents

Figures

Tables

Foreword

When we moved to Spain, I started learning padél, the hugely popular, trendy younger cousin in the racket sport family. I had played squash for years, so I walked onto the court with a quiet confidence in my abilities that turned out to be wildly misplaced. The small racquet felt weird. The tempo was strange. Shots off the glass that made perfect sense in squash suddenly had no use. Within a few minutes, I was awkward, off balance, and, if I am being completely honest, a bit embarrassed.

And then my mind kicked in with its usual commentary. "You should be better at this". "Why can't you learn quicker?" "Maybe you're too old to start a new sport". It was amazing how fast those old stories came back. I would make one mistake and spend the next few points replaying it, completely disconnected from what was actually happening in front of me.

But occasionally something different would happen as I continued to play. I would remember why I was there, what mattered to me – the joy of learning, the playfulness, the chance to move my body, and laugh with friends. When I connected with that, even briefly, the game changed. I relaxed. I paid attention again. I enjoyed it. It wasn't a Matrix-style shortcut to greater skill, but I felt more present, more alive in the moment.

It made me smile because this is exactly the kind of inner equipment I have spent most of my career helping people build. Not tricks to get rid of frustration or doubt, but ways of relating to those feelings so you can still act like the person you want to be. Sport demands this constantly. You can't hide from yourself in sport. Whatever stories or expectations you carry, they show up quickly.

This is one reason why ACT fits so naturally here. Sport is full of pressure and uncertainty. It pulls people into perfectionism and harsh self-judgement. It shapes identity in powerful and sometimes painful ways. ACT doesn't promise to clear away all of that, but it gives athletes tools to move with it rather than be driven by it. Tools that help them return to the moment and keep their behaviour aligned with their values, even when their mind is busy.

Traditional sport psychology has offered many helpful methods over the years. Mental skills training has real value, and for some athletes, it is exactly what they need. But there is also a clear gap that ACT helps fill. When an athlete is struggling with fear, or a jolt of shame, or the pressure of everyone watching, telling them to "think positive" or "control the nerves" often isn't enough. In fact, it can make them feel more stuck because they end up battling their own mind on top of everything else.

ACT gives athletes a different starting point. It normalises the messiness. It helps them see that doubt and discomfort are part of the territory, not signs of weakness. And it offers ways of responding that create more space rather than narrowing it. That frees people to compete with a sense of intention rather than fear of mistakes.

Importantly, this isn't just about performance moments. The lifespan of an athlete brings all sorts of challenges. Injury. Transitions. Identity shifts. The pressure that comes from being publicly evaluated. And the quieter pressure that comes from evaluating yourself. Many athletes end up with a sense that their entire worth is tied to their sport, and when that happens, things can unravel quickly.

Values help with that. Not values as slogans, but values as qualities you want to embody. When these are clear, sport becomes part of a life rather than the whole of it. It becomes a space where someone can explore who they want to be, not just what they can achieve. And that, in my view, is essential for well-being and long-term resilience.

This book speaks directly to the real world of sport. The chapters range widely, which is a sign of how far the field has come. Confidence work. Youth development. Coaching stress. Trauma. Team culture. Injury rehabilitation. Identity. Neurodivergence. These are not technical footnotes. They are the everyday challenges that athletes, coaches, and practitioners are actually dealing with.

What I appreciate is how the contributors take the core ideas of ACT and apply them in ways that feel grounded and practical. They are not trying to turn ACT into a set of slogans. They are working with the complexity of real environments and showing how psychological flexibility can be trained and supported across different roles and situations.

In many ways, this book marks a shift. We have moved past the early stage of "Can ACT be used in sport" and into a more interesting question. How do we apply ACT with precision, care, and creativity in settings that move fast and carry real consequences? That requires understanding the culture of each sport, the dynamics of teams, the expectations placed on athletes, and the pressures on coaches and support staff. It requires a model that can stretch without snapping. ACT can do that.

When I think back to those early weeks of learning padél, what I remember most clearly is the difference it made when I reconnected with why I was there. Nothing magical happened, but everything softened. I could move more freely.

The fun returned. I could make mistakes without falling apart. The game felt bigger than my frustration.

That is what good inner equipment does. It gives you room to move. It lets you be yourself in difficult moments. It lets you pursue your goals without losing the qualities that matter to you.

My hope is that this book helps athletes, coaches, and practitioners build and share that equipment in ways that make sport not only more effective but also more human. I am delighted to introduce it.

Dr Joe Oliver
26 November 2025

Acknowledgements

Samuel Wood

I have learned a tremendous amount while bringing this book to life. My aim from the outset was to unite academics and applied practitioners with expertise in using Acceptance and Commitment Therapy in sport. This project opened the door to new collaborations across these communities, and I'm grateful for the spirit of collegiality that shaped our work together. We gave our contributors the freedom to present their ideas in the ways they felt would best communicate their message, resulting in a rich variety of perspectives that we hope readers will value.

My sincere thanks go to my co-editor, Martin. This project simply would not have been possible without his guidance. He sets the highest standard for academic integrity and is, above all, an exceptionally decent person. I'm deeply appreciative of his mentorship and support. Our paths first crossed when I was a student on the MSc programme he led, and since joining Manchester Met, he has always made time to talk about all things sport psychology.

Most importantly, I thank my wife, Emily – my constant throughout everything. I dedicate this book to our daughter, who reminds me every day of the importance of a life lived beyond the textbooks.

Martin J. Turner

For Jayne and my dog Teddy.

Samuel Wood and Martin J. Turner

We are deeply grateful to each of the contributing authors for their time and effort in writing the chapters that make up this book. We offer our sincere thanks to Dr Joe Oliver for writing the Foreword to the book.

We extend our gratitude to Megan Smith, David Varely, and the wider team at Routledge (Taylor & Francis Group) for supporting the project and the development of the book.

About the Contributors

Luke Barnes is a Senior Lecturer in Sport and Exercise Psychology and Programme Leader for Sport and Exercise Sciences (BSc) at Leeds Trinity University. He is a Chartered Sport and Exercise Psychologist (BPS, HCPC Reg.) and Researcher, specialising in integrity development, mental health education, and the application of psychological principles in performance settings. Luke has completed extensive training in Acceptance and Commitment Therapy (ACT), which he applies to his work with elite sporting clients and organisations.

Richard Bennett works as a Clinical Psychologist and Cognitive Behavioural Psychotherapist. He holds a post as an Associate Professor of Psychology at the University of Birmingham. He worked in mental health services in the NHS for over 20 years before setting up Think Psychology, an independent practice offering therapy, supervision, and a training business, ACTivatingyourpractice.com. He is recognised as a British Association for Behavioural and Cognitive Psychotherapies (BABCP) accredited psychotherapist, supervisor, and trainer, an Associate Fellow, a certified Rational Emotive Behaviour Therapy (REBT) supervisor by the Albert Ellis Institute, and an Association for Contextual Behavioural Science (ACBS) Fellow and Peer-reviewed ACT trainer. He is the co-author of several ACT books and also hosts the podcast *Two Old Psychologists Talking About Stuff.*

Rebekah-Danielle Brockbank is a trainee Sport and Exercise Psychologist. Continuing the work from her undergraduate, master's, and PhD studies at Durham University, Rebekah specialises in motivational psychology and the influence of Achievement Goal Theory on athlete performance. Rebekah worked as a Motivational Performance Psychologist in the private school sector and continues to work with athletes using ACT and REBT.

Alban Dickson, PhD, is a Chartered Sport and Exercise Psychologist (BPS, HCPC) and Lecturer at the University of Stirling. His PhD explored methods to promote psychosocial development in young soccer players, having latterly worked almost exclusively in the sport at the professional level with players, coaches, and match officials. He is an active member of a variety of communities, including the BPS Division of Sport and Exercise Psychology, the Association for Contextual Behavioural Science, and the Talent Identification and Development Environments in Sport network.

Tracy C. Donachie is a Lecturer in Sport and Exercise Psychology at Newcastle University, a HCPC-Registered Sport and Exercise Psychologist, and a Chartered Psychologist (BPS). She is the Programme Director for the MSc Sport and Exercise Psychology. Tracy's research examines perfectionism and overthinking and their relationship with athletes' emotions, well-being, and performance, alongside developing and evaluating psychological interventions. She has over 25 years of experience across coaching, playing semi-professional football, and physical activity programmes for young people. Tracy works with athletes, teams, and organisations using ACT-based approaches to enhance performance, resilience, and psychological well-being.

Misia Gervis, PhD, holds a psychology degree from London, a master's degree in sport psychology from the United States, and a PhD from Brunel on emotional abuse in children's sport. A long-standing College member and recipient of the 2003 Vice Chancellor's Teaching Excellence Award, she has worked extensively as a sport psychologist with international athletes, coaches, and national bodies, including the British Olympic Association and the Football Association (FA). She supported England's women's national football team at major tournaments and developed programmes in the professional men's game. At Brunel, she leads postgraduate teaching and supervises trainee psychologists. Her current research focuses on safeguarding and emotional abuse in elite youth sport.

Aura Goldman is a Chartered Sport and Exercise Psychologist (BPS and HCPC-Registered) and an accredited psychotherapist with the National Counselling and Psychotherapy Society (NCPS). She specialises in mental health, performance under pressure, and trauma in high-performance environments, providing psychotherapy for athletes and other high-achieving individuals. Aura runs an independent practice and has worked with performers across a wide range of levels. Her work integrates philosophical perspectives, informed by training in philosophical counselling and broader study. She is also an independent researcher, focusing on trauma and generating practice-based evidence to help bridge the gap between frontline practice and research in sport and performance psychology.

Cheryl Grogan is currently working towards her sport and exercise psychology chartered status with Chartered Association of Sport and Exercise Sciences (CASES), with a specialist focus on supporting neurodivergent athletes and young people. She holds roles in both private practice and applied performance settings, including transition support, team cohesion, and performance well-being. Cheryl's work integrates ACT and DNA-V to strengthen psychological flexibility, values-based action, and consistent performance behaviours. She develops evidence-informed workshops for coaches, athletes, and young people and is currently creating neuro-affirmative resources to support coaches, teachers, and parents.

MeiLan Haberl is a writer who graduated from Yale University in December 2024 with a BS in psychology. At Yale, she was a research assistant (RA) in Dr. Jennifer Richeson's Social Perceptions and Communications Lab and worked for four years as Communication and Consent Educator, developing interventions and teaching workshops for students, athletes, and administrators on intergroup and interpersonal dynamics and sexual misconduct response and prevention. She has frequently worked with Dr Peter Haberl as an illustrator, editor, and, most recently, co-author. Since 2019, she has been a member of the Austrian Women's Senior National Ice Hockey Team.

Peter Haberl is a licensed psychologist, focused on mindfulness and ACT-based training approaches. The Paris 2024 Olympics marked Peter's 10th Games as a sport psychologist. He is in private practice and works with US and international teams in preparation for performing at the Olympic Games. He has lectured and given workshops on mindfulness and performing at the Olympic Games in Austria, Germany, Sweden, Japan, Denmark, Norway, Switzerland, China, Singapore, Iceland, and the United States. He is the recipient of the 2011 AASP Distinguished Professional Practice Award. Peter enjoys collaborating with his daughter and is blessed to use her illuminating artwork in his work.

Tom King is a Senior Lecturer in Sport Psychology at Wrexham University. He is an author, lecturer, researcher, and a Chartered Sport and Exercise Psychologist (BPS and HCPC). His background lies mainly in professional sport, particularly football and golf. Tom spent several years at Leicester City Football Club, where he supported academy players and those competing in Premier League 2. Over the past eight years, he has built a strong reputation on the professional golf circuit, working with players on the DP World Tour and the Professional Golfers' Association (PGA) Tour. His specialist area is the use of ACT to help athletes develop psychological flexibility, manage pressure, and perform with greater consistency and confidence.

Peter Olusoga, PhD, is a BPS Chartered Psychologist and Senior Lecturer in Psychology at Sheffield Hallam University, UK. Peter completed his PhD in 2012, focusing on stress and coping in elite sports coaching, and his current work focuses on burnout, well-being, and promoting sustainability in high-performance environments. He is an internationally recognised researcher, speaker, and regular guest on BBC Radio 4's *All in the Mind.*

He is also the producer and host of the award-winning psychology podcast, *Eighty Percent Mental.* Drawing on his extensive research and work with high-performance organisations, Peter focuses on the importance of organisational and cultural change for sustainable well-being.

David Price is a Senior Lecturer in Applied Sport Psychology at the University of Portsmouth and a HCPC-Registered Sport and Exercise Psychologist. Within his practice, David's preferred therapeutic approach is that of ACT, and he has extensive experience using this approach when working with individuals, teams, and organisations in sport. David currently divides his time across research, practice, and supervising trainee Sport and Exercise Psychologists on the Professional Doctorate pathway.

Laura D. Swettenham is a Senior Lecturer in Sport and Exercise Psychology at Liverpool John Moores University and an HCPC-registered practitioner psychologist. Her work centres on inclusive, neuroaffirmative practice in sport and esports, exploring how individuals with diverse minds experience and navigate performance environments. Laura combines applied practice with research spanning neurodiversity, equity, and the development of sport psychologists and coaches. In her applied work, she specialises in third-wave and trauma-informed approaches. She is the co-chair of the CASES Neurodiversity Special Interest Group, which aims to enhance support for neurodivergent athletes and practitioners across sport and esports.

Martin J. Turner, PhD, is a Reader in Psychology at Manchester Metropolitan University. He is a researcher, author, teacher, and Chartered Sport and Exercise Psychologist (BPS, HCPC Reg., CSci), specialising in well-being and performance under pressure and adversity. He is most known for his work examining the use of REBT within performance settings. Martin works within elite sport (Psychologist at Lincoln City FC) and private and public sector organisations.

Dean R. Watson is a Senior Lecturer in Psychology and an experienced researcher, author, and practitioner (HCPC-registered). His work centres on understanding how perfectionism can negatively impact athlete performance and well-being. He is recognised for his contribution to developing and evaluating evidence-based interventions aimed at reducing perfectionism in sport. Alongside his academic role, Dean brings over a decade of applied experience across diverse sporting environments, providing psychological support to athletes, coaches, and organisations.

Samuel Wood, PhD, is Lecturer in Sport Psychology at Manchester Metropolitan University. He is a Chartered (BPS) and registered practitioner sport and exercise psychologist (HCPC) with nine years of applied experience across developmental and high-performance sport. He has worked with national and world governing bodies of sport to enhance psychological flexibility among athletes, coaches, and support staff. Sam also supervises trainee sport and exercise psychologists on the BPS and CASES training pathways. As a researcher, his work centres on the application of ACT within sport, and assessing, identifying, and supporting neurodivergent individuals in sporting environments.

1 An Introduction to ACT for Sport and Performance

Samuel Wood and Martin J. Turner

Introduction

High-level performance inevitably brings individuals face-to-face with discomfort. In sport, athletes experience worry, rumination, doubt, and surges in anxiety before stepping into the spotlight (Casali et al., 2022; Rice et al., 2016). Navigating the emotional turbulence of performance can often result in trying to "fix" or eliminate challenges that might be considered normal human experiences. For example, consider a sprinter standing in the call room before a major championship final. Her heart is racing, her palms are clammy, and thoughts like "What if I false start?" or "Everyone expects me to medal" run through her mind. These reactions are entirely predictable responses to high stakes or uncertainty. Yet, like many athletes, she tries to slow her heartbeat, force herself to relax, or replace every anxious thought with a positive one – seeing her reactions as problems she needs to fix. The harder she works to suppress her anxiety, the more agitated she becomes. But in trying to eliminate her discomfort, she diverts attention away from the race itself and inadvertently undermines the very performance she is trying to protect.

Acceptance and Commitment Therapy (ACT – pronounced *act*) offers a compelling, evidence-based approach for helping athletes respond more effectively to the thoughts, emotions, and pressures that naturally arise in high-stress environments. Developed by Steven Hayes and colleagues (see Hayes et al., 1999), ACT emerged 25 years ago. In contrast to cognitive behavioural approaches that came before it (e.g., rational emotive behavioural therapy and cognitive therapy), ACT focuses on changing the function of thoughts rather than their form. Rooted in contextual behavioural science and decades of empirical development, ACT aims to promote psychological flexibility – the ability to stay present, open to experiences, and committed to meaningful action, even when internal experiences are difficult. Whereas approaches such as Rational Emotive Behaviour Therapy (REBT) and cognitive therapy might look to challenge, dispute, or replace unhelpful thoughts, ACT looks to change the performer's relationship with those thoughts so they can act effectively even when the thoughts

DOI: 10.4324/9781003515203-1

remain. This book, *ACT for Sport and Performance*, is written for practitioners (e.g., sport psychologists and performance coaches), trainee practitioners, students, and academics seeking to understand how ACT can be applied effectively to sport and performance contexts. Our goal is to bridge the gap between theory and applied practice by hosting clear explanations, real-world examples, practitioner-focused guidance, and actionable strategies grounded in evidence. The chapters that constitute this book have been offered by a diverse set of professionals, who have kindly and generously given their time, effort, and work to this book to help us as a field understand more about the application of ACT in sport. We thank them dearly.

The Changing Landscape of Sport and Performance Psychology

Early approaches to sport and performance psychology emphasised mental skills training – techniques such as imagery, positive self-talk, goal setting, and relaxation (Andersen, 2009). These approaches boast great evidence, remain valuable, and continue to play a central role in many athletes' routines. Yet athletes often experience intrusive thoughts at critical moments. Performers sometimes feel nervous, no matter how experienced they are. High-pressure environments produce physiological and emotional reactions that are not easily "switched off".

The introduction of ACT to sport marks a turning point in the field. This approach recognises that efforts to suppress or control internal experiences can, paradoxically, make them worse. Instead of trying to eliminate anxiety, performers can learn to carry it with them effectively. Instead of fighting negative thoughts, they can learn to relate to them differently. Instead of building a life and a training environment around emotional comfort, performers can focus on values and purposeful action. With a focus on psychological flexibility, ACT provides a robust framework for helping performers navigate the inherently uncertain, high-stakes, and emotionally charged environments in which they operate.

What Is ACT?

Although ACT will be explained in more detail later in the book, we provide a brief overview here. As highlighted earlier, ACT aims to increase psychological flexibility: the ability to act effectively in alignment with one's values, while remaining open to internal experiences, and engaging in the present moment. ACT is framed around six interrelated processes – termed the hexaflex model (Hayes et al., 2006) – which, together, support psychological flexibility. These are outlined in the following:

- Acceptance – the willingness to open up to difficult thoughts, emotions, and sensations, rather than struggle with, or avoid, them

- Cognitive defusion – focuses on altering the impact of thoughts by changing how one relates to them, rather than attempting to control or eliminate them
- Contact with the present moment – cultivating awareness, attentional flexibility, and engagement with what is happening right now
- Self-as-context – developing a stable sense of self that can hold experiences lightly, promoting perspective-taking, and reducing entanglement with internal content
- Values – clarifying the qualities of action that matter most, the "why" behind performance and commitment
- Committed action – building and sustaining behaviours that move the performer towards their values, even in the presence of challenge

These processes are not steps, but the mechanisms of ACT. When used flexibly and contextually, they help performers respond effectively to stress, stay connected to what matters most, and pursue excellence without becoming trapped in cycles of avoidance and internal struggle (Wood & Turner, 2025b). Importantly, ACT is not about "giving up", "accepting poor performances", or ignoring difficult internal experiences. Rather, ACT acknowledges that discomfort is an inevitable part of pursuing high performance. ACT aims to teach performers how to work with discomfort rather than against it.

Why ACT Is Suited to Performance Settings

Performance environments are inherently uncertain. They involve judgement, evaluation, risk, and often, public scrutiny. Furthermore, human beings are fallible, limited, and imperfect by nature. Together, these central truths create the conditions for fear, self-doubt, and anxiety. ACT aligns closely with the demands of performance. Psychological flexibility allows performers to act effectively under pressure, even when thoughts and emotions are intense and unpleasant. It promotes behaviour over internal state, allowing athletes to pursue valued actions regardless of how they feel. It integrates naturally with existing mental skills practices (Wood & Turner, 2025a), offering a process-based foundation rather than a replacement for other tools. Crucially, ACT is empirically supported. At the time of writing, there are over 1400 randomised control trials, over 500 reviews and meta-analytic papers (ACBS, n.d.), and even meta-meta-analytic data (Cheng et al., 2021; Gloster et al., 2020). Consequently, ACT appears effective in most areas where it has been applied and studied. The evidence base for ACT far outweighs that of broader mindfulness and acceptance-based approaches (see Noetel et al., 2019). This means that ACT is robust enough to address broader well-being concerns encountered in sport, such as burnout, motivation, identity issues, and career transitions.

The *What*, *Why*, and *Who* of This Book

Not long after ACT was introduced, Gardner and Moore (2007) created a sport-specific, manualised protocol for the application of parts of ACT, packaged as the Mindfulness, Acceptance, and Commitment (MAC) approach. The introduction of MAC to sport means that the documented application of ACT per se to sport is limited. This is a rather strange and surprising occurrence. Because of the popularity of ACT as an approach to sport psychology, it might seem as if there are reams and reams of documented applications of ACT in the literature – but there are not. This book provides an opportunity to pull together the applied work of practitioners in one resource in order to extend the reported use of ACT. We provide theoretical and example case-study accounts of experienced and qualified practitioners using ACT with athletes. As such, this book is for anyone interested in the theory and practice of ACT within sport psychology – although athletes are not the target audience of this book. Explanatory case studies offer a unique and detailed perspective on practitioners' work, offering insights into the application of ACT that are useful for qualified practitioners new to ACT and trainees alike.

This book is intended for a broad audience, including practitioners (e.g., applied sport psychologists and performance coaches) seeking to integrate ACT into their work, trainee and student practitioners looking to develop their applied skills within an evidence-based framework, and academics and researchers who wish to understand ACT within a performance setting. We assume varying levels of prior knowledge. Some readers may be new to ACT, while others may be familiar with the theory, but seeking deeper guidance on applied practice. This book is designed to meet readers at all levels, offering conceptual clarity alongside hands-on tools. However, we encourage readers not to treat ACT as a rigid manual or collection of techniques to be applied mechanically. Instead, ACT should be used flexibly, contextually, and with sensitivity to the unique environment and history of each performer. This book is intended to support that flexible, relational, context-driven approach.

How This Book Is Structured

This book is presented in two parts. The first focuses on the theoretical and philosophical underpinnings of ACT. Bennett (Chapter 2) provides an overview of the foundations of ACT, Wood and Turner (Chapter 3) explore where we are with ACT in sport psychology, Price and Dickson (Chapter 4) outline techniques for enhancing psychological flexibility in sport contexts, and Wood and Turner (Chapter 5) critically discuss the challenges and advances presented to the wider field in relation to evaluating ACT interventions in sport psychology.

The second part focuses on the application of ACT to sport. Watson and Donachie (Chapter 6) outline how ACT can support confidence and performance. Swettenham and Grogan (Chapter 7) outline the delivery of ACT with youth athletes. Barnes and Olusoga (Chapter 8) describe how ACT can navigate coach stress. Goldman and Gervis (Chapter 9) explore ACT's application to trauma in sport. Haberl (Chapter 10) outlines an applied example of using ACT with elite teams. Brockbank and Wood (Chapter 11) outline how ACT can support injury rehabilitation and the psychology of career transitions in sport. King (Chapter 12) explains how ACT interventions might support athletes' understanding of identity in sport. And, finally, Wood (Chapter 13) explores how ACT interventions might be delivered with neurodivergent athletes.

We hope readers enjoy both the variety of topics covered and the creativity with how authors present their work and ideas. We decided not to be restrictive with chapter authors and encouraged them to take creative approaches, whilst still meeting high academic standards. As such, not only will readers find the chapters fascinating and instructive, but they will also be able to read more deeply by exploring the references to other works provided by the authors throughout their chapters.

Conclusion

This introduction sets the stage for a process-based, flexible approach to enhancing performance and supporting people in the pursuit of excellence. We believe that ACT offers a powerful, evidence-based framework for helping performers thrive – not by eliminating discomfort, but by teaching athletes to navigate discomfort with openness, awareness, and commitment to what matters.

As you move through this book, we invite you to approach ACT experientially. Notice how the concepts resonate with your own professional practice, your own performances, and perhaps even your own internal experiences. Doing so, you will discover ACT's practical, sustainable, and compassionate way of relating to the challenges inherent in the pursuit of sporting performance.

References

Andersen, M. B. (2009). The "canon" of psychological skills training for enhancing performance. In *Performance psychology in action: A casebook for working with athletes, performing artists, business leaders, and professionals in high-risk occupations* (pp. 11–34). American Psychological Association. https://doi.org/10.1037/11876-001

Association for Contextual Behavioural Sciences. (n.d.). *State of the ACT evidence*. Retrieved November 05, 2025, from https://contextualscience.org/state_act_evidence

Casali, N., Ghisi, M., Jansen, P., Feraco, T., & Meneghetti, C. (2022). What can affect competition anxiety in athletes? The role of self-compassion and repetitive negative thinking. *Psychological Reports*, *125*(4), 2009–2028. https://doi.org/10.1177/00332941211017258

Cheng, D. K., Lai, K. S. P., Pico-Espinosa, O. J., Rice, D. B., Chung, C., Modarresi, G., & Sud, A. (2021). Interventions for depressive symptoms in people living with chronic pain: A systematic review of meta-analyses. *Pain Medicine*, *23*(5), 934–954. https://doi.org/10.1093/pm/pnab248

Gardner, F. L., & Moore, Z. E. (2007). *The psychology of enhancing human performance: The mindfulness-acceptance-commitment (MAC) approach.* Springer Publishing Company.

Gloster, A. T., Walder, N., Levin, M. E., Twohig, M. P., & Karekla, M. (2020). The empirical status of acceptance and commitment therapy: A review of meta-analyses. *Journal of Contextual Behavioral Science*, *18*, 181–192. https://doi.org/10.1016/j.jcbs.2020.09.009

Hayes, S. C., Strosahl, K. D., & Wilson, K. G. (1999). *Acceptance and commitment therapy* (Vol. 6). New York: Guilford Press.

Hayes, S. C., Luoma, J. B., Bond, F. W., Masuda, A., & Lillis, J. (2006). Acceptance and commitment therapy: Model, processes and outcomes. *Behaviour Research and Therapy*, *44*(1), 1–25. https://doi.org/10.1016/j.brat.2005.06.006

Noetel, M., Ciarrochi, J., Van Zanden, B., & Lonsdale, C. (2019). Mindfulness and acceptance approaches to sporting performance enhancement: A systematic review. *International Review of Sport and Exercise Psychology*, *12*(1), 139–175. https://doi.org/10.1080/1750984X.2017.1387803

Rice, S. M., Purcell, R., De Silva, S., Mawren, D., McGorry, P. D., & Parker, A. G. (2016). The mental health of elite athletes: A narrative systematic review. *Sports Medicine*, *46*(9), 1333–1353. https://doi.org/10.1007/s40279-016-0492-2

Wood, S., & Turner, M. J. (2025a). Integrating psychology skills training (PST) with acceptance and commitment therapy (ACT). *Journal of Sport Psychology in Action*, 1–12. https://doi.org/10.1080/21520704.2025.2472341

Wood, S., & Turner, M. J. (2025b). Using acceptance and commitment therapy with athletes. *Scandinavian Journal of Sport and Exercise Psychology*, *7*, 1–9. https://doi.org/10.7146/sjsep.v7i.150889

Part 1

Theoretical and Philosophical Underpinnings of ACT

2 Delving into the Theoretical and Philosophical Foundations of ACT

Richard Bennett

Learning Objectives

1. Gain an appreciation of the philosophical and theoretical background to ACT
2. Be introduced to the core concept of psychological flexibility and the six component processes that comprise it
3. Begin to consider how ACT might be applied within sporting contexts

Introduction

Any practitioner concerned with promoting adaptive behaviour change will, at some level, be interested in a model of how behaviour and the mechanisms of change can be understood. There is no shortage of candidates vying for their attention, from the latest miracle product, through the opinions of gurus and influencers, to ancient wisdom and numerous scientific theories. Which ideas end up taking root in the mind of the practitioner is something that is subject to a vast array of factors, many of which are often outside of conscious awareness. Certain ideas simply resonate, based on the lived experience and learning history of that practitioner. If that resonance seems to produce good outcomes, those ideas will persist and expand, influencing behaviour for as long as those outcomes are experienced as rewarding. At least, that is what the proponents of ACT would have you believe.

ACT suggests that we experience and respond to life from within our own verbal system, where language and cognition play a dominant role in shaping our behaviour and performance, based on our learning history (Ramnerö & Törneke, 2008). We may have some limited awareness of how our minds instruct our behaviour, and we may even be able to step out of that influence on occasion. However, the system is deeply embedded and self-sustaining, which means that most of the time, we get sucked in, whether we like it or not. To use the example of elite athletes, those struggling with their performance are not usually doing so out of a lack of knowledge or skill. Whilst there may be physiological or environmental constraints, it is frequently the case that the obstacles are internal.

DOI: 10.4324/9781003515203-3

They are the products of cognitive processes that the athletes do not themselves choose. In presenting an application of ACT to sport and exercise, this book aims to illuminate a model of behaviour change that provides a practical method for responding more effectively to those internal obstacles. To begin, this chapter will position ACT as a contemporary psychological approach that has amassed a significant evidence base attesting to its utility. The chapter will describe ACT's philosophical and theoretical underpinnings before exploring the central tenets of the model itself. It will start to explore how ACT principles can be applied by practitioners in the field of sport and exercise, a project that is continued throughout the remainder of this volume.

Background

In the 25 years that have passed since the first ACT textbook (Hayes et al., 1999) was published, a significant research program has established ACT as being at the forefront of the so-called "third wave" of cognitive behavioural therapy (CBT) (Hayes et al., 2022). CBT is often spoken about as if it were a unitary thing. However, it is much better thought of as a psychotherapeutic school of thought comprising several different perspectives united in their interest in the nature of the relationship between thoughts, emotions, physiological sensations, and behaviour. The "first wave" of CBT was characterised by an attempt to understand the form and function of human behaviour (e.g., Pavlov, 1927; Watson, 1929; Skinner, 1953). Building on this, the "second wave" of CBT marked a shift to focusing on the role of cognition in mediating behavioural responses, spearheaded by Albert Ellis' REBT (Ellis, 1962) and Aaron Beck's cognitive therapy (Beck, 1976). These, now more traditional, forms of CBT concentrated intervention efforts on changing thoughts in the service of producing more functional behaviour. In contrast, "third wave" CBT, including ACT, is more concerned with changing the function of thoughts rather than their form. ACT practitioners seek to help their clients examine their relationship to their thoughts, attending to thoughts that are helpful in terms of serving valued goals, while simply accepting the presence of, and paying less heed to, those that are not.

ACT begins from a place of seeing humans as purposeful, goal-directed organisms and seeks to help them maximise their potential. Based around the idea of increasing psychological flexibility, ACT offers a set of processes for promoting adaptive behaviour change, whatever the context that people find themselves in. This universal and non-diagnostic approach to human function has led to ACT being applied in a wide variety of contexts, including physical and mental health, occupational psychology, coaching, education, and sporting or other performance settings. It has amassed significant evidence base attesting to its efficacy across these and other contexts. At the time of writing, there are over 1400 randomised controlled trials (RCTs) and over 500 review and meta-analytic papers (ACBS, n.d.). Meta-meta-analytic data are now appearing (e.g., Gloster et al., 2020; Cheng et al., 2022), and the broad conclusion is that ACT is efficacious in most areas where it has been studied, demonstrating equivalence or superiority when compared to other active interventions. ACT is recommended by the health guidelines of an increasing number of nations and is also endorsed as an intervention for stress by the World Health Organisation (WHO, 2022).

Philosophy and Theory

Any approach to behaviour change will adopt a certain scientific or philosophical orientation, which involves making certain assumptions about the way the world works. ACT is informed by contextual behavioural science and the philosophical worldview of functional contextualism (Zettle et al., 2016). In brief, functional contextualism uses the "act-in-context" as its root metaphor, in that one cannot meaningfully separate the behaviour of an organism from the context in which that behaviour occurs. It assumes that practitioners cannot really facilitate effective behaviour without a consideration of how that behaviour functions within a specific context. For example, the behaviour of a fish makes no sense without also understanding that it lives in water. To use another example, imagine a sprint athlete stripping off, warming up, and then crouching down on the blocks at the starting line of a 100-m race. They do everything optimally, just as they have learned to do over many hours of training. In the context of starting the race, the behaviour works. Now imagine the same athlete doing the same behaviour in a local supermarket. It would likely elicit a very different set of reactions from other shoppers when compared to the audience in the stadium, and it would not work very well in terms of getting the weekly shopping done. This example illustrates that function and context are interdependent and that both need to be considered when examining a given behaviour. ACT intervention combines the principles of function and context to promote an increase in the frequency of behaviour that works. Examples of this that you will encounter throughout this book include changing the psychological context in which internal experiences arrive, perhaps through mindfulness and acceptance practices, or helping an athlete to consider that a certain behaviour does not work well in every situation they encounter.

Throughout ACT literature and practice, the notion of practitioners thinking more about function than form abounds. It is relatively easy to describe the form of any given thought or behaviour, although understanding its function (e.g., the consequences produced by that thought or behaviour) is a much more complex task. In the service of that task, functional analysis has long been at the heart of behavioural intervention. It is concerned with trying to isolate the factors that help to explain how a behaviour operates in its environment. Rooted in the work of Skinner (1953), behaviourally oriented practitioners are not simply interested in behaviour in isolation, but also in what precedes and follows it. This is frequently expressed as an ABC analysis as follows:

Antecedent (A) – Behaviour (B) – Consequence (C)

The key point is that in the context of a given situation (A), the consequences (C) of a certain behaviour (B) can increase or decrease the likelihood of that behaviour recurring in the future. Behaviour is more likely to be repeated if the consequences of it are experienced as pleasant or rewarding, and less likely to be repeated if it leads to unpleasant consequences. For example, if a golfer adopts a risky approach to a particular round, and that approach does not work well, they may be less likely to do it again, favouring a more conservative approach thereafter. This ABC analysis describes a central mechanism by which learning is acquired, often referred to as "learning by consequence", or, more formally, "operant conditioning". This theory is built on that of "learning by association" or "classical conditioning", popularised by Pavlov (1927).

In contrast to other species, humans have an additional form of learning at their disposal, the theory behind which is central to the practice of ACT. Whereas much learning in the rest of the animal kingdom takes place via classical and/or operant conditioning, humans can learn information simply by being told, that is, by listening to information that is relayed verbally (or using other symbolic means, such as the written word). This is a form of learning that has the power to transform all other types of learning, and once it begins to develop, which generally occurs in infancy, there is no going back. Relational frame theory (RFT; Hayes et al., 2001), which has grown and developed within a reticulated relationship with ACT, is a basic science that offers a behavioural account of the acquisition and function of human language. Whilst it might not be crucial for an aspiring ACT practitioner to plumb the depths of this theory, it can be argued that a working knowledge of it is important to be effective, and that many ACT interventions do not make much sense without it. In other words, a practitioner who knows what they are doing is likely to be less effective than a practitioner who also knows why they are doing it.

There are several texts that offer a comprehensive and accessible route into learning the theory and therapeutic applications of RFT (e.g., Törneke, 2010; Villatte et al., 2016). For the purposes of this chapter, a brief overview of how ACT relies on RFT will suffice. RFT describes the human ability to make sense of the world by understanding any stimulus in relation to another, and then by relating sets of relations together. To use a simple example, imagine you are shown a spherical object and are told that it is a "ball". The object and the sound "ball" will become related in a manner that is very easy to learn, and almost impossible to unlearn. Whenever you see such an object, you will think "ball", and whenever you hear the sound "ball", you will be able to imagine the object. Thus, the two stimuli have become forever related in a process known as "mutual entailment". The next developmental process after learning such "coordination" relations is to learn "distinction" relations, such that a "ball" is different from a "bat". Also, you will later learn that both "bat" and "ball" are the same, in the sense that they are both items of "sports equipment". An interesting aside here is that when you first read "bat" two sentences ago, you probably assumed that this word was referring to a cricket or baseball bat, rather than the small, winged mammal of the same name. This is a good illustration of the point made earlier in the chapter, namely, that context shapes the function of stimuli. Had this same word appeared in a wildlife textbook, it is probable that you would have related to "bat" quite differently.

As infants, most humans quickly master the ability to relate stimuli and then sets of relations, together in increasingly complex ways. In a few short years, young children can derive a myriad of complicated relations without even being shown the relevant stimuli. For example, many would be able to say that a gold medal is preferable to a bronze medal, even in the absence of the medals themselves. This is a uniquely human experience, defined by the ability to derive relations and therefore learn things without being shown. One remarkable fact about this is that most of what we learn and communicate to each other to make sense of the world is arbitrarily derived. For example, most sportspeople would hold the view that "winning is better than losing". This is a distinction relation, and the nature of the relationship between "winning" and "losing" is specified by the contextual cue "is better than". But it is only "better" because we have all agreed that it is. There is no law of the universe that demands it. If one cares to investigate, it soon becomes evident that sporting rules, teams, league tables, and so on are all completely arbitrary concepts. Nevertheless, they govern behaviour in all manner of complex ways.

Arbitrarily derived relational responding, or behaviour that is governed by verbal rules and relations, is an incredible ability that has elevated humanity to the dominant position it enjoys on the planet. For good or ill, we have been able to prevail over other animals despite our numerous physical disadvantages. Despite being relatively small and frail, being unable to fly, breathe underwater, or survive extreme temperatures, humans have conquered the Earth, bending the physical environment and other creatures in it to our will. This has been possible because of language and cognition, and it seems that evolution and survival have favoured the animal that could learn the most, communicate the best, and cooperate most flexibly, rather than those that were biggest, fastest, or strongest. However, for every evolutionary advantage, there is a trade-off (Dawkins, 2024), and our relational framing abilities have another side to them, which is that they sit at the heart of why it is so easy for us to experience distress and behavioural dysfunction. Leading RFT researcher, Yvonne Barnes-Holmes, has said about the acquisition of language, that "it starts simple, then it gets complex . . . and then it gets personal" (Barnes-Holmes, 2015). This is because the same normal developmental process of language that accounts for our ability to understand

and shape our response to the world in helpful ways matures in such a way that it is also the source of much suffering and maladaptive responding. For example, the coordination ability required to relate the term "ball" with a spherical object is precisely the same ability that allows us to relate the term "not good enough" with the concept of one's own self. If one can derive that a gold medal is preferable to a bronze one, then one can also derive that other people's qualities are preferable to mine. In relational terms, it is a short step from "winning is better than losing" through "winners are better than losers" to "I lost, I'm a loser, I'm not good enough, my worth is less, I'm *worthless*". In the same way, the feat of being able to derive relations without direct experience of the relevant stimuli might allow a netball team to prepare for a match against an opponent that they have never played before. However, it also allows them to anticipate a humiliating defeat that has not (and might never) happen, with all the subsequent anxiety and its negative impact on performance that can ensue. In summary, alongside their many benefits, the normal processes of language acquisition and relational responding make a tremendous amount of psychological pain and struggle possible. These forms of suffering are not in themselves pathological or indicative of any kind of disease process. They are ubiquitous across cultures and might be best thought of as an inescapable aspect of the human condition. They can, however, lead to behavioural dysfunction as people try to find ways of managing, suppressing, controlling, or otherwise avoiding this distress.

Psychological Flexibility

A knowledge of RFT provides a framework for understanding the importance of symbolic learning. This helps to explain how humans can become distressed or trapped in patterns of unhelpful behaviour, simply because of relating words and ideas together (Johnson & Bennett, 2023). Thus, as a model of human behaviour that leans on RFT, ACT can be understood as being principally concerned with two things: relating and the functions of that relating (Barnes-Holmes & McEnteggart, 2020). Relating stimuli does not occur in a vacuum, and in almost every waking moment, verbally able humans will experience the functions (or consequences) of that relating, such as orienting towards or attending to a stimulus and/or noticing whether that stimulus is appetitive, aversive, or neutral (Barnes-Holmes et al., 2020). This process is not linear, as relations and their functions work synergistically, influencing each other. For illustrative purposes, let us imagine an elite cyclist returning from a significant injury sustained following a mid-race collision in the middle of the pack. They might experience the thought "*being in the middle of the pack is dangerous*". In RFT terms, this is a coordination relation (this position in the pack = danger), which has the function of orienting the cyclist towards threat (and perhaps away from focusing on competitive technique). It also evokes an avoidant behavioural response (slowing down to let riders pass, thereby relinquishing a competitive advantage). Since the avoidant behaviour is negatively reinforced by a reduction in the sense of threat, it is likely to be repeated in a manner that could become problematic over time, given that the cyclist values competing to win.

Typically, in the presence of aversive stimuli, humans tend to rely on uncomplicated, narrow, and rigid behavioural responses, for example, running away from a more powerful aggressor. This is an essential survival mechanism, the roots of which lie deep in our evolutionary history. Indeed, even single-cell organisms have been noted to move away from toxins in the ocean (LeDoux, 2019). The problem for humans, particularly in the complex contexts of modern life, is that our minds tend to treat aversive internal experiences, such as critical thoughts or unwanted emotions like fear, as if they equate to external threats (Bennett & Oliver, 2025). Most of us do not face existential threats on a regular basis, yet our minds can respond as if that is exactly what is happening. To return to the cyclist outlined earlier, merely remembering something connected to the previous accident or imagining the possibility of a recurrence can lead to unwanted thoughts and feelings and the same kinds of narrow behavioural responses. Thus, a kind of psychological rigidity can take hold, which is frequently detrimental to people's purposes and goals. What an ACT practitioner would want to offer to this cyclist, in addition to a way to understand and normalise their behavioural response, is a method for reducing the ability of verbal relations to govern behaviour in unhelpful ways. Within the ACT literature, this method is most frequently referred to as having the aim of increasing *psychological flexibility*. This can be defined as assisting people to fully connect with their thoughts and experiences in any given moment and to interact more helpfully with them, such that those interactions serve valued ends (Hayes et al., 2012). This emphasis on changing the function of, or relationship with, thoughts, rather than their content or form, is perhaps the biggest point of divergence between ACT and more traditional forms of CBT, such as CT or REBT.

The Hexaflex Model

As a concept, psychological flexibility might be described as a "middle-level term", building a bridge between the more technical and scientific ideas of RFT and an everyday language that ACT practitioners can share with their clients (Bennett, 2023). Over time, the concept of psychological flexibility has been elaborated to include six key components that elucidate how ACT views psychopathology, and therefore what kinds of outcomes ACT practitioners are looking to achieve. The model outlined in Figure 2.1, first presented by Hayes et al. (2006), illustrates a conceptualisation of psychopathology based on the way that language and cognition interact with direct contingencies to produce behaviour that does not serve valued outcomes. The authors argued that such psychological inflexibility emerges from weak or unhelpful contextual control over language processes themselves and is not only inherently unhelpful but also serves to

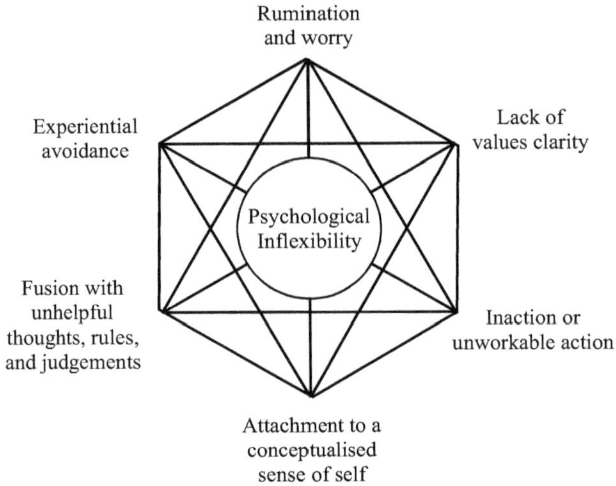

Figure 2.1 The Inflexahex (adapted from Bach and Moran, 2007).

exacerbate other pathological processes (e.g., the cyclist in the previous example can develop rigid judgements about their own avoidance).

Clearly, if psychological *rigidity* is seen as a problematic process, increased psychological *flexibility* describes the desired outcome of any ACT-informed intervention or procedure. Hayes et al. (2006) conceived the "Hexaflex" model of psychological flexibility as a means of outlining six adaptive skills that people can develop in the service of this outcome. These skills have also been described with reference to a "Triflex" model (e.g., Oliver et al., 2015), which groups the six skills under three simplified headings. The relationship between both ideas is illustrated in Figure 2.2 and will be expanded upon in the remainder of this chapter.

Openness to Experience

There are two common responses to the psychological discomfort that inevitably arises in the pursuit of a meaningful life and valued goals. Within the ACT literature, these are known as "experiential avoidance" and "cognitive fusion". Each of these will be discussed in turn.

Whilst avoidance is an adaptive response to threat or other aversive environmental stimuli, it is common for humans to respond similarly to aversive internal stimuli, such as unwanted thoughts or emotions. With reference to Figure 2.1, this is conceptualised within ACT as "experiential avoidance", which describes efforts to avoid one's own internal experience. Most people have wide and complex repertoires for achieving this, including distraction, numbing, intellectualising, suppression, as well as simple behavioural avoidance. Football fans who

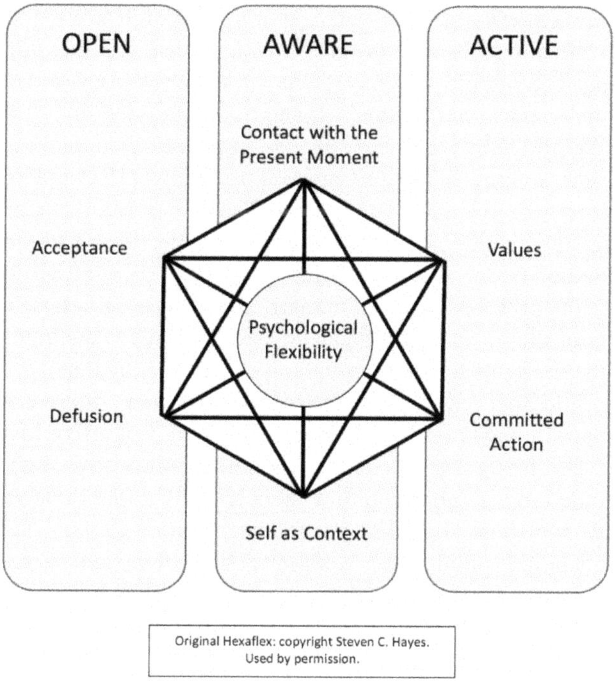

Figure 2.2 The Hexaflex and Triflex.

turn away when a penalty kick is being taken to alleviate tension are engaging this behavioural repertoire. Experiential avoidance is not intrinsically problematic, although it can easily become so if relied upon too often or too heavily. People who use experiential avoidance as their default strategy often find that their world becomes smaller as they avoid, escape, or retreat from more and more people, places, and activities.

As can be seen from its similar position in Figure 2.2 to that of experiential avoidance in Figure 2.1, “acceptance” is a skill that ACT promotes as an alternative to it. Acceptance involves the willing embrace of unwanted private events. Rather than seeing uncomfortable thoughts and emotions as some kind of enemy to be overcome or avoided, the emphasis within ACT is to allow experiences to come to and go without unnecessary attempts to change their frequency or form, especially when doing so has previously led a person to unhelpful outcomes. They might usefully be seen as messengers relaying important information. For example, if an athlete can learn to relate to the anxiety felt in the immediate buildup to a race as an indication of how much personal significance the race has, this is likely to be more functional than seeing it as some kind of weakness or as a sensation to be suppressed and avoided.

In addition to experiential avoidance, another common strategy for managing unwanted private events is to form rules or judgements around which behaviour can be organised. Examples might include "*in order to perform well tomorrow I must sleep for eight hours tonight*". It should be stressed that there is nothing inherently unhelpful about rules, and indeed, many rules can facilitate aspects of a purposeful life, so long as they are applied flexibly. Akin to the principles of a much older form of CBT, REBT (Ellis, 1962), ACT posits that rigid adherence to verbal rules or responding to them as if they were literal truths often leads to unworkable behaviour and undesirable outcomes. "Cognitive fusion" is the name given to the process by which humans can become so intertwined with the verbal content of their minds that it can become difficult to distinguish objective reality from the thoughts that we have about it. After all, whilst it would be great to get a solid eight hours of sleep before tomorrow's event, there is no law of the universe that predicts that it absolutely must happen. Cognitive fusion becomes problematic when thoughts exert such a regulatory impact over behaviour to the point that people pay less attention to what is actually going on around them. An example might be where an athlete pays more attention to their own perception of their coach's beliefs about them than they do to their coach's actual behaviour. Where ACT departs from traditional forms of CBT is in its assertion that the content of thoughts is less important than the process of becoming fused with them. Thoughts are not harmful, and they have no predictive power, so there is no imperative to change their content or think different thoughts. Rather, cognitive "defusion" interventions attempt to change the unhelpful functions of thoughts (or other private events), rather than trying to alter their form or frequency. This might be construed as changing the way people interact with, or relate to, their thoughts, in order to reduce the thoughts' unhelpful functions. Classic examples of defusion interventions include repeating an uncomfortable word or phrase until it loses its meaning or creating some distance from a painful thought by writing it down or ascribing physical characteristics to it (e.g., "this is a really old thought"; Blackledge, 2015). Such interventions are designed to provide some space between the thinker and the thought, such that, whilst there might be little choice about whether or not a thought appears, the thinker is able to more mindfully notice it and more carefully choose their response.

As a footnote, it is important to be clear that, from an ACT perspective, acceptance and defusion are not ends in themselves. Rather, they help foster an openness to experience that is useful to build as a method for increasing values-based action (Hayes et al., 2006).

Cultivating Present-Moment Awareness

The Hexaflex diagram in Figure 2.2 is drawn in such a way that each point is connected to every other point, indicating a relatedness between the six psychological flexibility skills. As an example of one such connection, it is self-evident that increasing openness to experience, as outlined earlier, necessarily involves improving the ability to notice experiences as they occur. ACT practitioners routinely promote the idea of cultivating present-moment awareness as a means of facilitating access to other points on the Hexaflex. With that as the aim, the central pillar of the model, encompassing "contact with the present moment" and "self-as-context", encourages the development of two skills: noticing and then noticing who is noticing.

One of the unhelpful consequences of cognition and language in verbal organisms is the way in which it can interrupt direct experience. We tend to experience external stimuli through the filter of language, and the functions of those stimuli can be transformed as a result. For example, if a football stadium is repeatedly described as "a fortress" or "a cauldron", it can elicit a feeling of anxious apprehension in visiting teams. The stadium itself is unchanged, although it has acquired intimidating functions, simply because of how it has been spoken about. Promoting the practice of bringing attention to the present moment can help clients to step out of these kinds of programmed or "autopilot" responses, experiencing the world more as it is, and less as their thoughts, beliefs, and judgements are telling them that it is. Segal et al. (2002) describe a "being" mode of mind, contrasting this with a "thinking" mode. In the same way, ACT promotes making non-judgemental contact with stimuli as they occur, in the hope of contacting the present moment more fully and experiencing it more directly. The aim here is for moment-to-moment behavioural responses to be more informed by direct experience and therefore both more flexible and more adaptive. Most ACT textbooks describe a range of formal and informal practices and interventions that can be employed to work towards this aim (e.g., Stoddard & Afari, 2014; Harris, 2019).

If the above describes sharpening the skill of noticing, "self-as-context", which has much in common with the Buddhist notion of the observing or transcendent self, refers to learning to pay attention to that part of us that is doing the noticing. One of the unfortunate aspects of the English language is the extent of its use of the verb "to be". Such instances include "I *am* fast" and "I *am* strong", although they also include "I *am* not good enough" and "I *am* a loser". Such statements effectively put an "equal" sign in between "I" and whatever comes next, and this kind of coordination relation can be very unhelpful and self-limiting. Therefore, it can be helpful to learn to relate "I" and the experiences that "I" have hierarchically, rather than as if they are coordinated. A simple way to illustrate this is with a container metaphor, such as the sky and weather. It would be odd to say, "the sky *is* the weather". Rather, it makes more sense to describe the sky as the place where the weather happens, or that the sky contains the weather. In the same way, people are not their thoughts and feelings. Rather, people *have* their thoughts and feelings.

There are many ACT interventions that seek to promote a hierarchical relationship between conscious awareness and the aspects of experience that awareness notices. Put more simply, just as there is a clear difference between a torch and the objects that the torch's beam illuminates, there is a difference between "I" and what "I" notice. Thus, an example "self-as-context" intervention might be to ask a team member experiencing the thought, "I'm letting the side down" to practice prefixing that thought with, "I'm noticing that I'm having the thought that . . . I'm letting the side down" and exploring with them whether this alters the thought's function in any way. "Self-as-context" is a somewhat abstract concept, and one that can be hard for ACT practitioners and their clients to fully grasp and embody. Fortunately, some excellent texts are available that provide detailed practical guidance on how best to understand and implement this skill (e.g., McHugh et al., 2019; McHugh & Stewart, 2012).

Engagement in Valued Activity

The Hexaflex is only one way in which the principles of ACT have been formulated. It is largely conceptual, and whilst useful for practitioners as a means of describing psychological flexibility, its practical utility is arguably limited. The ACT Matrix (Polk et al., 2016) and the Choice Point (Harris, 2019) are useful alternatives that are more accessible to clients. Another model, proposed by LeJeune and Luoma (2019), positions engagement in valued activity as the main outcome of ACT intervention, facilitated by the development of acceptance, defusion, present-moment awareness, and self-as-context skills. There is a lot to recommend their approach, and this is why engagement in valued activity has been left to last in this chapter. The argument here is that being more open to experience or more aware of the present moment is only desirable because they help a person move towards a life characterised by a greater emphasis on value-driven action. Hence, "values" and "committed action" within the Hexaflex really constitute ideas by which the impact of ACT interventions can be measured: has ACT work helped the client be clearer about what really matters to them, and are they using that clarity as a stimulus for ongoing action?

Within ACT, values are seen as qualities of purposive action that are best defined as a direction rather than a destination. Thus, they are distinct from goals, although they do describe how achieving the goal might be approached (e.g., "I want to win (goal), and I want to win honestly and fairly (values)"). The concept of values points to a quality within a person that they find intrinsically motivating and rewarding. It is the "why" behind wanting to be an athlete, rather than the "what" of any given sport. In behavioural terms, values serve as their own reinforcer, providing people with a reason for engaging in activity and are reflective of that person's fundamental desires, rather than any external demands or expectations.

ACT interventions in this area tend to focus on helping people clarify and connect with their values, since doing so helps provide meaning and purpose, helps clarify what people want to stand for in their lives, and helps motivate people around which challenges they want to pursue. This can be achieved in a variety of ways, including the use of values questionnaires, values card sort exercises, metaphors, or other techniques (see LeJeune and Luoma, 2019 for a comprehensive guide). The ultimate aim of values work is to increase the frequency with which people engage in value-driven behaviour, primarily because of the associations between this and other desirable life outcomes (Gloster et al., 2020).

Obviously, values clarification is of limited use unless it is embodied; there is no point in someone valuing fair play if that person does not then play fairly. This notion leads to the last skill on the Hexaflex, namely "committed action", which describes the behaviour of putting verbally construed values into action. It involves making a commitment to behave in a way that is consistent with one's values and then doing so. It also involves using techniques that might facilitate that action, and/or help manage internal barriers to it. In this way, committed action is inextricably linked to each of the other points of the Hexaflex, since taking value-driven action can often call for a present-moment focus or making room for discomfort. In terms of interventions, ACT practitioners are likely to help their clients identify behavioural goals, plan activities that broaden a person's repertoire of value-driven actions, and explore how best to manage any barriers to effective action.

Summary

This chapter has provided a philosophical and theoretical background to ACT as well as a description of the core concept of psychological flexibility. ACT interventions can be seen as a set of behavioural procedures delivered with the intention of helping people make more functional and flexible choices in any given moment. ACT aims to promote present-moment awareness and openness to experience to enable people to better engage in valued activity. In sporting contexts, ACT can be applied flexibly, perhaps being about helping people improve levels of performance or cope better with adversity. The remaining chapters of this book will illustrate examples of the application of ACT with reference to the foundational concepts described above.

References

Association for Contextual Behavioural Science. (n.d.). *State of the ACT Evidence*. Retrieved April 23, 2025, from https://contextualscience.org/state_act_evidence

Bach, P. A., & Moran, D. J. (2007). *ACT in practice: Case conceptualization in acceptance and commitment therapy*. Oakland, CA: New Harbinger.

Barnes-Holmes, D., Barnes-Holmes, Y., & McEnteggart, C. (2020). Updating RFT (more field than frame) and its implications for process-based therapy. *The Psychological Record, 70*, 605–624.

Barnes-Holmes, Y. (2015). *Supercharging your ACT or CBT practice using relational frame theory* [PowerPoint presentation]. British Association of Behavioural and Cognitive Psychotherapies, London.

Barnes-Holmes, Y., & McEnteggart, C. (2020). *Process-based behavior therapy week 1: Introduction to process-based behavior therapy, behavior analysis and functional analysis, and the concepts of updated RFT* [Course notes]. Perspectives Ireland.
Beck, A. T. (1976). *Cognitive therapy and the emotional disorders*. New York: Meridian Books.
Bennett, R. (2023). *Process, procedure, and outcome in ACT: Where have we been and where are we going?* [PowerPoint presentation]. Norsk Forening for Kognitiv Afterdsterapi ACT Konferansen, Trondheim.
Bennett, R., & Oliver, J. E. (2025). *Acceptance and commitment therapy: 100 key points and techniques* (2nd ed.). Abingdon: Routledge.
Blackledge, J. T. (2015). *Cognitive defusion in practice*. Oakland, CA: Context Press.
Cheng, D. K., Paris Lai, K. S., Pico-Espinosa, O. J., Rice, D. B., Chung, C., Modarresi, G., & Sud, A. (2022). Interventions for depressive symptoms in people living with chronic pain: A systematic review of meta-analyses. *Pain Medicine*, *23*(5), 934–954.
Dawkins, R. (2024). *The genetic book of the dead: A Darwinian reverie*. New York: Apollo.
Ellis, A. (1962). *Reason and emotion in psychotherapy*. New York: Citadel.
Gloster, A. T., Walder, N., Levin, M. E., Twohig, M. P., & Karekla, M. (2020). The empirical status of acceptance and commitment therapy: A review of meta-analyses. *Journal of Contextual Behavioural Science*, *18*, 181–192.
Harris, R. (2019). *ACT made simple: An easy to read primer on acceptance and commitment therapy* (2nd ed.). Oakland, CA: New Harbinger.
Hayes, S. C., Barnes-Holmes, D., & Roche, B. (2001). *Relational frame theory: A post-Skinnerian account of human language and cognition*. New York, NY: Plenum/Kluwer.
Hayes, S. C., Ciarrochi, J., Hofmann, S. G., Chin, F., & Sahdra, B. (2022). Evolving an idionomic approach to processes of change: Towards a unified personalized science of human improvement. *Behaviour Research and Therapy*, *156*, 104155.
Hayes, S. C., Luoma, J., Bond, F. W., Masuda, A., & Lillis, J. (2006). Acceptance and commitment therapy: Model, processes and outcomes. *Behaviour Research and Therapy*, *44*(1), 1–25.
Hayes, S. C., Strosahl, K. D., & Wilson, K. G. (1999). *Acceptance and commitment therapy: An experiential approach to behavior change*. New York: Guilford Press.
Hayes, S. C., Strosahl, K. D., & Wilson, K. G. (2012). *Acceptance and commitment therapy. Second edition: The process and practice of mindful change*. New York: Guilford Press.
Johnson, D., & Bennett, R. (2023). *Acceptance and commitment therapy: Responses to frequently asked questions*. Abingdon: Routledge.
LeDoux, J. (2019). *The deep history of ourselves: The four-billion-year story of how we got conscious brains*. New York: Viking.
LeJeune, J., & Luoma, J. B. (2019). *Values in therapy: A clinician's guide to helping clients explore values, increase psychological flexibility, and live a more meaningful life*. New Harbinger Publications.
McHugh, L., & Stewart, I. (2012). *The self and perspective taking: Contributions and applications from modern behavioural science*. Oakland: New Harbinger.
McHugh, L., Stewart, I., & Almada, P. (2019). *A contextual behavioural guide to the self*. Oakland: Context Press.
Oliver, J., Hill, J., & Morris, E. (2015). *Activate your life: Using acceptance and mindfulness to build a life that is rich, fulfilling and fun*. London: Constable & Robinson.
Pavlov, I. P. (1927). *Conditioned reflexes: An investigation of the physiological activity of the cerebral cortex*. Oxford: Oxford University Press.

Polk, K. L., Schoendorff, B., Webster, M., & Olaz, F. O. (2016). *The essential guide to the ACT matrix: A step-by-step approach to using the ACT matrix model in clinical practice*. Oakland: New Harbinger.
Ramnerö, J., & Törneke, N. (2008). *The ABCs of human behavior: Behavioral principles for the practicing clinician*. Oakland, CA: New Harbinger.
Segal, Z., Teasdale, J., & Williams, M. (2002). *Mindfulness-based cognitive therapy for depression*. New York, NY: Guilford Press.
Skinner, B. F. (1953). *Science and human behavior*. New York: The Free House.
Stoddard, J., & Afari, N. (2014). *The big book of ACT metaphors*. Oakland, CA: New Harbinger.
Törneke, N. (2010). *Learning RFT: An introduction to relational frame theory and its clinical application*. Oakland, CA: New Harbinger.
Villatte, M., Villatte, J. L., & Hayes, S. C. (2016). *Mastering the clinical conversation: Language as intervention*. New York, NY: Guilford Press.
Watson, J. B. (1929). *Psychology from the standpoint of the behaviourist* (3rd ed.). Philadelphia: Lippincott.
World Health Organisation. (2022). *Self-help plus (SH+): A group-based stress management course for adults*. Retrieved April 28, 2022, from www.who.int/publications/i/item/9789240035119
Zettle, R. D., Hayes, S. C, Barnes-Holmes, D., & Biglan, A. (2016). *The Wiley handbook of contextual behavioral science*. Chichester: Wiley-Blackwell.

3 Acceptance and Commitment Therapy in Sport Psychology

Where Are We Now?

Samuel Wood and Martin J. Turner

Learning Objectives

1. Critically evaluate the current evidence base for ACT in sport psychology, identifying key findings, methodological limitations, and future research directions
2. Apply key ACT principles within sport psychology practice, demonstrating how acceptance, mindfulness, and values-based approaches can be integrated into athlete and team interventions
3. Explain and illustrate how ACT conceptually aligns with established sport psychology frameworks to support both performance and well-being

Introduction

The work of applied sport psychology/performance practitioners (SPPs) has historically focused on the use of psychological skills training (PST; e.g., goal setting and imagery) to improve athlete performance (Andersen, 2009). As practitioners within the field have explored approaches beyond PST, the cognitive-behavioural tradition has become integral to SPPs' professional practice (Turner et al., 2023). The range of psychotherapeutic approaches that form theoretical orientations for practice delivery can be overwhelming for SPPs – both experienced and neophyte – to navigate (Tod & Eubank, 2020). Rather helpfully, SPPs have traditionally emphasised performance enhancement through cognitive control strategies (e.g., thought-stopping, reframing, and affirmations) in line with second-wave cognitive behavioural approaches like cognitive therapy and REBT (Turner et al., 2023). This stems from two related axiomatic principles that optimal performance requires either cognitive mediation or cognitive change to control internal experiences. This approach may work sometimes, but there are other psychotherapeutic approaches applied practitioners can explore.

DOI: 10.4324/9781003515203-4

Of the CBTs applied to sport, ACT, a so-called third-wave CBT, is gaining momentum (see Olusoga & Yousuf, 2023; Wood & Turner, 2025). ACT offers an alternative approach to second-wave CBTs, suggesting that performance can be enhanced not by controlling thoughts and feelings, but through accepting them and acting in accordance with one's values (Hayes et al., 2012b). High-pressure performance environments inevitably bring performers feelings of pressure, doubt, and discomfort. ACT encourages athletes to make room for these experiences, rather than fight them. In this way, ACT normalises the reality of performing while experiencing nerves and/or self-doubt, providing athletes with tools to navigate internal challenges, rather than avoid them (Wood & Turner, 2025).

Within this book, ACT's theoretical and mechanistic underpinnings are covered elsewhere very well by other authors, and we do not wish to repeat this content. So, the aim of this chapter is to synthesise the empirical evidence, current applications, integration with sport psychology frameworks, and the future directions of work in this area, exploring the application of ACT in sport settings. Doing so, this chapter examines the current landscape of ACT in sport psychology – and its implications for researchers, educators, and practitioners.

The Emergence of ACT in Sport Psychology

RFT and functional contextualism are discussed in detail in Chapter 2. However, we feel it is important to bring these alive here by applying them to a sport context. Let us take the example of a tennis player, Ruth, who experiences poor serves during critical match moments leading to lost points. Ruth might learn to connect serving with failure, telling herself, for example, "I always lose when I serve". This association – or relational framing – can lead to experiential avoidance, where Ruth avoids distressing thoughts and emotions related to serving. This would then impact how Ruth behaved. For example, she might opt for conservative serves to minimise anxiety, intrusive thoughts, and/or perceived risks, thereby hindering optimal performance and possibly even career progression.

Drawing on principles of contextual behavioural science, the broader focus of ACT interventions is to develop task-focused attention and acceptance of internal experiences as a natural part of the athletic and human experience, promoting values-driven behaviour (Harris, 2019; Wood & Turner, 2025). The central aim of ACT is psychological flexibility, which is perhaps best described as the ability to remain present and take value-directed action in the presence of difficult internal experiences (Hayes et al., 1999). This approach fits performance contexts well, where athletes are constantly managing pressure, expectations, and uncertainty.

A few years after the emergence of ACT, fundamental aspects of ACT were introduced to sport as MAC interventions (Gardner & Moore, 2012; Moore & Gardner, 2001). It is possible to see MAC as a bridge between ACT, historically applied in clinical settings, and performance enhancement. However, MAC is presented by the authors as a manualised, sport-specific programme for mindfulness and acceptance-based approaches, and something separate to ACT (Gardner & Moore, 2017; Moore, 2009). The literature on MAC has increased over recent years and is a well-supported approach to sport psychology. However, MAC and ACT are not equivalent, and evidence and discussion surrounding MAC cannot be taken to be referring to ACT. Indeed, there is a need to examine and communicate how ACT per se can be practiced in sport psychology.

Current Evidence for ACT in Sport

Overview of Research Evidence

Empirical studies on the use of ACT in sport are still relatively scarce. This might be surprising to some readers because ACT seems ubiquitous in sport psychology. We cover why this might be the case later in the chapter. In this part, we provide a brief overview of the research that has been conducted in this area.

Lundgren et al. (2020) conducted a feasibility study with 28 elite junior ice hockey players in Sweden. Delivering a four-session intervention during the competitive season against a control group, the authors showed that ACT significantly improved athletes' psychological flexibility and coach-rated performance compared to the control group. This demonstrated the feasibility and athlete acceptability of ACT in sport settings. Extending this work, Lundgren et al. (2021) conducted a randomised control trial over 4 weekly group sessions (plus homework), again with competitive ice hockey players in Sweden (n=34). Again, this study showed increased psychological flexibility and coach-rated performance, although this may be short-term, as effects were only partially maintained at a three-month follow-up. Watson et al. (2023) evaluated the effectiveness of an online ACT intervention for reducing perfectionism and improving pre-competition emotions in female soccer players through a randomised control trial. They concluded that online ACT interventions may be effective in reducing perfectionism but not necessarily improving pre-competition emotions. Finally, on the theme of performance enhancement, Reinebo et al. (2025) conducted a multiple-cohort intervention with Finnish ice hockey players and found preliminary effectiveness for their online, seven-week intervention. However, this clearly needs further evaluation in future trials. Nonetheless, taken together, these findings highlight the potential of ACT as a framework for enhancing athletic performance.

Aside from performance enhancement, sport-specific ACT interventions have proven effective for promoting the mental well-being of athletes (Ronkainen et al., 2025). Further, ACT has been shown to be effective in injury rehabilitation. For example, Mahoney and Hanrahan (2011) found that ACT improved athletes' commitment to rehabilitation behaviours when recovering from knee injuries. Moving into single-case study literature, Price et al. (2022) demonstrated that helping a youth snowboarder defuse from the thought "What if I get injured?" led to increased psychological flexibility and improved training engagement. Similarly, Wood and Turner (2023) applied ACT with a competitive figure skater experiencing fear of re-injury, and through defusion, mindfulness, and values work, the athlete became more able to tolerate discomfort and re-engage with performance goals. ACT interventions can therefore be used to address emotional recovery and support readiness for return to sport by helping athletes reconnect with a meaningful athletic identity and value-driven goals.

Methodological Trends and Gaps

Despite a large evidence base showing the effectiveness of ACT in clinical populations, the small samples in the empirical studies applying ACT to sport are a notable limitation. Other general limitations might include a lack of follow-up data once participants have completed an intervention, a dependence on self-report measures, and limited objective outcomes. However, in this section, we extend these general limitations, focusing on three important and often overlooked methodological trends and gaps: the somewhat inconsistent operationalisation of psychological flexibility; variable intervention fidelity; and the use of general psychometric measures for common presenting problems in sport psychology.

As previously discussed, psychological flexibility is the central construct of ACT – best described as the ability to contact with the present moment fully, and act in accordance with one's values, even in the presence of unwanted internal experiences (Hayes et al., 1999). However, how this construct is measured in sport research has varied considerably across studies. First, we highlight inconsistencies in the different measurement tools used. Some studies use the Acceptance and Action Questionnaire (AAQ-II; Bond et al., 2011), which was developed for general populations. Other studies use sport-adapted versions (e.g., AAQ for Sport; Lundgren et al., 2020), mindfulness scales, or emotional regulation questionnaires. These instruments assess different facets of flexibility – some focus on experiential avoidance, while others assess present-moment awareness or values-based action. Second, there is a diverse conceptual focus. Some studies see flexibility as mindfulness, whereas others see it as acceptance or even coping. This means psychological flexibility is sometimes operationalised narrowly (e.g., the ability to accept anxiety) or broadly (e.g., a composite of mindfulness and acceptance), making comparisons across studies quite difficult. Linked to this point, there is a lack of clarity around cognitive defusion, being discussed within the wider ACT literature as a procedure, process, and outcome. This creates ambiguity, decreases precision, and increases the chances of making category mistakes (Assaz et al., 2023). Defusion exercises aim to develop flexible thinking and encourage the athlete to experience thoughts and feelings simply as mental events, rather than seeing them as completely true or reflective of reality (Ruiz et al., 2023). Learning to observe thoughts non-judgementally, rather than removing or changing them, reduces the power (and negative impact) that unhelpful thoughts have on emotions and behaviours (Assaz et al., 2023). In this way, defusion encourages athletes to "unhook" from limiting narratives and unhelpful performance thoughts. Here, fusion and defusion can be seen as a continuum (Blackledge, 2007), with defusion best considered an outcome (Assaz et al., 2023). There is no agreed-upon taxonomy for categorising or linking cognitive defusion processes, and the ACT literature has yet to evidence the effectiveness of one approach over another (Ruiz et al., 2023).

Intervention fidelity – that is, the extent to which an intervention is delivered as intended (i.e., aligned with the theoretical model, structure, and core processes) – is often inconsistent or poorly reported in ACT-based sport research. For example, some studies use brief (two to three session) workshops, while others apply multi-week ACT interventions. Moreover, not all authors report which ACT processes were targeted (e.g., defusion and values work) or how much time was spent on each. Second, interventions are sometimes delivered by trained sport psychologists, sometimes by coaches or researchers with limited ACT-specific training. Few studies include fidelity checks (e.g., session recordings, adherence ratings, or supervision logs). Finally, sport adaptations are essential for ecological validity (e.g., using performance metaphors), but some studies simplify or omit key processes, reducing theoretical coherence. Without this fidelity data, it is unclear whether null or partial effects are due to the approach itself or how it was implemented. In summary, variable fidelity means that it is not always possible to determine whether positive outcomes stem from ACT-consistent processes (e.g., acceptance and defusion), from general supportive effects, or placebo factors. In conclusion, there is little research capturing the nuanced process of ACT in sport, with most meta-analyses in sport focused on mindfulness and acceptance approaches (Noetel et al., 2019; Ptáček et al., 2023).

The final issue we highlight is the aspect of measurement. This is discussed in more detail in Chapter 5.

Integrating ACT into Sport Psychology Practice

The research evidence for ACT in sport is still developing. However, we feel the effectiveness of ACT from other sectors – for which, at the time of writing, over 500 meta-analyses or systematic, scoping, and narrative reviews (ACBS, n.d.), including meta-analyses of meta-analyses exist – make the pursuit of ACT in sport a worthy endeavour. In this section, we outline how the core processes of ACT might apply to sport psychology practice.

The Working Alliance in ACT Interventions

First, we discuss the working alliance between practitioner and client during ACT interventions. With ACT, there is an emphasis on shared values and a willingness to explore discomfort together (Vilardaga & Hayes, 2010) to pursue valued living even while symptoms remain (Hayes et al., 2012a). Here, the practitioner might be seen as a co-traveller who models psychological flexibility and works "shoulder-to-shoulder" with the client (Plumb & Vilardaga, 2010). In some ways, then, the relationship is the intervention – a social scaling of the hexaflex model where real-time uses of ACT processes can repair alliance ruptures (Vilardaga & Hayes, 2010; Walser & O'Connell, 2021).

Acceptance over Control: Making Room for Unwanted Cognitions

The notion of challenging and changing unwanted thoughts seems ingrained in most performance contexts. This is because beliefs can lead to action. The prevalence of PST in sport means that cognitive behavioural approaches dominate sport psychology. Rather than focusing on changing the content of cognitions, ACT focuses on making room for – and accepting – these. It might be, at least in our experience, that athletes interpret acceptance as "rolling over" and "listening" to unhelpful thoughts within sport and performance contexts because it can be counterintuitive in performance contexts. At these times, it is important to highlight acceptance sits alongside value-based living.

Let us return to Ruth, the tennis player. Her inability to perform under pressure – often referred to as choking – is likely to be accompanied by a series of physical sensations and cognitions linked to the pressure of serving. Acceptance is about helping Ruth increase her openness to new experiences, including these internal experiences. It can be helpful for Ruth to reflect on her typical reactions to unhelpful thoughts in performance moments and the additional mental load that challenging and changing cognitions can bring, as well as her failed attempts to improve her performance by arguing with herself. Describing this approach as playing tug of war with her brain might encourage Ruth to see her brain as separate from her (and not always on her side). Equally, the passengers on the bus metaphor (see Harris, 2019) with a sporting focus can be helpful in framing discussions of how Ruth can still effectively execute her serve in pressured moments (i.e., driving the bus) even with a series of unhelpful thoughts (i.e., rowdy passengers). This can help Ruth come to see that thoughts can come and go – like trains passing through a station, or clouds passing overhead – without needing any attention (we discuss this further in the self-as-context section). This captures the essence of acceptance and links very closely to cognitive defusion, which we discuss next.

Defusion: Creating Space Between the Athlete and Their Thought(s)

For us, defusion separates ACT from other cognitive behavioural approaches applied to sport. It can be a complex idea to communicate with athletes because athletes might discuss a deep need to change unwanted cognitions. Embracing ACT's use of metaphors, we have come to explain defusion as follows:

> Imagine you're stood in a room with a bubble machine. Bubbles are all around you. Some of these bubbles pop in thin air. Some pop as they land on you. Some catch your attention. Some pass right by you. These bubbles are like your thoughts. Now imagine one of these bubbles lands on your arm. You try and shake it off, but it's stuck. You try and pop it, but it won't pop. You continue trying to go about watching bubbles, perhaps even chasing some, but this bubble stuck to your arm becomes distracting. You continue trying to shake it off, but it won't budge. This is like fusion. Defusion is about learning to continue with the bubble stuck to your arm, rather trying to get rid of it.

Importantly, ACT sees thoughts – pleasant and painful – as natural parts of being human, meaning the content of a thought – or bubble – is not automatically problematic. The focus is on the relationship we have with the thought (Twohig & Levin, 2017). So, a negative thought (e.g., "I'm a failure") is not automatically harmful, but, in ACT terms, it is our entanglement with that thought that causes suffering or maladaptive behaviour (Hayes et al., 2011a). Here, defusion captures this idea of noticing a thought, non-judgementally, and choosing how we respond (Harris, 2019).

Focusing on sport, an athlete might fuse with future-focused cognitions (e.g., "What if I fail?", "What if I do badly?", and "What if I do well?"), with their self-concept (e.g., "What if I'm not good enough?" and "Will I ever be good enough?"), or rules (e.g., pressure giving back to those who supported them). An SPP employing ACT will focus on helping the athlete defuse from performance cognitions that negatively impact their performance. Returning to Ruth and her thought, "I always lose when I serve", let us consider possible defusion exercises. First, the practitioner might encourage Ruth to shift her focus of the thought by increasing the salience of formal properties of each word. For example, Ruth could sing the words "I always lose when I serve" to the tune of happy birthday. Or repeat the words over and over in a silly voice, changing the pitch and tone of the sounds, speed up and slow down the pace of the repetitions, or elongate and/or shorten the sounds of the words. Similarly, Ruth could objectify her thoughts by arbitrarily attributing physical properties to her thought, seeing her thought as a "self-doubt" monster. Finally, Ruth might create distance by spatially and deictically framing thoughts. For example, Ruth could visualise the words of her thought on the tennis ball and then hitting the ball away. Academic evidence is yet to support the idea that this changes a thought's function, but we anecdotally know we respond differently to tragic events unfolding in our town or city versus those occurring on a different continent (Kross & Ayduk, 2017). Third, the SPP can encourage Ruth to see her thoughts as a verbal response from her "thinking self" – or her brain – that are separate to her as an individual and do not dominate her behaviour. This can encourage self-evaluation of Ruth as an untrustworthy thinker (Harris, 2019).

In our experience, given the lack of evidence supporting one approach to defusion over another (Ruiz et al., 2023), it might be best to explain multiple exercises to the athlete and leave them to practice a few to decide which is most effective for them. Doing so, we would advocate embracing the creativity ACT presents to the SPP, rather than seeing this as a daunting prospect. Of course, this becomes even more relevant when working in team sports. Covering a range of defusion exercises allows each team member to decide which approach sits best with them, rather than implementing a one-size-fits-all approach.

One challenge SPPs might encounter is the athlete incorrectly implementing these strategies. For example, the "thanks brain" response, which, in our experience, is perhaps the most popular approach, can see the athlete follow their "thanks brain, that's really helpful" comment with some form of performance-relevant self-talk. This might be motivational, such as "you've got this", or instructional, such as "eyes on the ball". Although this might not create too much of a negative impact, it highlights athletes' (sometimes) relentless need to tell themselves positive comments in attempts to push away unwanted thoughts (i.e., creative hopelessness; Harris, 2019). Here, the SPP should work with the athlete to ensure that if this is the case, these positive self-talk statements do not shift the focus from defusion to cognitive restructuring. We will revisit this point later in the Chapter.

Self-as-Context: Developing the Noticing Self

This encapsulates the idea that thoughts can be observed and can be an incredibly difficult aspect of the hexaflex model to discuss in the (often) fast-paced and diverse delivery environments of sport psychology (Britton et al., 2024). Quite simply, though, using metaphors again, we can discuss this with athletes like clouds passing overhead, or standing on a train platform watching trains come and go. The key is having the athlete deliberately increase their awareness and develop a stable sense of self amid continual change so that they come to realise that there is more to them than their body and mind (Harris, 2019). A useful metaphor here is comparing sporting performances to a stage show performance. Highlighting to the athlete that they can step back and watch the "show", take in the details – either the whole, bigger picture, or zoom in and/or out of specific aspects of the show – choosing where they place their focus, without being distracted by specific performers. More importantly, we can highlight that the play might change – from positive to negative, actors moving around the stage, different positions, different speeds – but the observer remains unchanged. Most of us can relate to the running commentary that plays in our heads. Having the athlete sit quietly, listening to their thoughts for 30 seconds or so, draws attention to their self-talk – highlighting what Harris (2019) terms the "thinking part" – that might change rather rapidly, and a part that listens – what Harris (2019) terms the "noticing part", which is more stable. This links to the broader idea of encouraging the athlete to understand a change in perspective.

Returning to Ruth and her thoughts about always losing when she serves, we can highlight that these thoughts come from Ruth's "thinking athlete". The aim would be to encourage Ruth not to over-identify with these thoughts, seeing that she sometimes fails at her serve, but this does not mean she is a failure as an athlete or as a person. Finally, returning to the concept of flow, we might encourage Ruth to consider how the thinking athlete disrupts her flow state and the negative impact this has on her performance.

Present Moment Awareness in Competitive Environments

It is likely that athletes will discuss instances of inflexible attention. They might recall times they have struggled with interactions with others – talking and listening, but not being fully present and struggling to connect. They might explain times they feel they have "missed out" on experiences, failing to savour or appreciate important and/or enjoyable elements of what they were doing – common when attending major events. Or they may discuss poor performances in training – generally being distracted and unfocused.

In our experience, most people involved with sport – athletes, coaches, parents, and SPPs – are familiar with the concept of achieving flow in sport performances; perhaps best considered as absolute, complete engagement in the here and now. This ability to flexibly notice here-and-now experience and narrow or broaden, sustain or redirect focus, as desired, is captured in the ACT hexaflex model as *contacting with the present moment*. Making links to flow states can be a helpful starting point when discussing this part of the hexaflex model in sport contexts. Having the athlete recall a time where they may have experienced flow, or a high-profile athlete discussing the concept, and the positive advantages this brings to sport performance, can be effective.

Returning to Ruth, it is likely that her unhelpful thoughts around her serve distract her from other parts of her game – that is, that her thoughts distract her from more than her serve. An effective strategy to help Ruth contact with the present moment during training and competition is the dropping anchor exercise (Harris, 2019). This exercise has three steps. First, Ruth is encouraged to acknowledge her thoughts, feelings, emotions, and memories – putting these into words, said silently or out loud – for example, "I'm noticing painful memories" or "I'm having a feeling of anger". Second, Ruth is encouraged to come back to the present moment by focusing on what she has the most control over when difficult thoughts and feelings are present. The SPP might devise a plan where Ruth moves, stretches, changes posture, alters her breathing, or pushes her feet into the ground. The aim here is to help Ruth focus on her physical self before considering physical action. Third, Ruth would be encouraged to engage with the world around her – focusing on her location and what she can see, hear, touch, taste, and smell. The aim here is not to distract her from her thoughts and feelings, but to notice what else is here in addition to them. This strategy can be integrated into pre- and mid-performance routines (Williams et al., 2010). We can highlight here, to Ruth, that when she is looking for control in uncertain situations, the present is the only time she truly has any power. Bringing her attention to this can be powerful for increasing her ability to handle unhelpful thoughts.

Values and Committed Action: Anchoring Performance in Meaning

Many athletes will be familiar with the concept of goal setting. It permeates nearly every aspect of life, because we are by nature a goal-directed species (Turner, 2022). Moving away from sport for a moment, let us take the goal of "travelling to the United States". This is possible. It has an endpoint. Once achieved, it's about thinking "what's next". Equally, several challenges might occur while achieving this goal that risk it not being achieved (Williamson et al., 2024). We are all perhaps familiar with the failures of achieving New Years' resolutions. If goal setting is not carefully managed, some would rather not set goals than set them and fail in pursuing them (Swann et al., 2021).

Values are different from goals. They are like a compass that directs behaviour. Returning to the above example, a value would be something like "travel West". This is possible but also never accomplished. Travelling West (from the United Kingdom) will mean we reach the United States. Yet when this is achieved, there is no "what's next". The focus would continue to be "travelling West". In this sense, compared to goals, values are non-specific and process-focused, more than outcome-focused, which can aid sustainable motivation, especially when faced with challenges and setbacks, which are inevitable in the pursuit of goals (Williamson et al., 2024). Performance environments often talk about controlling what is within your individual sphere of influence. In our experience, athletes positively receive the idea of values because values feel directly within their control – sometimes more so than goals.

Let us return to Ruth. Let us assume that, using a set of value cards, she identifies the value "brave" as important to her. From here, the SPP can encourage Ruth to focus on being brave in that moment when she notices her unhelpful thoughts around her serve, rather than focusing on executing a successful serve. This shift from goals focused on technical skill towards displaying a behaviour in a particular moment can be powerful and interpreted as more within Ruth's control. This approach is also observable and reinforced by coaches. Beyond this, having Ruth consider the tributes she would dream of hearing in her retirement – about her as an athlete and person – is a great exercise for identifying what she thinks is important. How "brave" looks in each moment links to the final part of the ACT hexaflex (see Figure 2.2): committed action. Having Ruth consider the behaviours she can exhibit in training and competition that align with her identified values becomes a focus leading into events, are helpful reminders during performances, and help shape positive performance reviews, tracking progress in line with values.

A Challenge to Applying ACT in Sport

Arguably, the notion of restructuring negative thoughts (e.g., cognitive therapy; Beck, 2011) is more established in applied sport psychology. Consequently, ACT's focus on prioritising workability of thoughts (i.e., "Will focusing on these thoughts take you closer to the athlete you want to be?") and seeing thoughts non-judgementally and less literally (i.e., accepting, rather than changing unhelpful thoughts) appears unusual. ACT's philosophy needs to be clearly communicated to sport organisations and athletes to navigate this difficult "sell". Acceptance can be (mis)interpreted as "rolling over" and "listening" to performance-hindering cognitions. Yet highlighting previous struggles with trying to control emotions (i.e., creative hopelessness) and how the high-pressure environment of sport can risk unhelpful cognitions resurfacing (Hayes et al., 1999) allows exploration of different strategies (i.e., acceptance and defusion).

Exploring Different Modalities for Employing ACT in Applied Sport Psychology

In this section, we aim to highlight how ACT interventions *might* be delivered across typical modalities an SPP might operate: individual consultations, brief and single-session therapy, and educational workshops. We are not prescriptive here, given the inherent flexibility of ACT. To provide context, we relate our examples to the hypothetical scenario of supporting an athlete with performance anxiety.

Individual Consultations

ACT is a flexible, principles-driven approach (Ong et al., 2024), meaning that it can be delivered within a range of professional philosophies, suited to both client-led and practitioner-led approaches to service delivery. It is important to note that there is no "correct" order for ACT interventions, a correct order to explore the ACT hexaflex model, or indeed a need to address all aspects of the hexaflex in equal measure within a single intervention (Wood & Turner, 2025). SPPs employing ACT might continually review treatment goals and complete tasks between sessions (Harris, 2019; Hayes et al., 2004). Below, we outline how ACT *might* be employed in individual consultations, across six sessions, supporting an athlete with performance anxiety.

Session 1

Explore the athlete's performance-hindering cognitions and label these to improve the athlete's ability to notice (and consequently become more aware of) their thoughts. For example, the athlete might be fusing with their self-concept, questioning if they "will ever be good enough".

Session 2

Explore the athlete's values and how these can be demonstrated. Let us assume the athlete values "growth", "curiosity", and "adventurousness". Demonstrating these through committing to, and being brave in, uncomfortable situations might help facilitate a focus on the process – and learning from experiences – more than the outcome of a season or career.

Session 3

Explore the behaviour(s) typically observed when the athlete experiences the cognitions they fuse with (i.e., experiential avoidance).

Sessions 4 and 5

Discuss with the athlete strategies that facilitate acceptance. For example, using the "thanks brain" response to defuse their thought "Will I ever be good enough?" and formal mindfulness activities to connect with the present moment, appreciating that not all thoughts need acting on (i.e., self-as-context).

Session 6

Summarise the work conducted, highlight growth in psychological flexibility, and review key techniques that proved useful. Reinforce values-based direction, discuss obstacles that remain, and co-create a plan for continued application of ACT principles beyond the intervention.

Brief and Single Session Interventions

The fast-paced environments that SPPs often operate require effective and impactful interventions within a single session (Bowman & Turner, 2022). Consequently, the use of brief and single-session CBTs in sport psychology is growing (Britton et al., 2024), with evidence supporting single sessions of ACT (e.g.,

Barreto & Gaynor, 2019). Using the outline provided by Turner (2022), below we present how a 15-minute interaction might look.

First Three Minutes

Build rapport and set an agenda for the session. Successful single-session interventions set realistic and appropriate goals for how the SP can best support the athlete in one session. Rather than squeezing multiple sessions into one, the SP should be selective, focusing support where needed. The ACT matrix might prove useful for structuring discussions (Schwabach et al., 2019).

Middle Ten Minutes

The SPP might choose to focus on thoughts the athlete is fusing with (e.g., "What if I do badly" and "What if I'm not good enough?"). The SPP might encourage the athlete to name their recurrent thoughts (e.g., "here's the 'I'm not good enough story' again"). The SP might then focus on the defusion strategy of "thanks brain". Next, the SP might educate the athlete on the importance of connecting with the present moment by physically moving (e.g., pressing their feet into the floor or stretching), or engaging their senses (e.g., "What can I see and hear?").

Last Two Minutes

Summarise and conclude the work done, referring to the ACT matrix and exercises discussed. As a takeaway, the practitioner might summarise

> You can't stop your mind from saying "What if I fail?" – but you can notice it, name it, and choose where to put your energy next. Each time you do, you're practicing psychological flexibility – the skill that helps you perform with presence and purpose, no matter what your mind is saying.

Workshops

Workshops might be termed Acceptance and Commitment *Training,* given their lack of therapeutic processes (Cihon et al., 2021). Yet ACT is an appropriate acronym (Hayes et al., 2011b), which we continue to use throughout this section. The experiential nature of ACT exercises lend themselves to workshop delivery. Psychoeducation grounded in ACT aims to help athletes understand how psychological flexibility and values-based action can enhance performance and well-being by learning to respond effectively to thoughts and emotions, rather than attempting to control or avoid them. With workshops typically forming a core part of applied sport psychology, we discuss here how an ACT workshop on performance anxiety might look within a sport context.

Starter Activity

Exercises that demonstrate mindfulness (e.g., colouring tasks, sudokus, crosswords, and puzzles) are all friendly ways to introduce the concept of "being present".

Psycho-Educational Element

Have the athletes recall a time they experienced flow in their sport experience(s). Explain the background of ACT, with as little technical language as possible, highlighting the evidence base for the effectiveness of being mindful during sport might be useful (Birrer et al., 2012).

Practical Activity

Formal mindfulness activity to encourage present moment awareness. Of course, as with all group delivery, it can sometimes be challenging to keep the group on task and to ensure that tasks are received by the group as intended.

Summary

Conclude the main points covered to connect practical activities with theory. Ask athletes what they have learned, leaving time for questions and feedback to evaluate if the workshop achieved its intended outcomes.

Conceptual Integration: Delivering ACT with PST

Within a sport psychology setting, PST is well established. We discuss the integration of ACT with PST in more detail elsewhere (see Wood & Turner, 2025) but provide a brief outline here of how each mechanism of the hexaflex model aligns with the different psychological skills. These are summarised in Table 3.1. This is because PST is likely to be familiar to most practitioners new to ACT, and this alignment might offer a friendly introduction to how ACT can be incorporated into sport psychology practice.

First, goal setting (i.e., the aim of action and what an individual is trying to achieve) aligns with the processes of values and committed action (i.e., identifying what is important to the athlete and associated behaviours needed to demonstrate this). Second, self-talk (i.e., a variety of techniques to refute negative consequences of unhelpful cognitions) aligns with defusing from unhelpful self-talk by changing the athlete's relationship with their self-talk, accepting unhelpful self-talk, or encouraging self-as-context so that the athlete observes self-talk nonjudgementally. Imagery (i.e., deliberate mental practice of sport performance) can facilitate defusion by visualising arbitrary physical properties to cognitions, acceptance of "bad" performances, visualising moving on from

Table 3.1 Aligning ACT processes with PST techniques

ACT process	*Related PST*
Values	Goal setting Concentration
Committed action	Goal setting Concentration Imagery
Acceptance	Self-talk Imagery
Defusion	Self-talk Imagery Concentration
Self-as-context	Self-talk Relaxation
Present moment awareness	Relaxation Concentration

errors in performance, and visualising the athlete delivering the performance that aligns with their committed action. Relaxation techniques (i.e., helping athletes maintain optimal arousal levels and manage psychological anxiety) align with ACT mechanisms that help the athlete connect with the present moment through a focus on here-and-now experiences, rather than past or future events (i.e., breathing and mindfulness exercises). Concentration (i.e., focusing attention on the task at hand and limiting the impact of external and internal stimuli) aligns with the notion of defusing from unhelpful cognitions to prevent the athlete becoming distracted by their cognitions, facilitating concentration through formal mindfulness activities to encourage contact with the present moment, and encouraging the athlete to focus on what is important to them in each moment (e.g., the athlete's values) can increase concentration.

Future Directions and Research Agenda

Looking ahead, we outline some key priorities for the field, as we see them. First, there is a need for more high-quality, multi-sport RCTs and replication studies. Second, research exploring the different mechanisms of ACT should focus on which ACT processes drive performance, and whether certain processes are more effective for youth athletes over others – especially, for example, with regard to the different routes to defusion. Third, there is scope to test the integration of ACT with developmental sport frameworks – as conceptually outlined above – as well as how ACT can relate with core psychological theories encountered in sport psychology, such as motivation and confidence. Fourth, there is the potential to explore the technology-based delivery of ACT interventions, for example, using apps or blended learning. Finally, future research should empirically explore cultural and developmental adaptations of ACT with different populations, whether any adaptations are needed, and, if they are, how these look. Overall, more research and applied work needs to be conducted and reported in this space, empirically demonstrating the role of ACT in promoting both performance excellence and athlete well-being. From here, research can begin to explore beyond athletes, exploring the intersection of ACT interventions with coach education and organisational culture.

Conclusion

Performance environments expose individuals to intense, chronic stress (Arnold et al., 2019). As such, SPPs supporting sport performers are likely to be presented with the reality of some stark statistics: athletes are twice as likely than the general population to experience anxiety and depression (Gouttebarge et al., 2019; Souter et al., 2018); eating disorders are common across sports, especially those that emphasise weight, aesthetics, or control (Mancine et al., 2020; Sundgot-Borgen & Torstveit, 2010); addiction – to painkillers, performance enhancers, or performance itself – is common (Rice et al., 2016); post-traumatic stress disorder-like symptoms are evident in athletes who have experienced dissociation (Aron et al., 2019; Aron & LeFay, 2022; Lynch, 2021); and mental ill health is far too common, especially following illness or injury (Lyon-Monk et al., 2025; Timpka et al., 2021).

Given these growing challenges, ACT offers SPPs a different approach to second-wave CBTs when supporting athletes; an approach focused on value-driven action and flexibility, rather than symptom reduction. The aim of this chapter was to highlight the application of ACT to sport. Acceptance is linked to reducing ironic rebound effects (Wegner, 1994) and reinvestment (Baumeister, 1984). Focusing on the present moment can facilitate automatic execution of performance (Gardner & Moore, 2012) and allow for goal-directed adjustments (Birrer et al., 2012). Finally, ACT embraces the idea that discomfort and struggle are part of sporting performance and part of achieving peak performance. Given the extensive evidence base for the effectiveness of ACT – despite the fact that it is still maturing as an approach in sport – we feel that exploring the application of ACT in sport is a worthy endeavour. ACT provides a coherent approach, linking mental health and performance enhancement. Its future in sport lies not in replacing existing methods, but in enriching them – fostering flexible, values-driven athletes and practitioners.

References

Andersen, M. B. (2009). The "canon" of psychological skills training for enhancing performance. In *Performance psychology in action: A casebook for working with athletes, performing artists, business leaders, and professionals in high-risk occupations* (pp. 11–34). American Psychological Association. https://doi.org/10.1037/11876-001

Arnold, R., Edwards, T., & Rees, T. (2019). Organizational stressors, social support, and implications for subjective performance in high-level sport. *Psychology of Sport and Exercise*, *39*, 204–212. https://doi.org/10.1016/j.psychsport.2018.08.010

Aron, C. M., Harvey, S., Hainline, B., Hitchcock, M. E., & Reardon, C. L. (2019). Post-traumatic stress disorder (PTSD) and other trauma-related mental disorders in elite athletes: A narrative review. *British Journal of Sports Medicine*, *53*(12), 779–784. https://doi.org/10.1136/bjsports-2019-100695

Aron, C. M., & LeFay, S. M. (2022). Post-traumatic stress disorder and other trauma-related disorders. In C. L. Reardon (Ed.), *Mental health care for elite athletes* (pp. 69–78). Springer International Publishing. https://doi.org/10.1007/978-3-031-08364-8_8

Assaz, D. A., Tyndall, I., Oshiro, C. K., & Roche, B. (2023). A process-based analysis of cognitive defusion in acceptance and commitment therapy. *Behavior Therapy*, *54*(6), 1020–1035.

Association of Contextual Behavioural Sciences. (n.d.). *State of the ACT evidence*. Retrieved November 05, 2025, from https://contextualscience.org/state_act_evidence

Barreto, M., & Gaynor, S. T. (2019). A single-session of acceptance and commitment therapy for health-related behavior change: Protocol description and initial case examples. *Behavior Analysis: Research and Practice*, *19*(1), 47–59. https://doi.org/10.1037/bar0000093

Baumeister, R. F. (1984). Choking under pressure: Self-consciousness and paradoxical effects of incentives on skillful performance. *Journal of Personality and Social Psychology*, *46*(3), 610–620. https://doi.org/https://psycnet.apa.org/doi/10.1037/0022-3514.46.3.610

Beck, J. S. (2011). *Cognitive behaviour therapy: Basics and beyond* (2nd ed.). Guildford Press.

Birrer, D., Röthlin, P., & Morgan, G. (2012). Mindfulness to enhance athletic performance: Theoretical considerations and possible impact mechanisms. *Mindfulness*, *3*(3), 235–246. https://doi.org/10.1007/s12671-012-0109-2

Blackledge, J. T. (2007). Disrupting verbal processes: Cognitive defusion in acceptance and commitment therapy and other mindfulness-based psychotherapies. *The Psychological Record*, *57*, 555–576.

Bond, F. W., Hayes, S. C., Baer, R. A., Carpenter, K. M., Guenole, N., Orcutt, H. K., . . . & Zettle, R. D. (2011). Preliminary psychometric properties of the Acceptance and Action Questionnaire–II: A revised measure of psychological inflexibility and experiential avoidance. *Behavior therapy*, *42*(4), 676–688.

Bowman, A. W., & Turner, M. J. (2022). When time is of the essence: The use of rational emotive behavior therapy (REBT) informed single-session therapy (SST) to alleviate social and golf-specific anxiety, and improve well-being and performance, in amateur golfers. *Psychology of Sport and Exercise*, *60*, 102167. https://doi.org/10.1016/j.psychsport.2022.102167

Britton, D., Wood, A. G., & Pitt, T. (2024). Having impact and doing it quickly: The place for brief and single-session cognitive-behavioral therapies in sport psychology practice. *The Sport Psychologist*, 1–10. https://doi.org/10.1123/tsp.2021-0146

Cihon, J. H., Ferguson, J. L., Leaf, J. B., Milne, C. M., Leaf, R., & McEachin, J. (2021). Acceptance and commitment training: A review of the research. *European Journal of Behavior Analysis*, *22*(2), 275–295. https://doi.org/10.1080/15021149.2021.1880688

Gardner, F. L., & Moore, Z. E. (2012). Mindfulness and acceptance models in sport psychology: A decade of basic and applied scientific advancements. *Canadian Psychology/Psychologie Canadienne*, *53*(4), 309.

Gardner, F. L., & Moore, Z. E. (2017). Mindfulness-based and acceptance-based interventions in sport and performance contexts. *Current Opinion in Psychology*, *16*, 180–184.

Gouttebarge, V., Castaldelli-Maia, J. M., Gorczynski, P., Hainline, B., Hitchcock, M. E., Kerkhoffs, G. M., Rice, S. M., & Reardon, C. L. (2019). Occurrence of mental health symptoms and disorders in current and former elite athletes: A systematic review and meta-analysis. *British Journal of Sports Medicine*, *53*(11), 700–706. https://doi.org/10.1136/bjsports-2019-100671

Harris, R. (2019). *ACT made simple: An easy-to-read primer on acceptance and commitment therapy* (2nd ed.). New Harbinger Publications.

Hayes, L., Boyd, C. P., & Sewell, J. (2011a). Acceptance and commitment therapy for the treatment of adolescent depression: A pilot study in a psychiatric outpatient setting. *Mindfulness*, *2*(2), 86–94. https://doi.org/10.1007/s12671-011-0046-5

Hayes, S. C., Pistorello, J., & Levin, M. E. (2012a). Acceptance and commitment therapy as a unified model of behavior change. *The Counseling Psychologist*, *40*(7), 976–1002. https://doi.org/10.1177/0011000012460836

Hayes, S. C., Stroshal, K. D., Luoma, J., Smith, A. A., & Wilson, K. G. (2004). ACT case formulation. In S. C. Hayes & K. D. Stroshal (Eds.), *A practical guide to acceptance and commitment therapy*. Springer.

Hayes, S. C., Strosahl, K. D., & Wilson, K. G. (1999). *Acceptance and commitment therapy* (Vol. 6). Guilford Press New York.

Hayes, S. C., Strosahl, K. D., & Wilson, K. G. (2011b). *Acceptance and commitment therapy: The process and practice of mindful change*. Guilford Press.

Hayes, S. C., Stroshal, K. D., & Wilson, K. G. (2012b). *Acceptance and commitment therapy: The process and practice of mindful change* (2nd ed.). Guildford Press.

Kross, E., & Ayduk, O. (2017). Chapter two – Self-distancing: Theory, research, and current directions. In J. M. Olson (Ed.), *Advances in experimental social psychology* (Vol. 55, pp. 81–136). Academic Press. https://doi.org/10.1016/bs.aesp.2016.10.002

Lundgren, T., Reinebo, G., Fröjmark, M. J., Jäder, E., Näslund, M., Svartvadet, P., Samuelsson, U., & Parling, T. (2021). Acceptance and commitment training for ice hockey players: A randomized controlled trial [Original Research]. *Frontiers in Psychology, Volume 12–2021*. https://doi.org/10.3389/fpsyg.2021.685260

Lundgren, T., Reinebo, G., Näslund, M., & Parling, T. (2020). Acceptance and commitment training to promote psychological flexibility in ice hockey performance: A controlled group feasibility study. *Journal of Clinical Sport Psychology*, *14*(2), 170–181. https://doi.org/10.1123/jcsp.2018-0081

Lynch, J. H. (2021). Posttraumatic stress disorder in elite athletes. *Current Sports Medicine Reports*, *20*(12).

Lyon-Monk, O., Arnold, R., Williams, S., Cleave, L. J., Cumming, S., Currie, A., Wass, J., & Moore, L. J. (2025). Understanding the bi-directional relationship between injury and mental ill-health in elite athletes: A six-year, retrospective cohort study. *Journal of Science and Medicine in Sport*. https://doi.org/10.1016/j.jsams.2025.10.002

Mahoney, J., & Hanrahan, S. J. (2011). A brief educational intervention using acceptance and commitment therapy: Four injured athletes' experiences. *Journal of Clinical Sport Psychology*, *5*(3), 252–273.

Mancine, R. P., Gusfa, D. W., Moshrefi, A., & Kennedy, S. F. (2020). Prevalence of disordered eating in athletes categorized by emphasis on leanness and activity type – A systematic review. *Journal of Eating Disorders*, *8*(1), 47. https://doi.org/10.1186/s40337-020-00323-2

Moore, Z. E. (2009). Theoretical and empirical developments of the Mindfulness-Acceptance-Commitment (MAC) approach to performance enhancement. *Journal of Clinical Sport Psychology*, *3*(4), 291–302.

Moore, Z. E., & Gardner, F. L. (2001, October). *Taking applied sport psychology from research to practice: Integrating empirically supported interventions into a self-regulatory model of athletic performance*. Annual Conference of the Association for the Advancement of Applied Sport Psychology, Orlando, Florida.

Noetel, M., Ciarrochi, J., Van Zanden, B., & Lonsdale, C. (2019). Mindfulness and acceptance approaches to sporting performance enhancement: A systematic review. *International Review of Sport and Exercise Psychology*, *12*(1), 139–175. https://doi.org/10.1080/1750984X.2017.1387803

Olusoga, P., & Yousuf, S. (2023). Acceptance and commitment therapy (ACT). In *Applying cognitive behavioural therapeutic approaches in sport* (pp. 26–43). Routledge.

Ong, C. W., Ciarrochi, J., Hofmann, S. G., Karekla, M., & Hayes, S. C. (2024). Through the extended evolutionary meta-model, and what ACT found there: ACT as a process-based therapy. *Journal of Contextual Behavioral Science*, *32*, 100734. https://doi.org/10.1016/j.jcbs.2024.100734

Plumb, J. C., & Vilardaga, R. (2010). Assessing treatment integrity in acceptance and commitment therapy: Strategies and suggestions. *International Journal of Behavioral Consultation and Therapy*, *6*(3), 263–295. https://doi.org/10.1037/h0100912

Price, D., Wagstaff, C. R., & Thelwell, R. C. (2022). "What if I get injured?": An acceptance and commitment therapy approach for fear of injury with a semielite youth snowboarder. *Case Studies in Sport and Exercise Psychology*, *6*(1), 12–20.

Ptáček, M., Lugo, R. G., Steptoe, K., & Sütterlin, S. (2023). Effectiveness of the mindfulness – Acceptance – Commitment approach: A meta-analysis. *International Journal of Sport and Exercise Psychology*, 1–19. https://doi.org/10.1080/1612197X.2023.2180070

Reinebo, G., Jansson-Fröjmark, M., Parling, T., Andersson, G., Lindner, P., & Lundgren, T. (2025). Internet-based acceptance and commitment therapy (I-ACT) for elite ice hockey players: A quasi-experimental multiple-cohort intervention study. *International Journal of Sport and Exercise Psychology*, 1–21.

Rice, S. M., Purcell, R., De Silva, S., Mawren, D., McGorry, P. D., & Parker, A. G. (2016). The mental health of elite athletes: A narrative systematic review. *Sports Medicine*, *46*(9), 1333–1353. https://doi.org/10.1007/s40279-016-0492-2

Ronkainen, H., Lundgren, T., Metsä, G., Ihalainen, J. K., Kalaja, S., Valtonen, M., & Lappalainen, R. (2025). A sport-specific ACT group intervention for promoting athletes' mental well-being: A randomized controlled trial. *Journal of Applied Sport Psychology*, 1–26. https://doi.org/10.1080/10413200.2025.2521267

Ruiz, F. J., Gil-Luciano, B., & Segura-Vargas, M. A. (2023). Cognitive defusion. In M. P. Twohig, M. E. Levin, & J. M. Petersen (Eds.), *The Oxford handbook of acceptance and commitment therapy* (pp. 206–229). Oxford University Press.

Schwabach, J., Bartley, J., & Polk, K. (2019). Sorting it out: A framework for increasing mental flexibility and valued action in athletes using the ACT matrix. *Journal of Sport Psychology in Action*, *10*(4), 208–213.

Souter, G., Lewis, R., & Serrant, L. (2018). Men, mental health and elite sport: A narrative review. *Sports Med Open*, *4*(1), 57. https://doi.org/10.1186/s40798-018-0175-7

Sundgot-Borgen, J., & Torstveit, M. K. (2010). Aspects of disordered eating continuum in elite high-intensity sports. *Scandinavian Journal of Medicine & Science in Sports*, *20*(s2), 112–121. https://doi.org/10.1111/j.1600-0838.2010.01190.x

Swann, C., Rosenbaum, S., Lawrence, A., Vella, S. A., McEwan, D., & Ekkekakis, P. (2021). Updating goal-setting theory in physical activity promotion: A critical conceptual review. *Health Psychology Review*, *15*(1), 34–50. https://doi.org/10.1080/17437199.2019.1706616

Timpka, T., Spreco, A., Dahlstrom, O., Jacobsson, J., Kowalski, J., Bargoria, V., Mountjoy, M., & Svedin, C. G. (2021). Suicidal thoughts (ideation) among elite athletics (track and field) athletes: Associations with sports participation, psychological resourcefulness and having been a victim of sexual and/or physical abuse. *British Journal of Sports Medicine*, *55*(4), 198–205. https://doi.org/10.1136/bjsports-2019-101386

Tod, D., & Eubank, M. (2020). *Applied sport, exercise, and performance psychology: Current approaches to helping clients*. Routledge.

Turner, M., Jones, M., & Wood, A. (2023). *Applying cognitive behavioural therapeutic approaches in sport*. Taylor & Francis.

Turner, M. J. (2022). *The rational practitioner: The sport and performance psychologist's guide to practicing rational emotive behaviour therapy*. Routledge.

Twohig, M. P., & Levin, M. E. (2017). Acceptance and commitment therapy as a treatment for anxiety and depression: A review. *Psychiatric Clinics*, *40*(4), 751–770.

Vilardaga, R., & Hayes, S. C. (2010). Acceptance and commitment therapy and the therapeutic relationship stance. *European Psychotherapy*, *9*, 117–139.

Walser, R. D., & O'Connell, M. (2021). Acceptance and commitment therapy and the therapeutic relationship: Rupture and repair. *Journal of Clinical Psychology*, *77*(2), 429–440. https://doi.org/10.1002/jclp.23114

Watson, D. R., Hill, A. P., Madigan, D. J., & Donachie, T. (2023). Effectiveness of an online acceptance and commitment therapy programme for perfectionism in soccer players. *Sport, Exercise, and Performance Psychology*, Advance online publication. https://doi.org/ 10.1037/spy0000333

Wegner, D. M. (1994). Ironic processes of mental control. *Psychological Review*, *101*(1), 34.

Williams, J. M., Nideffer, R. M., Wilson, V. E., Sagal, M.-S., & Peper, E. (2010). Concentration and strategies for controlling it. In J. M. Williams (Ed.), *Applied sport psychology: Personal growth to peak performance* (6th ed., pp. 336–358). McGraw-Hill.

Williamson, O., Swann, C., Bennett, K. J. M., Bird, M. D., Goddard, S. G., Schweickle, M. J., & Jackman, P. C. (2024). The performance and psychological effects of goal setting in sport: A systematic review and meta-analysis. *International Review of Sport and Exercise Psychology*, *17*(2), 1050–1078. https://doi.org/10.1080/1750984X.2022.2116723

Wood, S., & Turner, M. J. (2023). Using an acceptance and commitment therapy approach for fear of (re)injury with a competitive figure skater. *Case Studies in Sport and Exercise Psychology*, *7*(1), 150–157. https://doi.org/10.1123/cssep.2023-0033

Wood, S., & Turner, M. J. (2025). Using acceptance and commitment therapy with athletes. *Scandinavian Journal of Sport and Exercise Psychology*, *7*, 1–9. https://doi.org/ 10.7146/sjsep.v7i.150889

4 Bringing ACT to Life

Six Techniques for Enhancing Psychological Flexibility in Sport and Performance Contexts

David Price and Alban Dickson

Learning Objectives

1. Gain an awareness of creative hopelessness and metaphors when using ACT in sport and performance contexts
2. Develop an understanding of how to use the ACT matrix to conceptualise a client's "stuckness" and six techniques for enhancing psychological flexibility when working with individuals and teams in sport and performance contexts
3. Critically reflect on the utility of ACT in sport and performance contexts through applied practice reflections

Introduction

Intervention techniques are a salient feature in the service delivery of sport, exercise, and performance psychology professionals (SEPPPs) (Keegan, 2016). Typically grounded in a therapeutic approach, SEPPPs may employ a broad array of intervention techniques. One therapeutic approach that has gained popularity in sport and performance contexts is ACT (Hayes et al., 2012). ACT is referred to as a third-wave CBT approach derived from the contextual behavioural sciences, which is founded on the philosophical worldview of functional contextualism and the theoretical framework of RFT (see Chapter 2). The aim of ACT is to promote psychological flexibility, which is defined as "the ability to contact the present moment more fully as a conscious human being, and to change or persist in behaviour when doing so serves valued ends" (Hayes et al., 2006, p. 7). To increase psychological flexibility, SEPPPs implement intervention techniques that target the six core processes of the hexaflex model, namely, acceptance, cognitive defusion, self-as-context, contact with the present moment, values, and committed action (see Chapter 1).

Despite the growing number of publications in recent years concerning the application of ACT in sport and performance contexts (Watson et al., 2024; Wood & Turner, 2025), SEPPPs are required to carefully tailor interventions to suit the clients they work with (e.g., athlete, coach, and organisation), the context

DOI: 10.4324/9781003515203-5

they operate in (e.g., sport, military, and healthcare), developmental stage (e.g., age), and cultural background (e.g., Western vs. Eastern traditions). Notably, ACT practitioners draw on experiential exercises and metaphors to *bring to life* the core tenets of ACT and promote psychological flexibility. In the preceding chapter, we aim to first provide a brief background of creative hopelessness and metaphors, before outlining how the ACT matrix can be a useful starting point to conceptualise a client's "stuckness" through a fictitious case study example. We will then offer techniques from our practice that target the six core processes of the hexaflex model when working with individuals and teams in sport and performance contexts. We conclude the chapter with reflections from our experiences as ACT practitioners and offer future research recommendations.

Overview of ACT Interventions

ACT interventions are understood to contribute to sporting performance by targeting the interplay of attention, cognition, and emotions (Noetel et al., 2019). In recent times, such programmes have been implemented across multiple sporting contexts, ranging from Olympic athletes to professional sports teams (see Henriksen et al., 2019). To enhance the performance of individuals and teams, SEPPPs may draw on creative hopelessness techniques and metaphors as mechanisms for reducing a client's "stuckness" and promoting psychological flexibility.

Creative Hopelessness

One technique used early on with clients is creative hopelessness, which is defined as the process of validating a client's experience of being caught in a struggle with their own thoughts and feelings, helping them recognise the futility of this, and setting the stage for creatively identifying more workable ways forward (Luoma et al., 2007). Put differently, creative hopelessness aims to illuminate the workability of current techniques to control their internal states and the short-term gains versus the long-term costs of engaging in such actions. To illustrate further, previous research by Ruiz and Luciano (2012) with international-level chess players found that promoting creative hopelessness in the context of valued action appeared to provide the foundations in which acceptance and cognitive defusion techniques could be implemented to enhance performance. Therein, creative hopelessness techniques are critical in the early stages when using ACT that enable the exploration of core processes to promote psychological flexibility.

The Role of Metaphor

Metaphors in therapeutic settings may help an individual by validating their experiences, conducting functional analysis, and enhancing awareness through observational distance (Foody et al., 2014). With metaphors commonplace in everyday language, cognitive fusion through literalisation can be addressed by this same linguistic technique (Törneke, 2017). An effective metaphor will serve as a representation of a person's situation, providing a safe environment for exploration in which understanding may be gained and solutions identified (Törneke, 2017). It may translate an abstract experience – where a person may feel "stuck" – into a more concrete and therefore workable form (Villatte et al., 2014). Metaphors can be particularly useful for SEPPPs working in sport settings by transferring experiences from one domain into another, which may liberate an individual's thinking from the parameters of their training and competition context. Further, experiential metaphors can be deployed which may translate well into the physical world many athletes and sportspeople are already more familiar and comfortable with (Villatte et al., 2014).

To deploy metaphors in therapeutic settings, a target concept must be functionally reflected in a source (Villatte et al., 2014). These two elements must share corresponding features and be relevant to the individual, thus transferring the experience from one domain into a comparable other (Törneke, 2017). A metaphor could be caught in conversation, or carefully constructed through collaboration between an individual and their practitioner. Co-creation of a metaphor may help illustrate a predicament, and also permits opportunities for cultural translation into a way that makes it relatable to the individual (Masuda et al., 2023; Villatte et al., 2014). Especially when co-created, metaphors offer a memorable method of engagement with sport psychology (Törneke, 2017). Nevertheless, it is important to be cognizant that metaphors are contextualised to sport and performance domains to ensure they are relatable and thus more impactful. For example, the "passengers on the bus" exercise is a well-known metaphor; however, its application to a sporting context might be futile. Instead, contextualising the metaphor to the client's sporting domain might help translate the underpinning meaning conveyed by the metaphor (see self-as-context). An illustration of this could apply to the sport of rowing. An athlete may be familiar with listening to a coxswain whose role is to shape the navigation of the boat or guide the team towards their objectives. However, the same athlete could be situated beside another rower who continually expresses pessimism, doubt, and complaints of fatigue. In such a case, the athlete may notice the two contrasting voices but decide to align their actions to the more helpful source – the coxswain – thereby demonstrating defusion. By adapting the "passengers on the bus" metaphor to a more familiar context, the principles of ACT may become clearer to an athlete.

The ACT Matrix in Sport and Performance Contexts

When working with individuals and teams, a useful starting point is to conceptualise their "stuckness" and use creative hopelessness techniques to identify their unworkable behaviours. The ACT matrix (Polk & Schoendorff, 2014), also referred to as the point-of-view exercise, is an effective framework that provides a visual representation of the client's actions and internal experiences. Given the widespread use of the ACT matrix within a range of contexts, there has also been increasing support for its use within sport and performance domains (Gutman & Gottlieb, 2024; Price et al., 2022b). To demonstrate its utility in sport and performance contexts, we provide a fictitious case when using the ACT matrix with individuals. Nevertheless, it should be highlighted that although we present an illustration of using the ACT matrix with individuals, it can be used when working with teams.

ACT Matrix Case Study Example

Melissa is a 100-m sprinter who competes internationally and holds ambitions of medalling at the upcoming Olympic Games. Informal conversations with Melissa indicate that she is struggling with performance anxiety, evidenced through intense somatic anxiety (i.e., increased heart rate and muscle tension) and cognitive anxiety (i.e., "What if I don't get a good start off the blocks" and "I don't want to let my coaches and family down") symptoms. Melissa reports that her previous attempts to control these symptoms (e.g., reframing the thoughts positively, feigning injury, and withdrawing from the event) are ineffective and only reduce the symptoms temporarily. Instead, these symptoms frequently return and intensify, leading to a recent performance slump. As a result of Melissa's attempts to control her performance anxiety, she experiences meta-cognitions (e.g., "If I can't control this anxiety my career is over") and meta-emotions (e.g., frustrated about being anxious), exacerbating her "stuckness". The ACT matrix can serve as a useful technique to visually represent Melissa's "stuckness" and provide the foundations to implement ACT techniques that aim to promote psychological flexibility, subsequently enhance her performance, and achieve her aspirations.

Step 1 – Introducing the ACT Matrix

When working with a client, whether that be an individual or a team, a useful starting point is to introduce the ACT matrix and explain its purpose. Here, it is important to clarify that the ACT matrix represents their point of view and does not claim to be the right point of view or the only point of view. Once the purpose of the ACT matrix has been clarified, the SEPPP draws a vertical line, writing "five-sense experiencing" at the top and "mental experiencing" at the bottom. To discriminate between the two experiences, the practitioner invites the client to engage in an experiential exercise called the "pen exercise".

While the "pen exercise" is a popular method, we advocate that SEPPPs contextualise the exercise to suit the client. In the context of this case, a SEPPP could replace the pen with a running shoe to make this more applicable to Melissa.

Next, the client is invited to experience the object through their five senses (i.e., see, hear, taste, touch, and smell), although some senses (i.e., taste) might not be appropriate depending on the object used. The client is then asked to put the object aside and mentally experience the object using their five senses. This provides the opportunity for the SEPPP to now pose the question "Do you notice a difference between the two experiences?" to discriminate between "five-sense experiencing" and "mental experiencing".

The next step involves drawing a horizontal line bisecting the vertical line and writing "away" on the left-hand side and "towards" on the right-hand side". The SEPPP now asks "Can you recall a time when you moved towards something that was important to you?" and "Can you recall a time when you moved away from something that showed up internally that was uncomfortable?" to clarify towards and away moves. On completion of these exercises, the client and SEPPP can now work through the ACT matrix.

Step 2 – Values Identification

In keeping with the underlying principles of ACT, the matrix offers clients flexibility with which quadrant they want to start with (Bennett & Lindsay, 2016). For the purpose of this illustration, we will start in the bottom right-hand quadrant, which is a common starting place. The bottom right-hand quadrant represents values with the purpose of eliciting the important values that a client holds. A useful question to stimulate reflection regarding one's values is for the SEPPP to ask the client, "who and what matters to you?" Subsequently, values can be explored further by engaging in a discussion about their values, asking questions such as "why is dedication a value for you?" or "what does dedication as a value mean to you?"

Relating to the case, the SEPPP working with Melissa may encourage her to reflect on sporting and non-sporting experiences to elicit the values she holds. It is important to state that values are freely chosen, and therefore, the SEPPP should not imply that there is a right or wrong value to hold. When posed the question "who is important to you?", Melissa may respond with "partner" or her "coach". A follow-up question from the SEPPP on "what is important to you?" might reveal an underlying value of "courage" or "determination". Through further reflection and discussion, values can be clarified in what they mean to Melissa and how they would show up in her sport.

Step 3 – Cognitive Fusion

Once values have been elicited, the client can transition to the bottom left-hand quadrant, which represents cognitive fusion. The mnemonic "TIMES", which stands for thoughts, images, memories, emotions, and sensations, can be helpful when reflecting on the internal states a client is cognitively fused with. A

SEPPP may ask a client, "what stuff shows up and gets in the way of you engaging in your sport?" Within the case, Melissa highlighted how she experiences intense cognitive and somatic anxiety symptoms prior to competition as well as meta-cognitions and meta-emotions following ineffective attempts to control her performance anxiety. Through exploring the uncomfortable internal states Melissa experiences, we can begin to see the away moves taken which cause her to deviate from the athlete and person she wants to be.

Step 4 – Experiential Avoidance

Now, we have gained an understanding of the internal states the client fuses with, SEPPPs can explore the top two quadrants which represent observable behaviours. The next step would be to move to the top left-hand quadrant, known as experiential avoidance. Here, the SEPPP aims to explore the unworkable behaviours the client engages in to control their internal states that result in moving away from the athlete or person they want to be. As noted earlier, creative hopelessness techniques are used to assess the workability of their behaviours (e.g., "how is this behaviour working for you?") in relation to the short-term gains (i.e., symptom reduction) and long-term costs (i.e., missing out on competing at an international event). SEPPPs could pose the question "What can we see you do when this stuff shows up?" or "When anxiety is in the driving seat, what might I see you do?" Again, the metaphor of internal states being in the driving seat could be contextualised to sport to help resonate with the client (e.g., "when anxiety is calling the plays, what might I see you do?").

Step 5 – Committed Action

Now, three of the four quadrants have been explored; we can begin to orientate to the final quadrant, which is in the top right-hand corner and represents committed action. The purpose here is to identify the value-driven behaviours that one can engage in, despite the presence of unwanted internal states. The SEPPP may pose the question "What could/can we see you doing when you are moving towards what's important to you?" or "When your values are in the driving seat, what might I see you do that lead you towards who and what is important to you?" In the context of Melissa, she may respond to the above questions by saying that a value-driven behaviour would be focusing on her pre-race routines, discussing strategies with her coach, and giving everything she has to the race despite the uncomfortable stuff that shows up.

Step 6 – Relational Framing and Noticing

Once all quadrants are completed, the SEPPP can draw relational frames between quadrants. While it is beyond the scope of the book chapter to discuss the different types of relational frames, we direct interested readers to the work of Hayes et al. (2001) for a full overview. To provide an example, a frame of coordination can be created between cognitive fusion and values by asking the question, "What would you have to not care about, to never experience this discomfort?" or "If suffering were the mere cost of valuing, would you still pay that cost to continue valuing?" In the aforementioned case example, SEPPP may pose these questions when discussing the performance anxiety symptoms Melissa experiences to draw a frame of coordination between her symptoms and the value of dedication. This would serve to highlight that her symptoms are a result of holding the value of dedication, and in order to hold the value of dedication, then these symptoms will show up. In other words, the SEPPP is trying to demonstrate that the two are inextricably linked.

To conclude the ACT matrix, the SEPPP can ask the client, "who is the one person who notices all that is going on?" to target the core process of self-as-context. The client is the only one who can choose values and how they respond or notice the internal states that show up in a given situation. Although the ACT matrix is now complete (see Figure 4.1), clients can continually return to, update, or even complete a new matrix for a different context. What follows in the preceding section are six techniques for individuals and teams that can be employed by SEPPPs to increase psychological flexibility.

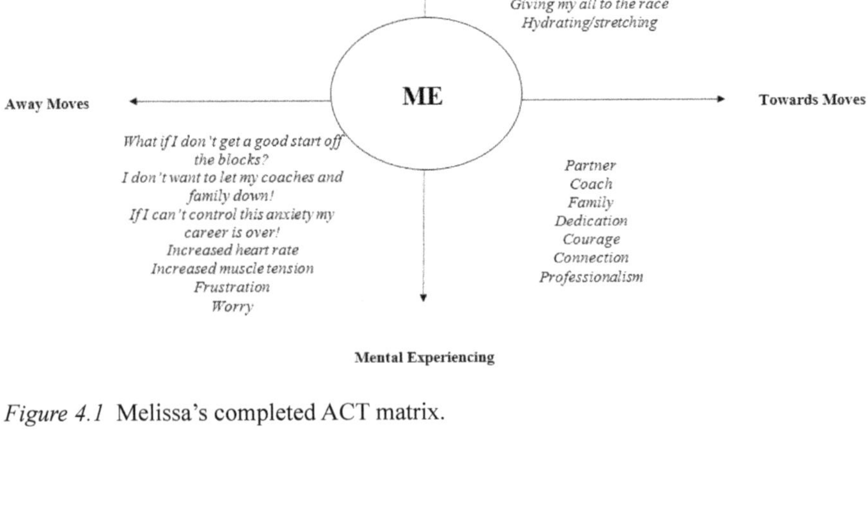

Figure 4.1 Melissa's completed ACT matrix.

Six Techniques for Enhancing Psychological Flexibility in Sport and Performance

Before outlining six techniques that we employ when working with individuals and teams in sport and performance contexts to enhance psychological flexibility, it is important to highlight that we do not believe these to be the only ACT techniques available. Instead, we encourage readers to be curious about the full spectrum of creative techniques SEPPPs can employ within their own practice. As illustrated in the following, ACT offers opportunities for adaptation to the context of sport and performance settings. Practitioners should consider careful yet creative adjustments that may bring a metaphor or experiential activity to life by translating its principles into the world of their client. We would also like to draw attention to the reader that while we present these techniques independently, they are often used in collaboration to target multiple processes of the hexaflex model.

Acceptance

Often, when people hear the term "acceptance", there are negative connotations associated, such as giving in or waving a white flag. In the context of ACT, the term refers to opening up to one's own internal experiences, even if that means they are unpleasant, to move towards valued actions (Bennett & Oliver, 2019). According to evolutionary psychology, humans have a default response to problem-solve when encountered with a difficult experience, which, in some cases, can lead to unworkable behaviours and be the root cause of their "stuckness" (Hayes et al., 2012). In contrast, acceptance represents a paradoxical approach that encourages individuals to step into their discomfort in the service of what matters.

One common technique that represents acceptance is the finger trap exercise, which can be used with individuals and teams. Simply put, the finger trap represents our internal states (e.g., performance anxiety) and acts as a metaphor and experiential exercise for acceptance by highlighting the dominant control agenda. First, the client is invited to insert both their index fingers at either end of the finger trap and notice the automatic reaction (i.e., pull away) when the trap tightens. Relational frames are then drawn between the discomfort felt when the finger trap tightens and the discomfort felt in their lives. The client is then encouraged to try a counterintuitive approach of acceptance (i.e., push in) and notice the difference between opening up to discomfort and their dominating need to control their internal states. Within a sporting context, an athlete could keep the finger trap in their kit bag as a reminder of accepting the internal states they are experiencing prior to competition.

Cognitive Defusion

Cognitive defusion techniques aim to alter the way a person relates to undesirable functions of thoughts and other internal events, rather than trying to alter their form, frequency, or situational sensitivity (Hayes et al., 2006). In other words, cognitive defusion may help to decrease the believability of, or attachment to, internal events (Hayes & Plumb, 2007). The "I notice I am having the thought . . ." exercise is useful for targeting cognitive defusion by creating psychological distance from their thoughts (Hayes et al., 2006). For example, if a client was fused with the thought "What if I make a mistake", the client would be invited to label the process of their thinking by first adding "I am having the thought, what if I make a mistake". Second, the athlete could be encouraged to add, "I notice, I am having the thought, what if I make a mistake", to create even more separation from their thoughts. By increasing the layers of verbal context around each thought, clients report becoming more detached from their thoughts and reduce the literal believability of the thought (Bennett & Oliver, 2019).

Another experiential exercise to illustrate defusion involves physicalising the source of cognitive fusion. This exercise can work well in a team setting – using a volunteer – yet equally be demonstrated in an individual session. The athlete is asked to simply walk from one spot to another, usually across the room (and potentially in front of their peers). After a successful first attempt, the volunteer walks again, but this time, the SEPPP places a chair in front of them to block their path. If the athlete stops, the SEPPP highlights this as a consequence of fusion; the unwanted experience has delayed or prevented them from moving forwards. If the athlete navigates around the chair, they have shown cognitive defusion. These options can then be explored and discussed. It is also worth highlighting or demonstrating that pretending the chair is not there will also hinder their journey, therefore illustrating how acceptance of the obstacle is important.

Contact with the Present Moment

Contact with the present moment is often used synonymously with being in the here and now, being present, or flexible attention and is a core process of the hexaflex model that forms as part of the aware pillar. Specifically, contact with the present moment is defined as mindful focus on the here and now, as opposed to being pulled into the conceptualised past or worrying about what will happen in the future, thus allowing an individual to appreciate the full range of choices in front of them (Olusoga & Yousuf, 2023, p. 28). Although there is a broad array of techniques that target contact with the present moment, mindfulness is one technique that has grown exponentially in sport and performance contexts over the last few decades (Gardner & Moore, 2017).

When working with an individual client, a SEPPP may wish to introduce an informal mindfulness exercise to promote contact with the present moment, known as the focus circle exercise. Previously employed by Team Denmark (Hansen & Haberl, 2019), the focus circle exercise aims to increase the client's awareness of their attention (i.e., present, past, or future) and whether they adopt a judgemental or non-judgemental stance to their attention. To illustrate, clients would be invited to register, label, and categorise their thoughts and attention using a colour-coded system. The client has autonomy over what these colours represent with distinctions being made between a non-judgemental awareness in the present moment versus a judgemental awareness in the past or future (Price et al., 2022b). For example, focusing on the task at hand might be labelled as green to indicate laser focus, whereas comparing performances to opponents might be labelled as red to indicate a judgemental awareness. The focus circles can act as a check-in for clients to determine where their focus and attention is, providing them an opportunity to refocus on the present moment (see Figure 4.2).

Similarly, informal mindfulness can be implemented when working with a team. The warm-up prior to training or competitions can serve as an opportune moment to embed informal mindfulness by engaging in multidisciplinary practice. Specifically, as a SEPPP, you could work with and through a strength and conditioning coach to deliver informal mindfulness whereby the clients are encouraged to notice the stretching of their muscles when performing an exercise. For example, when performing a hamstring stretch, the strength and conditioning coach could encourage the soccer team to direct their focus inwardly in a non-judgemental and curious manner, paying specific attention to the feel of the muscles contracting and relaxing throughout the stretch.

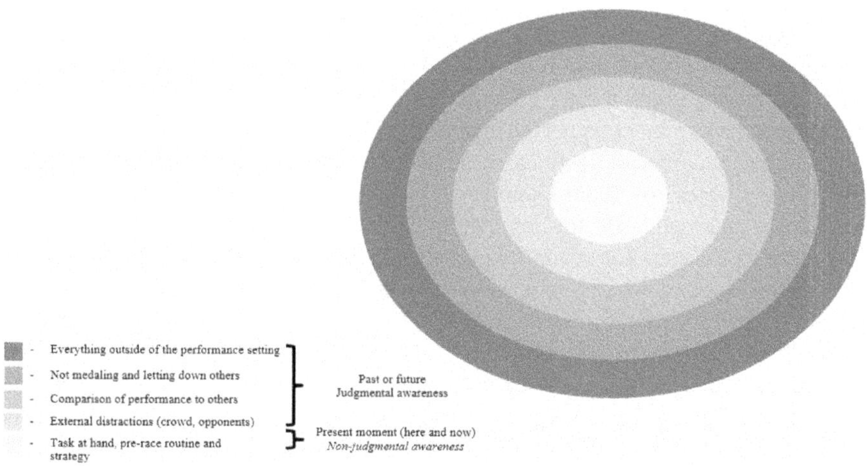

Figure 4.2 Melissa's focus circle example.

Self-As-Context

Self-As-Context guides a person to adopt the stance of the observing self, who may notice what they are experiencing (White et al., 2021). Traditional methods advocate for the use of metaphors to explain Self-As-Context, describing a chessboard, stage show, or even leaves on a stream (Harris, 2019; Hegarty & Huelsmann, 2020). These principles are important for facilitating defusion and awareness, though they may not resonate so well with athletes. An alternative depiction adopts the venue of an athlete's sport: a tennis court, swimming pool, football pitch, and so forth. The metaphor is established by describing the setting, which could even be enhanced by asking the athlete to identify any particular sights, sounds, or smells they would associate. The scene is then set to introduce the occasion of a difficult match. The athlete is guided to imagine looking at the venue, hearing the crowd noises, and seeing the competition occurring in front of them. Shaping a vivid experience for the athlete is helpful at this point, with the opportunity to portray a narrative of a gruelling contest.

When the situation is described at its most vibrant, the SEPPP then suggests the contest concluding; competitors and attendees leave, lights go out, and the venue is reset. The athlete is questioned with "what happens next"? The SEPPP then guides the athlete to consider how, even after the most challenging of events, the venue itself remains constant. It simply hosts the sport. The players who take to the metaphorical field can be equated to the experiences (thoughts, feelings, images, and memories) which come – but ultimately go – in our sporting pursuits. Here, the mind is related to the venue, and the athlete is encouraged to observe how the activity they bear witness to does not itself or alter its host.

Values

Understanding what is important to a person, and the free choice they have in articulating this, offers a strong foundation of ACT in practice, upon which later developments can be constructed (Harris, 2019). An excellent illustration of the central role occupied by values in a sport context can be found in the Sport Psychology Model of Team Denmark (Diment et al., 2020). Values and "how I want to be as an athlete" are depicted as an integral element of mental strength and serve as a means for grounding when difficult experiences are encountered.

To elicit values, an athlete is invited to imagine themselves in the future, in receipt of commendations from their sport governing body, club, or federation in celebration of their achievements. Should this seem too distal, a localised alternative could be the end-of-season "Player of the Year" awards night. As may be common at such events, the athlete is invited to imagine their favourite peers, family, and coaches describe them as a person. It is emphasised that the athlete should pick out what they would wish these important people to say, not predict what they might say (Hegarty & Huelsmann, 2020). As the athlete reflects on example words they would wish to hear (common examples may include "hard-working", "determination", or "caring"), the SEPPP can probe further, asking for definitions, examples, or alternative words. Once a small set has been captured, the SEPPP may enquire as to how universal these pursuits are and explore how these may be values that the athlete feels represent them at their very best.

Committed Action

The concept of goal-setting is familiar in sporting and performance contexts (Locke & Latham, 1985; Williamson et al., 2025). Often encapsulated in athletic development plans or presented as a fundamental psychological skill, the notion of setting specific, achievement, targets that are within our control has a long history in sport psychology (Swann et al., 2023; Williamson et al., 2025). Committed action might be thought of as goal setting in the ACT lexicon. It is important to distinguish this, as committed action should reflect values, and may therefore be more nuanced than setting process, performance, or outcome goals. Committed action has been described as the patterns of behaviours that demonstrate an individual's values (Berger et al., 2021). Goals may be checkpoints as an individual pursues their personal values, rather than as destinations in which their values must guide them towards (Chase et al., 2013). This distinction between values and goals could be illustrated to an athlete using a hypothetical question: if winning a game is your goal, would you be willing to cheat if your values included integrity or honesty?

Athletes could be introduced to this interpretation through a graphical illustration of drawing a simple golf hole on a sheet of paper. The "pin" should represent a chosen value (not a goal per se), with various "strokes" depicting examples of tangible steps – committed actions – that allow the golfer to get closer to the green. This could include actions taken should the ball land off the fairway or in a sand trap. For example, an athlete could be aspiring towards their value of "leadership" in their sport. Their drive off the tee could represent "embracing opportunities to be vocal and commanding", their bunker shot could represent dealing with a setback such as being dropped; "always driving standards in training", their fairway shot could be "seeking feedback from coaches to improve this quality", and so on. Critically, every stroke – whether a long drive or a short chip – is highlighted as taking them closer to the green.

Reflections

Throughout our practice, we have regularly drawn on ACT when working with individuals and clients to optimise performance and well-being in sport and performance contexts. In the following, we share two salient reflections to shed light on the realities of using ACT techniques in the world of sport.

Performance Environments Perpetuating a Control Agenda

Sport and performance environments are highly demanding, with it being socially inferred that to be successful, one must control their internal states. This narrative perpetuates a dominant control agenda, thus making it challenging to implement the underlying principles of ACT. In our applied experience, we have found that using creative hopelessness techniques and devoting significant time to exploring the unworkability of their behaviours is critical to challenging the dominant control agenda. Further, operating at a systems level to challenge the dominant control agenda and educate key stakeholders in the system regarding ACT principles is an effective method of working alongside individual- and team-level work.

Using ACT Online: Opportunities and Considerations

The way in which SEPPPs operate is constantly evolving with an increasing movement towards working online due to the geographically dispersed nature of clients, for example, clients competing at international events or supporting a client when not attending a training camp (Price et al., 2022a). Further, given the pressing need for engaging in more sustainable practices, working online could be a more carbon-friendly alternative to traditional in-person service delivery methods. Therein, working online presents numerous opportunities when implementing ACT techniques. Specifically, drawing on creative functions that online platforms offer, such as the whiteboard function, has enabled us to collaborate with our clients when working through the ACT matrix. Further, working online has provided the opportunity to be creative when using visuals and different media to engage clients, particularly youth athletes (Price et al., 2022b). Yet working online has provided its challenges, and we have learnt to be cognizant of the need to assess the client's technological literacy and accessibility to online platforms. Therefore, we contend that working online should be viewed as an adjunct to in-person delivery, not as an alternative.

Future Research Directions

Despite a growing body of evidence on ACT in sport, the majority are applied practice case studies, with only a few experimental studies existing. Nevertheless, in a recent systematic review, Noetel et al. (2019) rated the current evidence base as low quality, meaning that caution must be exercised when interpreting the data. To advance the evidence base on ACT in sport and performance contexts, we encourage scholars to conduct high-quality research using randomised control trials to assess the effectiveness and efficacy of ACT techniques. We do, however, appreciate the logistical challenges of conducting this type of research and, therefore, call for robust longitudinal single-case experimental designs that enable the effectiveness of ACT interventions to be tracked over a period of time. Given the growing popularity of diverse methodologies, scholars should also consider using participatory action research as a way of actively involving participants throughout the whole research design process to ensure that ACT metaphors and techniques are culturally sensitive and relevant. Finally, ACT research in sport and performance contexts would benefit from research being conducted across levels (e.g., recreation vs. elite), developmental stages (e.g., youth vs. adult), and cross-culturally (e.g., Eastern and Western populations).

Conclusion

ACT continues to be a popular therapeutic approach adopted by SEPPPs in sport and performance contexts. Underpinned by the hexaflex model, ACT techniques are employed to promote psychological flexibility and enhance performance and well-being when working with individuals and teams. To date, there exists a plethora of ACT techniques for SEPPPs to draw on, namely, creative hopelessness, experiential exercises, and metaphors. Further, the ACT matrix can be a useful technique to conceptualise a client's "stuckness" and provide the foundations in which SEPPPs can draw on a range of creative ACT techniques. Despite ACT's popularity in sport and performance contexts, there are a number of challenges and opportunities for SEPPPs when implementing such techniques. To advance the evidence base further, SEPPPs are encouraged to share case studies to illuminate the realities of using ACT and conduct high-quality research to address the current shortcomings.

References

Bennett, J., & Lindsay, P. (2016). Case Study 3: An acceptance commitment and mindfulness based intervention for a female hockey player experiencing post injury performance anxiety. *Sport & Exercise Psychology Review*, *12*, 36–45.

Bennett, R., & Oliver, J. E. (2019). *Acceptance and commitment therapy: 100 key points and techniques*. Routledge.

Berger, E., Garcia, Y., Catagnus, R., & Temple, J. (2021). The effect of acceptance and commitment training on improving physical activity during the COVID-19 pandemic. *Journal of Contextual Behavioral Science*, *20*, 70–78. https://doi.org/10.1016/j.jcbs.2021.02.005

Chase, J. A., Houmanfar, R., Hayes, S. C., Ward, T. A., Vilardaga, J. P., & Follette, V. (2013). Values are not just goals: Online ACT-based values training adds to goal setting in improving undergraduate college student performance. *Journal of Contextual Behavioral Science*, *2*(3), 79–84. https://doi.org/10.1016/j.jcbs.2013.08.002

Diment, G., Henriksen, K., & Larsen, C. H. (2020). Team Denmark's sport psychology professional philosophy 2.0. *Scandinavian Journal of Sport and Exercise Psychology*, *2*, 16–32. https://doi.org/10.7146/sjsep.v2i0.115660

Foody, M., Barnes-Holmes, Y., Barnes-Holmes, D., Törneke, N., Luciano, C., Stewart, I., & McEnteggart, C. (2014). RFT for clinical use: The example of metaphor. *Journal of Contextual Behavioral Science*, *3*(4), 305–313.

Gardner, F. L., & Moore, Z. E. (2017). Mindfulness-based and acceptance-based interventions in sport and performance contexts. *Current Opinion in Psychology, 16*, 180–184. https://doi.org/10.1016/j.copsyc.2017.06.001

Gutman, T., & Gottlieb, A. (2024). Performance mindfulness: Integrating ACT matrix, imagery and mindfulness for performance enhancement. *Journal of Sport Psychology in Action*, 1–17. https://doi.org/10.1080/21520704.2024.2422820

Hansen, J., & Haberl, P. (2019). Helping athletes be present when performing under pressure. In K. Henriksen, J. Hansen, & C. H. Larsen (Eds.), *Mindfulness and acceptance in sport: How to help athletes perform and thrive under pressure* (pp. 47–58). Routledge.

Harris, R. (2019). *ACT made simple: An easy-to-read primer on acceptance and commitment therapy* (2nd ed.). New Harbinger Publications.

Hayes, S. C., Barnes-Holmes, D., & Roche, B. (Eds.). (2001). *Relational frame theory: A post-Skinnerian account of human language and cognition*. Springer Science & Business Media.

Hayes, S. C., Luoma, J. B., Bond, F. W., Masuda, A., & Lillis, J. (2006). Acceptance and commitment therapy: Model, processes and outcomes. *Behaviour Research and Therapy, 44*(1), 1–25. https://doi.org/10.1016/j.brat.2005.06.006

Hayes, S. C., & Plumb, J. C. (2007). Mindfulness from the bottom up: Providing an inductive framework for understanding mindfulness processes and their application to human suffering. *Psychological Inquiry, 18*(4), 242–248. https://doi.org/10.1080/10478400701598314

Hayes, S. C., Strosahl, K. D., & Wilson, K. G. (2012). *Acceptance and commitment therapy: The process and practice of mindful change* (2nd ed.). Guilford Press.

Hegarty, J., & Huelsmann, C. (2020). *ACT in sport: Improve performance through mindfulness, acceptance, and commitment*. Dark River.

Henriksen, K., Hansen, J., & Larsen, C. H. (2019). *Mindfulness and acceptance in sport: How to help athletes perform and thrive under pressure*. Routledge.

Keegan, R. (2016). *Being a sport psychologist*. Palgrave Macmillan.

Locke, E. A., & Latham, G. P. (1985). The application of goal setting to sports. *Journal of Sport Psychology, 7*(3), 205–222.

Luoma, J. B., Hayes, S. C., & Walser R. D. (2007). *Learning ACT: An acceptance and commitment therapy skills training manual for therapists*. New Harbinger Publications.

Masuda, A., Morgan, L., Spencer, S. D., Qina'au, J., & Jo, D. (2023). Cultural adaptations of acceptance and commitment therapy. In M. P. Twohig, M. E. Levin, & J. M. Petersen (Eds.), *The Oxford handbook of acceptance and commitment therapy* (p. 0). Oxford University Press. https://doi.org/10.1093/oxfordhb/9780197550076.013.30

Noetel, M., Ciarrochi, J., Van Zanden, B., & Lonsdale, C. (2019). Mindfulness and acceptance approaches to sporting performance enhancement: A systematic review. *International Review of Sport and Exercise Psychology, 12*(1), 139–175.

Olusoga, P., & Yousuf, S. (2023). Acceptance and commitment therapy (ACT). In M. Turner, M. Jones, & A. Wood (Eds.), *Applying cognitive behavioural therapeutic approaches in sport* (pp. 26–43). Routledge.

Polk, K. L., & Schoendorff, B. (2014). *The ACT matrix: A new approach to building psychological flexibility across settings and populations*. New Harbinger Publications.

Price, D., Wagstaff, C. R., & Thelwell, R. C. (2022a). Opportunities and considerations of new media and technology in sport psychology service delivery. *Journal of Sport Psychology in Action, 13*(1), 4–15. https://doi.org/10.1080/21520704.2020.1846648

Price, D., Wagstaff, C. R., & Thelwell, R. C. (2022b). "What if I get injured?": An acceptance and commitment therapy approach for fear of injury with a semielite youth snowboarder. *Case Studies in Sport and Exercise Psychology, 6*(1), 12–20. https://doi.org/10.1123/cssep.2021-0020

Ruiz, F. J., & Luciano, C. (2012). Improving international-level chess players' performance with an acceptance-based protocol: Preliminary findings. *The Psychological Record, 62*(3), 447–462. https://doi.org/10.1007/BF03395813

Swann, C., Jackman, P. C., Lawrence, A., Hawkins, R. M., Goddard, S. G., Williamson, O., Schweickle, M. J., Vella, S. A., Rosenbaum, S., & Ekkekakis, P. (2023). The (over)use of SMART goals for physical activity promotion: A narrative review and critique. *Health Psychology Review, 17*(2), 211–226. https://doi.org/10.1080/17437199.2021.2023608

Törneke, N. (2017). *Metaphor in practice: A professional's guide to using the science of language in psychotherapy*. New Harbinger Publications.

Villatte, M., Villatte, J. L, & Monestes, J. L. (2014). Understanding and using relational frame theory in experiential clinical practice. In J. Stoddard & N. Afari (Eds.), *The big book of ACT metaphors: The complete guide to ACT metaphors and experiential exercises* (pp. 13–28). New Harbinger Publications.

Watson, D. R., Hill, A. P., Madigan, D. J., & Donachie, T. C. (2024). Effectiveness of an online acceptance and commitment therapy programme for perfectionism in soccer players: A randomized control trial. *Sport, Exercise, and Performance Psychology, 13*(1), 5–22. https://psycnet.apa.org/doi/10.1037/spy0000333

White, R. G., Bethell, A., Charnock, L., Leckey, S., & Penpraze, V. (2021). *Acceptance and commitment approaches for athletes' well-being and performance: The flexible mind*. Springer International Publishing. https://doi.org/10.1007/978-3-030-64942-5

Williamson, O., Swann, C., Jackman, P. C., Bennett, K. J. M., & Bird, M. D. (2025). "It's not handcuffing the athlete to success or failure": Sport psychology practitioners' use of nonspecific goals in applied contexts. *Journal of Applied Sport Psychology*, 1–22. https://doi.org/10.1080/10413200.2025.2457986

Wood, S., & Turner, M. J. (2025). Using acceptance and commitment therapy with athletes. *Scandinavian Journal of Sport and Exercise Psychology, 7*, 1–9. https://doi.org/10.7146/sjsep.v7i.150889

5 Measuring What Matters

Challenges and Advances in Evaluating ACT Interventions in Sport

Samuel Wood and Martin J. Turner

Learning Objectives

1. Identify key methodological challenges in evaluating ACT's effectiveness in sport and performance contexts
2. Critically appraise existing outcome measures for assessing psychological flexibility and performance-related change
3. Design robust and context-sensitive strategies for measuring the impact of ACT-based interventions in sport settings

Why Measurement Matters in ACT and Sport

Measurement in sport psychology is essential to validate interventions and inform practice (Vealey et al., 2019). In ACT, effectiveness is not defined by symptom reduction but by increased psychological flexibility – the capacity to behave in accordance with one's values while accepting difficult internal experiences (Hayes et al., 2012b). In the sport context, this means helping athletes perform in alignment with their personally held values, even in the presence of performance-hindering cognitions and feelings of debilitative anxiety, fatigue, or self-doubt (Wood & Turner, 2025).

In sport, performance is more than a goal; it's a daily endeavour. This means assessing the impact of ACT becomes a deeper test – one that asks if athletes both feel better and perform better when it counts. Athletes can do everything right – train relentlessly, prepare strategically, and cultivate mental strength – yet still face forces beyond their control: a referee's call, a teammate's slip, a sudden downpour, a hostile crowd, and a travel delay. Sport doesn't always reward preparation; it also tests adaptability amid chaos. Effectiveness, therefore, is arguably measured by increased engagement in values-consistent behaviours (even under pressure); improved functionality in sport contexts (e.g., recovery from errors, maintaining focus); evidence

DOI: 10.4324/9781003515203-6

of enhanced process-related variables such as acceptance, defusion, and present-moment awareness; and demonstrated transfer of psychological skills across settings (e.g., from training to competition). This functional and contextual emphasis distinguishes ACT from traditional approaches (e.g., cognitive therapy) that typically focus on symptom reduction. As such, evaluating ACT interventions in these environments demands tools and strategies that are both theoretically coherent and contextually sensitive. Yet systematic monitoring and evaluation of interventions to evidence the effectiveness of ACT in sport is a prominent challenge. This chapter outlines key issues in measuring ACT's impact in sport, reviews current approaches, and offers recommendations for advancing the field.

Quantitative Measurements of Effective ACT Interventions

First, and a rather crucial point to start our discussion here, some processes of ACT within the ACT hexaflex intentionally forsake precision in favour of pragmatic utility (Hayes et al., 2012b). For example, fusion and defusion have been discussed within the wider literature using multiple definitions (Ruiz et al., 2023) *and* as a procedure, process, and outcome (Assaz et al., 2023). This risks confusion across practitioners, making the measurement of changes in ACT processes more challenging, causing a variety of experiences for athletes (and practitioners) engaging in ACT interventions. We do not wish to propose new definitions here, but workable, consistent definitions for key ACT processes are important to establish and facilitate accurate measurement of these ACT processes.

Sport psychology is littered with quantitative measures to assess psychological theories and concepts in applied (and research) settings. Typically, in applied practice, these are used pre- and post-intervention to attempt to evaluate the effectiveness of an intervention – and, ultimately, increase confidence in claiming that the intervention is responsible for observable changes (Anderson et al., 2002). However, this requires some additional thought with ACT interventions. Some sport and performance psychologists might see changes in anxiety or self-confidence as markers of change. In contrast, ACT interventions focus on increasing psychological flexibility – an athlete's ability to remain present, open, and committed to values-based actions, even in the presence of discomfort.

This raises critical questions: should we measure changes in symptoms (e.g., anxiety), in processes (e.g., cognitive defusion), or in outcomes (e.g., performance)? Well, from an ACT perspective, symptom reduction is not the goal, although it may be a secondary outcome. Here, a practitioner employing ACT might teach acceptance, meaning the athlete might come to accept their anxiety, which means the idea of reporting a reduction in anxiety on a scale like the Sport Anxiety Scale-2 (SAS-2; Smith et al., 2006) is not aligned. One reason for this is that these measures are rooted in second-wave CBT approaches. This means that, for example, items on the SAS-2 like "I worry I will not play well" or "I worry I will let others down" are cognitions that athletes are likely to experience before and after an ACT intervention. This means that, despite differences in the impact of these thoughts on performance pre- and post-intervention, there may be no change in SAS-2 scores because ACT did not aim to change these cognitions, but rather the athlete's relationship with them. Consequently, it is unhelpful to evaluate the effectiveness of ACT in sport using some psychometric measures (see Wood & Turner, 2024).

Several clinically-focused ACT psychometric measures exist that evaluate various ACT concepts, including: adaption to stressful events (the Cognitive Flexibility Inventory; Dennis & Vander Wal, 2010); consistency of acting in line with values (the Valuing Questionnaire; Smout et al., 2014); mindfulness (the Five Facet Mindfulness Questionnaire; Baer et al., 2006); believability of thoughts (the Automatic Thoughts Questionnaire-Believability; Netemeyer et al., 2002); and fusion with cognitions (the Cognitive Fusion Questionnaire [CFQ-7]; Gillanders et al., 2014). Finally, we might consider measuring psychological flexibility as a central construct of ACT, for which several measures exist. For example, the AAQ-II (Bond et al., 2011) is perhaps the most used: a seven-item scale assessing experiential avoidance and cognitive fusion. Despite its popularity, it has been critiqued for poor discriminant validity and for overlapping with measures of distress (Tyndall et al., 2019). Further, it is arguable that in sport contexts, athletes may score high not because they are psychologically inflexible, but because they are under high stress – which is a norm in elite sport. Put simply: elite athletes might score high on this measure not because they're rigid or avoidant – but because they live in a pressure cooker where high stress is the baseline. To address these limitations, Francis et al. (2016) developed the CompACT (Comprehensive Assessment of ACT Processes), which measures openness to experience, behavioural awareness, and valued action. Though promising, this measure has not been widely validated in sport populations. Focused on general populations, these measures can be disengaging for athletes when applied to a sports context. With this in mind, the Athlete Mindfulness Questionnaire (Zhang et al., 2017), with several subscales that are close to ACT processes (connecting with the present moment, awareness, and acceptance), might be the most appropriate questionnaire for measuring the effects of ACT interventions in sport.

Beyond Standardised Measures: Values, Meaning, and Context

When performance in sport is public, high-stakes, and personally meaningful, understanding change through the lens of values and meaning can be effective. This is because athletes often define success not just through external results but through how well they stay true to what matters in the face of adversity (Hayes et al., 2012b). Moreover, because ACT processes can manifest in subtle, context-bound ways, they may not translate into quantifiable, measurable metrics. Here, qualitative measurement might be more suitable, capturing the richness of any changes brought about by the ACT intervention.

Within the sport domain, ACT interventions can also be evaluated through changes in performance-relevant behaviours and psychological processes, rather than performance outcomes alone. Although ACT is not primarily targeted at athletic performance, it facilitates conditions that may enhance performance by reducing experiential avoidance and increasing values-based action. Yet this presents one of the most challenging aspects of evaluating ACT interventions in sport because there is an indirect, often non-linear, relationship between psychological flexibility and observable performance outcomes. This is because ACT emphasises contextual behavioural changes, particularly an individual's ability to persist or change behaviour in the service of personally meaningful goals, even in the presence of difficult internal experiences (Hayes et al., 2012b). Ultimately, this means we should measure the effectiveness of ACT interventions in terms of their goal and how well an individual can pursue valued action in the presence of difficult internal experiences.

In sport, performance is often measured using objective outcomes, such as win–loss ratios, scoring, statistics, or physiological indicators (e.g., reaction time and endurance metrics). Yet sport performance is broader than objective outcomes alone (Höner et al., 2021; Saw et al., 2016). Further, while we understand the reality of sport is that performance is often evaluated through these measures, they often fail to reflect the psychological processes ACT targets. For example, an athlete may perform poorly in a game but have demonstrated significant growth in values-consistent behaviour – a key part of ACT. If working in a systemic way, being able to communicate ACT's approach – and finding different ways to measure success – with those around the athlete (e.g., coaches and, possibly, parents) is important. In addition, encouraging those who support the athlete to capture behaviour change that is not always evident in statistics – for example, staying engaged after a poor start or maintaining leadership presence under stress. Here, subjective performance measures assess how athletes believe they performed – that is, how they experience performance – rather than simply how they objectively performed. Possible options here include the perceived performance in team sport questionnaire (Gershgoren et al., 2021) or the subjective training quality scale (Shell et al., 2023). Video analysis of performance would be helpful here as it allows the systematic coding of behavioural responses, such as visible recovery strategies (e.g., breathing and posture resetting), behavioural persistence despite fatigue or frustration, and non-verbal indicators of engagement or withdrawal. Here, behavioural coding frameworks can be useful (and adapting) to reflect ACT-relevant constructs such as values-based action, present moment awareness, and acceptance of difficult stimuli (Gross et al., 2018).

Another approach might be to have the athlete self-rate their confidence, presence, and values alignment before, during, and after performance events to reveal patterns of psychological flexibility, or record shifts in what they are doing and why, through diary entries, perhaps framed using the ACT matrix (Polk & Schoendorff, 2014). Structured reflective journaling like this invites the athlete to consider "what values did I act on today, and how?", "what uncomfortable thoughts or feelings showed up before and during training?", and "how did I respond to unhelpful inner experiences – did I make room for them, or avoid them?" This increases athletes' self-monitoring and self-awareness. Conducted over time, these entries can highlight longitudinal changes in the athlete's behavioural patterns and internal narratives. This also provides an opportunity to identify instances where the athlete might be successfully executing ACT mechanisms, regardless of changes in performance.

Considering Process-Based Evaluation of ACT

The concept of effectiveness in ACT is inherently process-oriented (Ong et al., 2024). Consequently, ACT emphasises process over outcome, advocating for assessment approaches that track change mechanisms over time. This shifts the focus from pre/post evaluation towards process-based tracking. In this section, we discuss some process-based strategies that can be used to evaluate ACT interventions.

First, we propose a rough measure of how a psychological concept (e.g., confidence) can be rated against the mechanisms of the hexaflex model, where athletes could rate themselves on a Likert scale (see Figure 5.1). Second, we highlight how session-by-session tracking, using tools like the Session Rating Scale (Duncan et al., 2003), can assess the athlete's experiences of the therapeutic alliance, allowing real-time monitoring of the athlete–practitioner relationship. This can track the athlete's perceived engagement in the session as the techniques and strategies discussed – a vital precursor to behavioural change. Third, the ACT matrix (Polk & Schoendorff, 2014; Schwabach et al., 2019) provides a visual tool for session reflection, tracking shifts in key ACT processes. Fourth, process-based therapy (PBT: Hofmann & Hayes, 2019) proposes tailoring interventions to core psychological processes. This enables individualised

Rate your confidence in how well you embodied each skill today in training/ competition, from 1 (not at all) to 7 (consistently and confidently).

ACT Process	*Statement*	*1–7 Rating*
Acceptance	I allowed discomfort, pressure, and difficult feelings without fighting or avoiding them.	___
Cognitive Defusion	I noticed unhelpful thoughts without getting hooked or controlled by them.	___
Present-Moment Awareness	I stayed focused on the here-and-now, rather than dwelling on mistakes or future outcomes.	___
Self-as-Context	I saw myself as more than my thoughts, emotions, and performance today.	___
Values Connection	I remembered what matters to me as an athlete and acted in line with it.	___
Committed Action	I made deliberate, values-driven effort, even when it was hard.	___
Psychological Flexibility	I adapted effectively to challenges and stayed engaged with what mattered.	___ *(average of above or athlete rating)*

Scoring idea:

- 1–2 = Struggling / dominated by stress or thoughts
- 3–4 = Partial awareness / inconsistent application
- 5–6 = Strong engagement / flexible responding
- 7 = High psychological flexibility under pressure

Figure 5.1 Rough ACT hexaflex self-rating scale for athletes.

assessment and tracking of intervention effectiveness by acknowledging that: psychological flexibility may manifest differently across athletes, depending on the sport, context, and the athlete's personal values; athletes may benefit from distinct combinations of processes (e.g., some may need greater work on self-as-context, while others benefit from enhancing committed action); and measurement tools and intervention strategies should evolve in real-time, based on progress across these processes. Further, PBT advocates the monitoring of shifts in process variables using ecological momentary assessment, behavioural tracking, and client-generated metrics to reveal how key processes influence each other over time (Shiffman et al., 2008).

Research Design Considerations in Sport Settings

Although this book focuses on the application of theory to practice, we feel it is important when discussing the measurement of ACT interventions to discuss how measurement ties with research in this area. Of course, rigorous research to evaluate ACT interventions in sport needs consideration of design choices, measurement strategies, and the nature of psychological change targeted by ACT with a population of people (i.e., athletes) who operate in high-stakes environments with unique demands.

RCTs are the gold standard in clinical research, with limited examples of their application in elite sport settings (see Munnik et al., 2024; Nejati et al., 2024). The niche nature of elite sport dictates small sample sizes. Yet ACT's focus on functional, context-sensitive change lends itself to more flexible and responsive research designs. For example, single-case experimental designs are especially suitable for applied sport psychology (Barker et al., 2013). Repeated measures across baseline, intervention, and follow-up phases can detect changes and link them to intervention components (Onghena & Edgington, 2005). Equally, crossover designs, where participants receive both the ACT intervention and a comparison condition, can help control for expectancy and order effects. Of course, both single-case experimental and crossover designs can be measured using quantitative and qualitative data methods (see Barker et al., 2011; Deen et al., 2017; Harwood & Steptoe, 2013; McDougall, 2013). In summary, having robust ways of measuring changes brought about by ACT interventions is crucial for demonstrating the effectiveness of ACT in both research and applied contexts.

Future Directions and Recommendations

The future of ACT evaluation in sport lies in innovation, integration, and context sensitivity. As ACT interventions expand into diverse sporting domains – from elite competition to youth development – measurement practices must evolve accordingly. Crucially, ACT-informed sport psychologists must be trained not only in delivery but also in assessment literacy. Practitioners should be equipped to use and interpret measures designed to evaluate ACT processes, facilitate reflective discussions, and adapt protocols based on individual athlete needs. Collaborative evaluation, where practitioners work with athletes (and coaches) to co-construct success criteria, would ensure contextual fit and ethical transparency (Gardner & Moore, 2007).

While tools such as the CFQ-7, AAQ-II, and CompACT are foundational, they require refinement for sport-specific use. Future research should aim to develop modular assessments that target distinct ACT processes (e.g., defusion and values clarity) relevant to specific performance contexts. Further, exploring the combination of self-report, behavioural observation, coach/peer ratings, and biometric data (e.g., heart rate variability and cortisol levels) would provide converging evidence of intervention impact. Triangulating data improves reliability and paints a fuller picture of functional change (Kazdin, 2011). Additionally, combining idiographic and nomothetic methods supports both theoretical development and applied relevance. Indeed, it is important to note that short-term gains may not reflect the enduring benefits of psychological flexibility. Longitudinal designs that track athletes across training cycles, competitions, and transitions (e.g., injury and retirement) will provide insight into sustained ACT outcomes. Here, ecological momentary interventions (i.e., digitally delivered ACT prompts embedded in athletes' routines) have the potential to simultaneously support practice and generate rich, real-time data (Heron & Smyth, 2010). Finally, evaluation tools must reflect cultural and contextual diversity within sport. Athletes' definitions of values and success are not universal. As ACT grows globally, culturally adapted assessments and inclusive qualitative methods will be critical to ensure ethical and meaningful measurement (Hayes et al., 2012a).

Conclusion

Evaluating ACT interventions in sport requires more than adapting clinical measures to athletic settings. It demands a philosophical shift – from seeking standardised change across populations to illuminating meaningful, individualised transformation. The central question becomes not "Did symptoms reduce?" but "Did this athlete gain greater freedom to act on what matters in their sport, despite adversity?" By integrating process-based, idiographic, and contextually grounded methods, we can more accurately assess the complex realities of psychological flexibility in high-performance environments. Doing so ensures that ACT remains both scientifically rigorous and personally relevant – helping athletes not just perform, but live and compete in line with their values.

References

Anderson, A. G., Miles, A., Mahoney, C., & Robinson, P. (2002). Evaluating the effectiveness of applied sport psychology practice: Making the case for a case study approach. *The Sport Psychologist*, *16*(4), 433–454. https://doi.org/10.1123/tsp.16.4.432

Assaz, D. A., Tyndall, I., Oshiro, C. K., & Roche, B. (2023). A process-based analysis of cognitive defusion in acceptance and commitment therapy. *Behavior Therapy*, *54*(6), 1020–1035.

Baer, R. A., Smith, G. T., Hopkins, J., Krietemeyer, J., & Toney, L. (2006). Using self-report assessment methods to explore facets of mindfulness. *Assessment*, *13*(1), 27–45. https://doi.org/10.1177/1073191105283504

Barker, J., McCarthy, P., Jones, M., & Moran, A. (2011). *Single-case research methods in sport and exercise psychology*. Routledge.

Barker, J. B., Mellalieu, S. D., McCarthy, P. J., Jones, M. V., & Moran, A. (2013). Special issue on single-case research in sport psychology. *Journal of Applied Sport Psychology*, *25*(1), 1–3. https://doi.org/10.1080/10413200.2012.729378

Bond, F. W., Hayes, S. C., Baer, R. A., Carpenter, K. M., Guenole, N., Orcutt, H. K., . . . & Zettle, R. D. (2011). Preliminary psychometric properties of the Acceptance and Action Questionnaire–II: A revised measure of psychological inflexibility and experiential avoidance. *Behavior therapy, 42*(4), 676–688.

Deen, S., Turner, M. J., & Wong, R. S. K. (2017). The effects of REBT, and the use of credos, on irrational beliefs and resilience qualities in athletes. *The Sport Psychologist, 31*(3), 249–263. https://doi.org/10.1123/tsp.2016-0057

Dennis, J. P., & Vander Wal, J. S. (2010). The cognitive flexibility inventory: Instrument development and estimates of reliability and validity. *Cognitive Therapy and Research, 34*(3), 241–253. https://doi.org/10.1007/s10608-009-9276-4

Duncan, B. L., Miller, S. D., Sparks, J. A., Claud, D. A., Reynolds, L. S., Brown, J., & Johnson, L. D. (2003). The session rating scale: Preliminary psychometric properties for a "working" alliance measure. *Journal of Brief Therapy, 3*(1), 3–12.

Francis, A. W., Dawson, D. L., & Golijani-Moghaddam, N. (2016). The development and validation of the comprehensive assessment of acceptance and commitment therapy processes (CompACT). *Journal of Contextual Behavioral Science, 5*(3), 134–145. https://doi.org/10.1016/j.jcbs.2016.05.003

Gardner, F. L., & Moore, Z. E. (2007). *The psychology of enhancing human performance: The mindfulness-acceptance-commitment (MAC) approach.* Springer Publishing Company.

Gershgoren, L., Blatt, A., Sela, T., & Tenenbaum, G. (2021). Does the league table lie? The development and validation of the perceived performance in team sports questionnaire (PPTSQ) [Original Research]. *Frontiers in Psychology, Volume 11–2020.* https://doi.org/10.3389/fpsyg.2020.615018

Gillanders, D. T., Bolderston, H., Bond, F. W., Dempster, M., Flaxman, P. E., & Campbell, L. T. (2014). The development and initial validation of the cognitive fusion questionnaire. *Behavioural Therapy, 45*(1), 83–101. https://doi.org/10.1016/j.beth.2013.09.001

Gross, M., Moore, Z. E., Gardner, F. L., Wolanin, A. T., Pess, R., & Marks, D. R. (2018). An empirical examination comparing the mindfulness-acceptance-commitment approach and psychological skills training for the mental health and sport performance of female student athletes. *International Journal of Sport and Exercise Psychology, 16*(4), 431–451. https://doi.org/10.1080/1612197X.2016.1250802

Harwood, C., & Steptoe, K. (2013). The integration of single case designs in coaching contexts: A commentary for applied sport psychologists. *Journal of Applied Sport Psychology, 25*(1), 167–174. https://doi.org/10.1080/10413200.2012.690361

Hayes, S. C., Pistorello, J., & Levin, M. E. (2012a). Acceptance and commitment therapy as a unified model of behavior change. *The Counseling Psychologist, 40*(7), 976–1002. https://doi.org/10.1177/0011000012460836

Hayes, S. C., Stroshal, K. D., & Wilson, K. G. (2012b). *Acceptance and commitment therapy: The process and practice of mindful change* (2nd ed.). Guildford Press.

Heron, K. E., & Smyth, J. M. (2010). Ecological momentary interventions: Incorporating mobile technology into psychosocial and health behaviour treatments. *British Journal of Health Psychology, 15*(1), 1–39. https://doi.org/10.1348/135910709X466063

Hofmann, S. G., & Hayes, S. C. (2019). The future of intervention science: Process-based therapy. *Clinical Psychological Science, 7*(1), 37–50. https://doi.org/10.1177/2167702618772296

Höner, O., Murr, D., Larkin, P., Schreiner, R., & Leyhr, D. (2021). Nationwide subjective and objective assessments of potential talent predictors in elite youth soccer: An investigation of prognostic validity in a prospective study. *Frontiers in Sports and Active Living, Volume 3–2021.* https://doi.org/10.3389/fspor.2021.638227

Kazdin, A. E. (2011). *Single-case research designs: Methods for clinical and applied settings* (2nd ed.). Oxford University Press.

McDougall, D. (2013). Applying single-case design innovations to research in sport and exercise psychology. *Journal of Applied Sport Psychology*, *25*(1), 33–45. https://doi.org/10.1080/10413200.2012.720640

Munnik, J. B., van Niekerk, R. L., & Turner, M. J. (2024). A cluster randomized trial of a rational emotive behavior therapy (REBT) program and a mindfulness-acceptance-commitment (MAC) program, with South African adolescent rugby players. *Psychology of Sport and Exercise*, *75*, 102706. https://doi.org/10.1016/j.psychsport.2024.102706

Nejati, M., Farsi, A., Moteshareie, E., Miller, A., & Turner, M. J. (2024). The effects of rational emotive behaviour therapy on performance under pressure in adolescent soccer athletes: A randomised control design. *International Journal of Sport and Exercise Psychology*, *22*(1), 123–140. https://doi.org/10.1080/1612197X.2022.2152852

Netemeyer, R. G., Williamson, D. A., Burton, S., Biswas, D., Jindal, S., Landreth, S., Mills, G., & Primeaux, S. (2002). Psychometric properties of shortened versions of the automatic thoughts questionnaire. *Educational and Psychological Measurement*, *62*(1), 111–129. https://doi.org/10.1177/0013164402062001008

Ong, C. W., Ciarrochi, J., Hofmann, S. G., Karekla, M., & Hayes, S. C. (2024). Through the extended evolutionary meta-model, and what ACT found there: ACT as a process-based therapy. *Journal of Contextual Behavioral Science*, *32*, 100734. https://doi.org/10.1016/j.jcbs.2024.100734

Onghena, P., & Edgington, E. S. (2005). Customization of pain treatments: Single-case design and analysis. *The Clinical Journal of Pain*, *21*(1), 56–68. https://doi.org/10.1097/00002508-200501000-00007

Polk, K. L., & Schoendorff, B. (2014). *The ACT matrix: A new approach to building psychological flexibility across settings and populations*. New Harbinger Publications.

Ruiz, F. J., Gil-Luciano, B., & Segura-Vargas, M. A. (2023). Cognitive defusion. In M. P. Twohig, M. E. Levin, & J. M. Petersen (Eds.), *The Oxford handbook of acceptance and commitment therapy* (pp. 206–229). Oxford University Press.

Saw, A. E., Main, L. C., & Gastin, P. B. (2016). Monitoring the athlete training response: Subjective self-reported measures trump commonly used objective measures: A systematic review. *British Journal of Sports Medicine*, *50*(5), 281–291. https://doi.org/10.1136/bjsports-2015-094758

Schwabach, J., Bartley, J., & Polk, K. (2019). Sorting it out: A framework for increasing mental flexibility and valued action in athletes using the ACT matrix. *Journal of Sport Psychology in Action*, *10*(4), 208–213.

Shell, S. J., Slattery, K., Clark, B., Broatch, J. R., Halson, S. L., & Coutts, A. J. (2023). Development and validity of the subjective training quality scale. *European Journal of Sport Science*, *23*(7), 1102–1109. https://doi.org/10.1080/17461391.2022.2111276

Shiffman, S., Stone, A. A., & Hufford, M. R. (2008). Ecological momentary assessment. *Annual Review of Clinical Psychology*, *4*(2008), 1–32. https://doi.org/10.1146/annurev.clinpsy.3.022806.091415

Smith, R. E., Smoll, F. L., Cumming, S. P., & Grossbard, J. R. (2006). Measurement of multidimensional sport performance anxiety in children and adults: The sport anxiety scale-2. *Journal of Sport and Exercise Psychology*, *28*(4), 479–501. https://doi.org/10.1123/jsep.28.4.479

Smout, M., Davies, M., Burns, N., & Christie, A. (2014). Development of the valuing questionnaire (VQ). *Journal of Contextual Behavioral Science*, *3*(3), 164–172.

Tyndall, I., Waldeck, D., Pancani, L., Whelan, R., Roche, B., & Dawson, D. L. (2019). The acceptance and action questionnaire-II (AAQ-II) as a measure of experiential avoidance: Concerns over discriminant validity. *Journal of Contextual Behavioral Science*, *12*, 278–284. https://doi.org/10.1016/j.jcbs.2018.09.005

Vealey, R. (1986). Conceptualisation of sport-confidence and competitive orientation: Preliminary investigation and instrument development. *Journal of Sport Psychology*, *8*, 221–246.

Vealey, R. S., Cooley, R., Nilsson, E., Block, C., & Galli, N. (2019). Assessment and the use of questionnaires in sport psychology consulting: An analysis of practices and attitudes from 2003 to 2017. *Journal of Clinical Sport Psychology*, *13*(4), 505–523. https://doi.org/10.1123/jcsp.2019-0012

Wood, S., & Turner, M. J. (2024). Using an acceptance and commitment therapy approach to overcome distractive overthinking with a high school baseball player. *Case Studies in Sport and Exercise Psychology*, *8*(1), 8–15. https://doi.org/10.1123/cssep.2023-0036

Wood, S., & Turner, M. J. (2025). Using acceptance and commitment therapy with athletes. *Scandinavian Journal of Sport and Exercise Psychology*, *7*, 1–9. https://doi.org/10.7146/sjsep.v7i.150889

Zhang, C.-Q., Chung, P.-K., & Si, G. (2017). Assessing acceptance in mindfulness with direct-worded items: The development and initial validation of the athlete mindfulness questionnaire. *Journal of Sport and Health Science*, *6*(3), 311–320. https://doi.org/10.1016/j.jshs.2015.09.010

Part 2

Applying ACT in Sport

6 Applying ACT to Support Confidence and Performance

Dean R. Watson and Tracy C. Donachie

Learning Outcomes

1. Implement an ACT intervention with an athlete to enhance their confidence and performance
2. Identify and explain core ACT processes relevant to enhancing athletic confidence and performance
3. Understand relevant research and theory in addressing psychological (in) flexibility

Context for the Chapter

Both authors are HCPC-registered Sport and Exercise Psychologists working in the United Kingdom. The first author brings over a decade of experience as an SPP, working across various levels (e.g., amateur, national, and international), sports (e.g., tennis, football, and gymnastics), and age groups (e.g., youth and senior). In addition, the first author has applied ACT with athletes for four years, supported by continuous professional development (CPD) and accredited training in ACT. The second author has 25 years of experience in sport, initially as a coach and a semi-professional football player, and later as an SPP, with experience across various levels (e.g., amateur, national, and international), sports (e.g., football, racket sports, and basketball), and age groups (e.g., youth and senior). The second author has applied ACT in sport for over three years, drawing on ACT-based supervision, CPD, and applied work with athletes, coaches, and teams.

From our experiences of using ACT, athletes have found its techniques to be useful, often more so than other cognitive-behavioural approaches that rely on changing thoughts (e.g., Cognitive Therapy). A growing body of case examples demonstrates how ACT can be applied in sport (e.g., Wood & Turner, 2024), alongside broader evidence supporting ACT's effectiveness (see -Ptáček et al., 2024). As explained in previous chapters, ACT encourages acceptance of thoughts rather than attempting to control or eliminate them. In

DOI: 10.4324/9781003515203-8

our experience, athletes appear to prefer this approach – choosing to acknowledge and let difficult thoughts pass rather than engage with or analyse them. This shift may help to explain why ACT can be beneficial for both confidence and performance.

ACT, Confidence, and Performance Enhancement

ACT is a modern behavioural approach grounded in RFT (Hayes, 2004) designed to enhance psychological flexibility: the ability to stay present, openly experience difficult thoughts or emotions, and take action in line with personal values (Ong & Eustis, 2023). Unlike traditional cognitive-behavioural approaches that focus on disputing negative thoughts, ACT promotes acceptance of internal experiences and the ability to defuse from unhelpful cognitive patterns. In sport settings, this means helping athletes to recognise thoughts as natural and non-threatening, thereby reducing their influence on behaviour (Wood & Turner, 2025). This is achieved through six interrelated core processes: acceptance, cognitive defusion, present-moment awareness, self-as-context, values clarification, and committed action. Collectively, ACT offers a functional contextual model of behaviour change, aiming to promote adaptable, values-driven behaviour even in the presence of performance-relevant stress.

Confidence plays a significant role in how athletes perform (e.g., Thomas et al., 2011b). Sport confidence is conceptualised as a multidimensional set of enduring positive beliefs related to success in competitive sport (Thomas et al., 2011a). Rather than relying solely on the presence of confidence, ACT encourages athletes to develop psychological flexibility, which enables them to unhook from self-critical or unhelpful thoughts and take committed action guided by personal values. This approach is particularly beneficial for perfectionistic athletes, who often struggle with low confidence due to rigid standards and fear of failure. For example, Watson et al. (2023) found that teaching perfectionistic athletes to live more consistently with their values led to reduced self-criticism and, in turn, enhanced confidence. Similarly, Wood and Turner (2024) demonstrated that an ACT-based intervention helped a competitive figure skater with autism spectrum disorder defuse from perfectionistic thoughts and internal pressure, and in turn, increased confidence.

Performance is a central focus in sport, often regarded as the key measure of success, progress, and the realisation of athletic potential (e.g., Gulbin et al., 2013; Wachsmuth et al., 2024). Psychological flexibility has been shown to enhance performance. Meta-analytical evidence supports the use of ACT-based protocols for improving performance outcomes (see -Ptáček et al., 2024). In two examples, De Petrillo et al. (2009) found that elite athletes who received ACT training performed more effectively compared to a waitlist control group. Similarly, Gross et al. (2018) found that athletes who engaged in an ACT-based programme demonstrated improvements in coach-rated performance, psychological flexibility, and emotion regulation, compared to those receiving traditional PST. Together, these findings highlight the potential of ACT as a framework for enhancing athletic performance.

Injury can be a psychologically distressing experience for athletes, often resulting in fear, avoidance, and identity disruptions (Tranaeus et al., 2024). By targeting experiential avoidance and psychological inflexibility, ACT offers a framework to support athletes through injury rehabilitation (e.g., Cecil, 2020). Also, ACT helps athletes accept distressing internal experiences (e.g., pain and fear of re-injury) while committing to rehabilitation behaviours aligned with personal values. For example, Mahoney and Hanrahan (2011) found that ACT improved athletes' commitment to rehabilitation in athletes recovering from knee injuries. In another example, Price et al. (2022) demonstrated that helping a youth snowboarder defuse from the thought "What if I get injured?" led to increased psychological flexibility and improved training engagement. Finally, Wood and Turner (2023) applied ACT with a competitive figure skater experiencing fear of re-injury and through defusion, mindfulness, and values work. The athlete became more able to tolerate discomfort and re-engage with performance goals. ACT interventions can therefore address emotional recovery and support readiness for return to sport by helping athletes reconnect with a meaningful athletic identity and value-driven goals (Tranaeus et al., 2024).

A Case Example of an Athlete

To illustrate the process of using ACT, we present a case study based on an athlete previously supported by the lead author. This account follows the Hexaflex model of ACT (Bach & Moran, 2008) and describes key phases of the intervention. To protect the athlete's identity, a pseudonym (e.g., Mia) has been used, and minor details have been altered or omitted. Nevertheless, the case accurately reflects the support provided.

Case Description

The first author was initially contacted by the athlete's parent following recent performance concerns. Mia is a 17-year-old gymnast who has been training and competing at a high level for many years, including national-level competitions. She faces high expectations from her coaches, who anticipate she will progress to an elite level. However, in the past year, Mia has been recovering from knee surgery, which has led to a significant decline in her confidence and performance. She has started to struggle with skills she previously found easy (e.g., roundoff), leading to frustration and self-doubt.

In conversations with both Mia and her mother, several key concerns emerged. Mia explained that she was worried about her knee, but also about her self-belief, stating, "I'm just not good enough anymore". She described hesitancy about executing certain floor routines and admitted to pulling out of a particular move part-way through execution. This has contributed to a decline in performance, with her scores for routines reflecting this. Mia also reported avoiding harder routines out of fear that she would be unable to execute them to her desired standard. Mia's mother explained that she would normally accomplish these "harder" routines with ease. They both shared concerns that younger gymnasts appear to be progressing more quickly and that this raises fears that Mia may be de-selected in the future.

In surmising Mia's challenges, the lead author explained to Mia that she is likely experiencing psychological blocks towards certain routines, partially stemming from her previous knee injury. The fear of re-injury is contributing to hesitancy and increased mistakes during routine execution. This fear is directly affecting Mia's confidence and overall performance (e.g., increased technical errors). In addition, Mia is comparing herself to other gymnasts, leading to concern over her ability. As a result, she does not feel good enough, and her self-efficacy has significantly declined. In the following section, we present how we conceptualised the needs of Mia and how this was informed by a theoretical framework.

Case Formulation of the Challenges

Following the initial assessment of Mia's needs, it was important to ground our understanding with a working framework (Harris, 2019). We employed the ACT Hexaflex model, which has been used previously in sport (e.g., Wood & Turner, 2025). The ACT Hexaflex focuses on understanding a client's psychological challenges through the lens of the six core ACT processes, aiming to enhance psychological flexibility (Harris, 2019). Psychological flexibility is achieved by facilitating defusion, acceptance, values clarification, being present, self as context, and committed action. To understand and conceptualise Mia's psychological flexibility (or inflexibility), we used a Sport Specific Case Conceptualisation Worksheet (see Table 6.1). This resource was adapted and amended from Harris' *Getting unstuck in ACT: A clinician's guide to overcoming common obstacles in acceptance and commitment therapy* (Harris, 2013).

Using both of these resources helped conceptualise Mia's unworkable actions and identify her psychological inflexibility. In addition, it allowed us to understand Mia's avoidance towards distressing experiences (e.g., fear, doubt, and anxiety). Mia has many self-critical thoughts, such as "I'm not good enough" and "I'll never perform well again". She believes that these negative thoughts define her ability as a gymnast, leading to emotional distress and avoidance behaviours. Rather than challenging or stepping back from these thoughts, she treats them as absolute truths, which further reinforces her struggles. Mia needed to reduce this struggle in order to be less self-critical and irrational towards herself (Young & Turner, 2023).

Table 6.1 Sport-specific case formulation for ACT

WHAT DOES THE ATHLETE WANT FROM SPORT PSYCHOLOGY? What does the athlete describe as the main performance or well-being challenges? Examples: performance anxiety, perfectionism, confidence, returning from injury, fear of mistakes, motivation, and balancing sport and life.
EXTERNAL/STRUCTURAL BARRIERS Are there any non-psychological barriers affecting performance or well-being? (e.g., injury status, selection issues, coach–athlete relationship difficulties, time demands, financial pressures, academic/workload, and travel schedule)
UNWORKABLE ACTION (behaviours keeping the athlete stuck) **What is the athlete doing that makes performance or well-being worse?** Examples: overtraining, avoiding feedback, withdrawing in training, arguing with coach/teammates, excessive self-criticism after mistakes, and unhealthy coping (alcohol and poor sleep). **Avoidance of people, places, situations, or performance moments** Examples: avoiding competitions, avoiding key skills in training, procrastinating on reviews or video analysis, and avoiding conversations with coaches.
FUSION (thought entanglement impacting performance) **PAST AND FUTURE THINKING** (e.g., replaying past mistakes, worrying about selection, catastrophising competition outcomes, "what if I mess up?", and "if only I had . . .") **SELF-DESCRIPTION/ATHLETE IDENTITY** (e.g., "I'm not mentally strong", "I can't perform under pressure", "I need to be perfect", and "I'm only valuable when I perform well".) **REASONS/JUSTIFICATIONS FOR NOT CHANGING** (e.g., "There's no point working on mental skills unless I'm playing well", "I can't relax or I'll lose my edge", and "Coaches won't pick me anyway".) **RULES/SHOULD STATEMENTS** Look for rigid performance rules: (e.g., "I must never make mistakes", "I should always be the best", "I have to earn my place", "I shouldn't show emotion", and "I can't take rest days".) **JUDGEMENTS** Negative or positive evaluations of self, others, performance, or body: (e.g., "I'm useless", "everyone is better than me," and "coaches don't rate me".) **OTHER UNHELPFUL COGNITIONS** Any other beliefs or assumptions that create pressure or fear: (e.g., "If I don't perform well, I'll lose everything" and "Failure means I'm weak".)
EXPERIENTIAL AVOIDANCE **THOUGHTS/IMAGES/MEMORIES** (e.g., flashbacks to poor games, negative feedback loops, and fear imagery) **FEELINGS/SENSATIONS/URGES** (e.g., tight chest before competition, urge to withdraw, anxiety, and fear of judgement)

(*Continued*)

Table 6.1 (Continued)

VALUES AND COMMITTED ACTION SPORT LIFE DOMAINS What domains are most important to the athlete? Competition, training, recovery, team relationships, leadership, academic/life balance, and family. VALUES IN THOSE DOMAINS Examples: effort, courage, growth, professionalism, teamwork, resilience, and learning. GOALS AND ACTIONS What goals is the athlete currently pursuing? What values-aligned actions does the athlete want to commit to next? (short-term: actions in upcoming training/competition; long-term: career pathway and development focus) NEED FOR SKILLS TRAINING What skills would benefit the athlete? Examples: confidence routines, competition coping plans, grounding and attention control, self-reflection, assertive communication, and sleep/recovery habits. ATTENTION TRAINING Can the athlete: Focus on task despite emotions? Shift attention back when distracted? Stay engaged in the present moment in pressure situations? **RESOURCES** What strengths or supports does the athlete already have that we can leverage? (Mental toughness, strong routines, supportive coach/parents, performance analysts, physio, S&C, etc.)
PERSONAL BARRIERS (for practitioner) What emotions, assumptions, or biases show up for me as the psychologist that could influence the support process?
NEXT SESSION BRAINSTORM What interventions, metaphors, exercises, or tools may be useful in the next session? (e.g., performance profiles, ACT matrix, defusion exercises, values clarification, imagery routines, cognitive reframing, breathing, and focus training)

Adapted and amended from Harris' *Getting unstuck in ACT: A clinician's guide to overcoming common obstacles in acceptance and commitment therapy* (Harris, 2013).

Mia engages in experiential avoidance, characterised by trying to suppress or escape uncomfortable emotions (Wood & Turner, 2024). She avoids fully engaging in training and routines due to her fear of re-injury, which prevents her from rebuilding confidence in her skills. Instead of allowing herself to experience anxiety and discomfort as natural responses, she fights against these feelings, which paradoxically amplifies their impact. Her attempts to control or push away these emotions make them even more overwhelming, creating a cycle of fear and avoidance. Facilitating Mia's acceptance of these internal experiences could help reduce their influence and enable her to re-engage with training and gradually rebuild confidence in her skills. Furthermore, Mia struggles with present-moment awareness, often becoming preoccupied with fears about the future or past failures rather than focusing on the execution of her routines. This scattered attention negatively affects her performance, leading to increased mistakes and further doubt about her abilities. Instead of immersing herself in the present and responding to her movements with focus, she is consumed by worries that disrupt her ability to perform at her best. Increasing her psychological flexibility will support Mia to be in the present moment more often, leading to greater awareness of skill execution.

Finally, Mia's lack of committed action is preventing her from progressing and developing as a gymnast. Her hesitation, driven by fear, stops her from fully engaging in practice. Instead of taking purposeful steps towards improving her skills, she holds back, limiting her ability to regain confidence. This avoidance-based behaviour reinforces her self-doubt and prevents her from making the meaningful progress needed to overcome her challenges. Next, there is a description of the six ACT sessions that were delivered to Mia. Each session explains what was done and why.

Description of the ACT Intervention

Session 1 – Being Present

The first session of the intervention focused on the ACT principle of being present, which involves consciously attending to the here and now with openness and curiosity. Mia was introduced to the concept of mindfulness and how it can help her manage distractions, pressure, and unhelpful thoughts during performance. She engaged in practical exercises such as mindful breathing – focusing her attention on the natural rhythm of her breath – and a body scan to develop greater awareness of physical sensations. Mia also completed the "leaves on a stream" exercise (Harris, 2019), where she practised observing her thoughts as if they were leaves floating by on water, acknowledging them without becoming entangled in them. These exercises aimed to strengthen her ability to stay grounded in the present moment and respond more flexibly to internal experiences during both training and competition.

Session 2 – Defusion

The second session of the intervention focused on defusion, which involves learning to observe thoughts without becoming entangled in them or automatically reacting to them (Hayes et al., 2022). During the session, Mia was guided through exercises designed to help her notice her thoughts as passing mental events rather than absolute truths. For example, metaphors, such as imagining thoughts as clouds drifting across the sky, were used to create psychological distance from unhelpful thinking patterns. Techniques like labelling thoughts ("I am having the thought that . . .") helped Mia see her thoughts more objectively. This practice encourages greater mental flexibility, allowing Mia to respond more adaptively to her experiences rather than being overwhelmed or controlled by negative or distressing thoughts.

Session 3 – Self

The third session of the intervention focused on Self (or Self-as-Context). Self-as-context in ACT refers to the ability to observe one's experiences – thoughts, feelings, and sensations – without being defined or overwhelmed by them (Bennett & Oliver, 2019). During the session, Mia was guided to notice that there is a part of herself that is consistent and stable, separate from the changing thoughts and emotions she experiences. Through exercises like the "observer" metaphor, Mia practiced stepping back and observing her inner experiences. This helped her recognise that she is more than her thoughts or feelings, creating a sense of perspective and calm. By strengthening this sense of self-as-context, Mia can better manage difficult emotions and maintain a steady sense of who she is, which supports her confidence and well-being.

Session 4 – Acceptance

The fourth session of the intervention focused on acceptance, which involves allowing uncomfortable thoughts and feelings to be present without trying to avoid, eliminate, or change them. Acceptance in ACT involves learning to accept difficult emotions and feelings without trying to avoid, fight, or change them. During the session, Mia was guided to notice and make space for uncomfortable emotions such as anxiety or self-doubt instead of struggling against them. The "quicksand" metaphor was used to illustrate how trying to fight or push away difficult emotions can actually make them stronger – like struggling in quicksand causes you to sink deeper. Through this process, Mia learned that accepting these experiences can reduce their impact and help her focus more on her values and goals. Developing acceptance supports Mia in responding to challenges with greater calm and flexibility, ultimately enhancing her confidence and overall performance.

Session 5 – Values

The fifth session of the intervention focused on values, which are guiding principles connected to patterns of behaviour that give life meaning and help direct actions (LeJeune & Luoma, 2019). Values are like a compass that keeps us headed in a desired direction by identifying what really matters. During the session, Mia explored her core values, which included personal growth and meaningful relationships, and clarified how these values can guide her goals and decisions. She was encouraged to connect with these values to create motivation and direction, helping her stay focused even when facing setbacks or difficult emotions. Exercises involved reflecting on past experiences where she felt most fulfilled and identifying the underlying values in those moments. By aligning her actions with her values, Mia can create a purposeful path forward that supports her confidence.

Session 6 – Commitment

The final session of the intervention focused on commitment, which involves making a deliberate choice to take actions that align with values (Hayes et al., 2006). During the session, Mia identified that building self-confidence and improving her performance were important to her core values. She worked on setting concrete, achievable goals such as speaking up more during team meetings and practicing positive self-talk before training sessions. The session included exercises where Mia reflected on past situations where she felt confident and what helped her in those moments. She also practiced committing to small daily actions, such as setting a goal to try one new technique in practice or reminding herself of her strengths when negative thoughts arise. This commitment process supports Mia in moving forward with purpose, despite discomfort, helping her develop greater confidence and persistence.

Case Study Evaluation

To evaluate the case study, we used a multi-method approach to track Mia's progress throughout the intervention. First, regular sessional reflections and practitioner notes were analysed to identify qualitative changes in Mia's emotional responses, behavioural patterns, and engagement with core ACT processes. For example, pre-intervention, Mia often became overwhelmed by anxious thoughts before training, frequently leading to avoidance behaviours such as withdrawing from practice. By the midpoint of the intervention, practitioner notes highlighted moments where Mia acknowledged the presence of these thoughts ("I'm not good enough to be here") but chose to attend training regardless – demonstrating early signs of defusion and values-based action. In one reflection, she described "thanking her mind" when unhelpful thoughts appeared and focusing on her breathing to ground herself before walking to practice. By the final session, Mia reported using values clarification to guide her choices, such as being more vocal in team meetings despite discomfort, because she recognised this behaviour aligned with her personal values. These qualitative entries indicated a meaningful shift in how she related to difficult internal experiences, moving from avoidance and control to acceptance and purposeful engagement.

Second, standardised outcome measures, specifically the AAQ-II (Bond et al., 2011), were administered pre- and post-intervention to assess psychological flexibility. This quantitative data helped track shifts in Mia's experiential avoidance and willingness to engage with previously avoided thoughts and feelings. For example, Mia's pre-intervention AAQ-II score was 34, indicating a moderate to high level of experiential avoidance and psychological inflexibility. She frequently reported struggling to control or suppress distressing thoughts related to performance. By the end of the intervention, her AAQ-II score had decreased to 24, reflecting a marked improvement in her ability to accept uncomfortable thoughts and feelings without letting them dictate her behaviour. These changes suggest enhanced psychological flexibility, with Mia showing greater openness, awareness, and values-based action.

Finally, feedback from Mia during the final session was incorporated to evaluate subjective perceptions of change and intervention relevance. Mia described the ACT sessions as "different to anything I've done before" and shared that the focus on values and learning to "make space" for uncomfortable thoughts helped her feel less trapped by anxiety. She identified the defusion techniques as particularly helpful, noting that being able to label her thoughts as just "mental chatter" allowed her to shift attention back to her goals rather than getting stuck in rumination. Mia also reflected on the "values compass" exercise, which she said helped clarify what truly mattered to her beyond immediate performance outcomes, such as being a supportive teammate and growing her confidence. Together, these mixed-method approaches allowed for a comprehensive understanding of the intervention's impact, highlighting improvements in Mia's ability to stay present, psychological flexibility, and ability to act in line with personally meaningful values.

Practical Advice for SPPs

This chapter offers several recommendations for SPPs seeking to integrate ACT into their applied work. First, practitioners are encouraged to utilise a range of appropriate measures to assess psychological flexibility. Employing multiple assessment methods (e.g., self-report questionnaires, behavioural observations, and interviews) allows for a more comprehensive understanding of an athlete's cognitive, emotional, and behavioural processes (Taylor, 2017). Also, this multimodal approach enables more tailored and effective ACT intervention. In the present case study, this approach allowed for a clearer demonstration of Mia's progress, particularly in terms of improved confidence and performance levels.

Second, SPPs should remain abreast of the evidence base when designing ACT interventions to address confidence and performance in athletes. The evidence for using ACT interventions is still in its infancy, particularly in regard to supporting confidence and performance in athletes. As such, the field is still developing, and best practices continue to emerge. SPPs can keep up to date with the evidence base by regularly engaging with peer-reviewed journals, attending relevant conferences and workshops, subscribing to professional newsletters, and participating in CPD activities. They can also engage in supervision, join professional networks or special interest groups, and follow key researchers. Staying informed ensures that interventions are grounded in the most effective, evidence-informed techniques.

Finally, SPPs should not be overly structured when working from the Hexaflex model. While the six core processes offer a valuable framework, rigidly adhering to them in a linear or overly prescriptive manner can limit the flexibility and responsiveness needed to meet the unique and dynamic needs of each athlete. Instead, the Hexaflex should be used as a guiding map rather than a fixed sequence, integrating processes fluidly and contextually based on the athlete's presenting concerns, readiness for change, and performance environment. This flexible and context-sensitive application aligns with the spirit of ACT, which prioritises psychological flexibility and functional change over strict linear protocols (Hayes et al., 2012).

Concluding Comments

This chapter has demonstrated how ACT can be effectively applied within sport psychology practice to address confidence and performance-related challenges in athletes. Using a case example of a female athlete recovering from injury, we highlighted how psychological inflexibility can be meaningfully addressed through the six core ACT processes. The intervention targeted processes such as defusion, self-as-context, and committed action and supported the athlete in developing greater present-moment awareness, accepting difficult internal experiences, and reconnecting with her values. This led to measurable improvements in psychological flexibility. These findings align with the growing body of evidence and case examples of ACT in sport (e.g., Wood & Turner, 2025).

The key takeaway from this chapter is that ACT offers a practical framework for supporting athletes' confidence and performance. Rather than focusing solely on eliminating doubt or boosting self-belief, ACT equips athletes to accept discomfort, unhook from unhelpful thoughts, and take meaningful action aligned with their values. For athletes like Mia, who face fear of re-injury and reduced confidence, this shift in perspective can allow for fuller engagement in training and competition. As ACT encourages athletes to redefine confidence as not the absence of fear but the willingness to move forward in its presence, SPPs can use ACT to help athletes to embrace fear and help them perform with greater resilience and purpose.

References

Bach, P., & Moran, D. (2008). ACT in practice: Case conceptualization in acceptance and commitment therapy. New Harbinger Publications.

Bennett, R., & Oliver, J. E. (2019). *Acceptance and commitment therapy: 100 key points and techniques*. Routledge.

Bond, F. W., Hayes, S. C., Baer, R. A., Carpenter, K. M., Guenole, N., Orcutt, H. K., . . . & Zettle, R. D. (2011). Preliminary psychometric properties of the acceptance and action questionnaire – II: A revised measure of psychological inflexibility and experiential avoidance. *Behavior Therapy*, *42*(4), 676–688.

Cecil, S. (2020). Less control, more flexibility: Using acceptance and commitment therapy with injured athletes. In R. Wadey (Eds.), *Sport injury psychology* (pp. 197–206). Routledge.

De Petrillo, L. A., Kaufman, K. A., Glass, C. R., & Arnkoff, D. B. (2009). Mindful sport performance enhancement: An application of mindfulness and acceptance strategies in sport. Journal of Clinical Sport Psychology, 3(4), 291–303.

Gross, M., Moore, Z. E., Gardner, F. L., & Wolanin, A. T. (2018). An empirical examination comparing the mindfulness-acceptance-commitment approach and psychological skills training for the mental health and sport performance of female student athletes. International Journal of Sport and Exercise Psychology, 16(4), 431–451.

Gulbin, J. P., Croser, M. J., Morley, E. J., & Weissensteiner, J. R. (2013). An integrated framework for the optimisation of sport and athlete development: A practitioner approach. *Journal of Sports Sciences*, *31*(12), 1319–1331.

Harris, R. (2013). *Getting unstuck in ACT: A clinician's guide to overcoming common obstacles in acceptance and commitment therapy*. New Harbinger Publications.

Harris, R. (2019). ACT made simple: An easy-to-read primer on acceptance and commitment therapy (2nd ed.). New Harbinger Publications.

Hayes, L. L., Ciarrochi, J. V., & Bailey, A. (2022). What makes you stronger: How to thrive in the face of change and uncertainty using acceptance and commitment therapy. New Harbinger Publications.

Hayes, S. C. (2004). Acceptance and commitment therapy, relational frame theory, and the third wave of behavioral and cognitive therapies. *Behavior Therapy*, *35*(4), 639–665.

Hayes, S. C., Luoma, J. B., Bond, F. W., Masuda, A., & Lillis, J. (2006). Acceptance and commitment therapy: Model, processes and outcomes. *Behaviour Research and Therapy*, *44*(1), 1–25.

Hayes, S. C., Pistorello, J., & Levin, M. E. (2012). Acceptance and commitment therapy as a unified model of behavior change. *The Counseling Psychologist*, *40*(7), 976–1002.

LeJeune, J., & Luoma, J. B. (2019). *Values in therapy: A clinician's guide to helping clients explore values, increase psychological flexibility, and live a more meaningful life*. New Harbinger Publications.

Mahoney, J., & Hanrahan, S. J. (2011). A brief educational intervention using acceptance and commitment therapy: Four injured athletes' experiences. *Journal of Clinical Sport Psychology*, *5*(3), 252–273.

Ong, C. W., & Eustis, E. H. (2023). Psychological flexibility. In M. P. Twohig, M. E. Levin, & J. M. Petersen (Eds.), *The Oxford handbook of acceptance and commitment therapy* (pp. 169–181). Oxford University Press.

Price, D., Wagstaff, C. R., & Thelwell, R. C. (2022). "What if I get injured?": An acceptance and commitment therapy approach for fear of injury with a semielite youth snowboarder. *Case Studies in Sport and Exercise Psychology*, *6*(1), 12–20.

Ptáček, M., Šťastná, K., Vančurová, I., & Novotný, M. (2024). Effectiveness of acceptance and commitment therapy: A systematic review and meta--analysis-. Frontiers in Psychiatry, 15, 1403718.

Taylor, J. (2017). Importance of assessment in sport psychology consulting. In J. Taylor (Eds.), Assessment in applied sport psychology (pp. 3–14). Human Kinetics.
Thomas, O., Lane, A., & Kingston, K. (2011a). Defining and contextualizing robust sport-confidence. *Journal of Applied Sport Psychology*, *23*(2), 189–208.
Thomas, O., Murphy, S., & Hardy, L. (2011b). On the link between self-confidence and sport performance: A meta-analytic review. Journal of Sports Sciences, 29(7), 675–686.
Tranaeus, U., Gledhill, A., Johnson, U., Podlog, L., Wadey, R., Wiese Bjornstal, D., & Ivarsson, A. (2024). 50 years of research on the psychology of sport injury: A consensus statement. *Sports Medicine*, *54*(7), 1733–1748.
Wachsmuth, S., Feichtinger, P., Bartley, J., & Höner, O. (2024). Psychological characteristics and future success: A prospective study examining youth soccer players at different stages within the German talent development pathway. *Journal of Applied Sport Psychology*, *36*(2), 276–300.
Watson, D. R., Hill, A. P., Madigan, D. J., & Donachie, T. (2023). Effectiveness of an online acceptance and commitment therapy programme for perfectionism in soccer players. Sport, Exercise, and Performance Psychology, 13(1), 5–22.
Wood, S., & Turner, M. J. (2023). Using an acceptance and commitment therapy approach for fear of (re)injury with a competitive figure skater. Case Studies in Sport and Exercise Psychology, 7(1), 150–157.
Wood, S., & Turner, M. J. (2024). Using acceptance and commitment therapy to develop self-confidence in a neurodivergent athlete. Case Studies in Sport and Exercise Psychology, 8(1), 37–46.
Wood, S., & Turner, M. J. (2025). Using acceptance and commitment therapy with athletes. Scandinavian Journal of Sport and Exercise Psychology, 7, 1–9.
Young, P., & Turner, M. J. (2023). To (i) B or not to i (B), that is the question: On the differences between Ellis' REBT and Beck's CT. *The Cognitive Behaviour Therapist*, *16*, 1–10.

7 Performing with Vitality

Using DNA-V with Young Athletes

Laura D. Swettenham and Cheryl Grogan

Learning Objectives

1. To understand what DNA-V is and how it can help you to deliver effective support for young athletes
2. Gain insight into the core components of DNA-V, and how you can practically explore these areas with an athlete
3. To practice viewing an athlete case through a DNA-V lens, providing you with a starting point to conduct your own DNA-V case formulation

Why Do We Need DNA-V?

DNA-V (Discoverer, Noticer, Advisor – Values) is a contextual behaviour science approach and an adaptation of ACT (Liu et al., 2023). DNA-V was developed by Dr Louise Hayes and Dr Joseph Ciarocchi after observing the challenges ACT trainees faced when applying ACT processes with young people. ACT is often assumed to fit child and adolescent development, but Hayes and Ciarrochi (2020) emphasise that while ACT is used to support adults to move towards their values and committed action to live with (or lessen) pain and suffering, a developmental approach must focus on teaching, modelling, and shaping flexible thoughts, feelings, and actions before psychological inflexibility occurs. Hayes and Ciarrochi (2020) note how ACT practitioners need developmental knowledge to adapt ACT for young people or otherwise risk developmentally insensitive interventions.

Of course, all is not lost for the use of ACT with young people! There are likely some of you reading this who have delivered successful ACT interventions with young athletes. This may be because you have adapted ACT to be appropriate for young clients. There are interventions and resources for developmentally appropriate use of ACT, such as InTER-ACT (Samuel et al., 2021). However, there will be some of you reading this who have become stuck using ACT with young people and may have noted the lack of literature in this area. This is where DNA-V comes in.

DNA-V is developmentally informed and integrates contextual behavioural science principles, with empirical research suggesting that DNA-V interventions

DOI: 10.4324/9781003515203-9

contribute to improved mental health outcomes, reduced stress, and enhanced coping strategies (Shao et al., 2024). Importantly, the DNA-V model is not a one-to-one translation of the hexaflex to children and adolescents, but a model that provides practical and direct guidance for psychologists to use contextual behaviour science, ACT, and psychological flexibility processes within their work with adolescents (Hayes & Ciarrochi, 2015). A lack of psychological flexibility can negatively impact experiences of anxiety, depression, and quality of life when faced with challenges in sport (Johles et al., 2020). Both ACT and DNA-V focus on developing psychological flexibility through mindfulness, acceptance, and values-based actions; however, DNA-V incorporates positive psychology, process-based therapy (PBT), mindfulness-based interventions, self-determination theory, attachment theory, and evolutionary science (Hayes et al., 2022).

Contextualising the Authors

We're excited to share DNA-V with you and give you some insights into what this can look like in sport! Before we dive into the details surrounding DNA-V, we'd like to introduce ourselves as the authors. I am Laura, a sport and exercise psychologist. I have used ACT in my practice for five years and started to integrate DNA-V into my applied practice after searching for approaches for working with adolescents. I recall a supervision session two years ago where I was detailing my thoughts as to whether I was using ACT in an "adolescent-friendly" way. My supervisor at the time mentioned DNA-V, and since then, I have been down a DNA-V rabbit hole and using it in my applied practice.

I am Cheryl, a sport and exercise psychologist in training, working towards chartered status. Like Laura, I developed an interest in ACT early in my training while exploring different approaches. Laura, who is my supervisor, introduced me to DNA-V, and we booked onto the same online training. When I attended the training, the way Louise Hayes explained the approach made it feel accessible and practical, particularly for working with young children and adolescents. Since then, I've been using DNA-V in my applied practice, delivering workshops and during one-to-one sessions with athletes.

To be upfront, we would like to highlight that there is no current literature exploring the application of DNA-V within applied sport psychology practice. While we know of sport and exercise psychologists implementing DNA-V in their applied work, this chapter will largely draw on our own experiences of translating DNA-V literature from traditional psychology into a sporting setting. More research on the application of DNA-V within sporting contexts is required. We hope that sharing our understanding and experiences of using DNA-V within sport will encourage others to explore how the model may be used to benefit adolescent athletes and even help us and other DNA-V researchers and practitioners to develop the literature base!

Components of the DNA-V Model and Sport-Specific Applications

The acronym DNA-V represents four behavioural processes, which, when working with a client, can be referred to as skills: Discoverer, Noticer, Advisor, and Value (see Figure 7.1). Integrating these skills within a values-driven

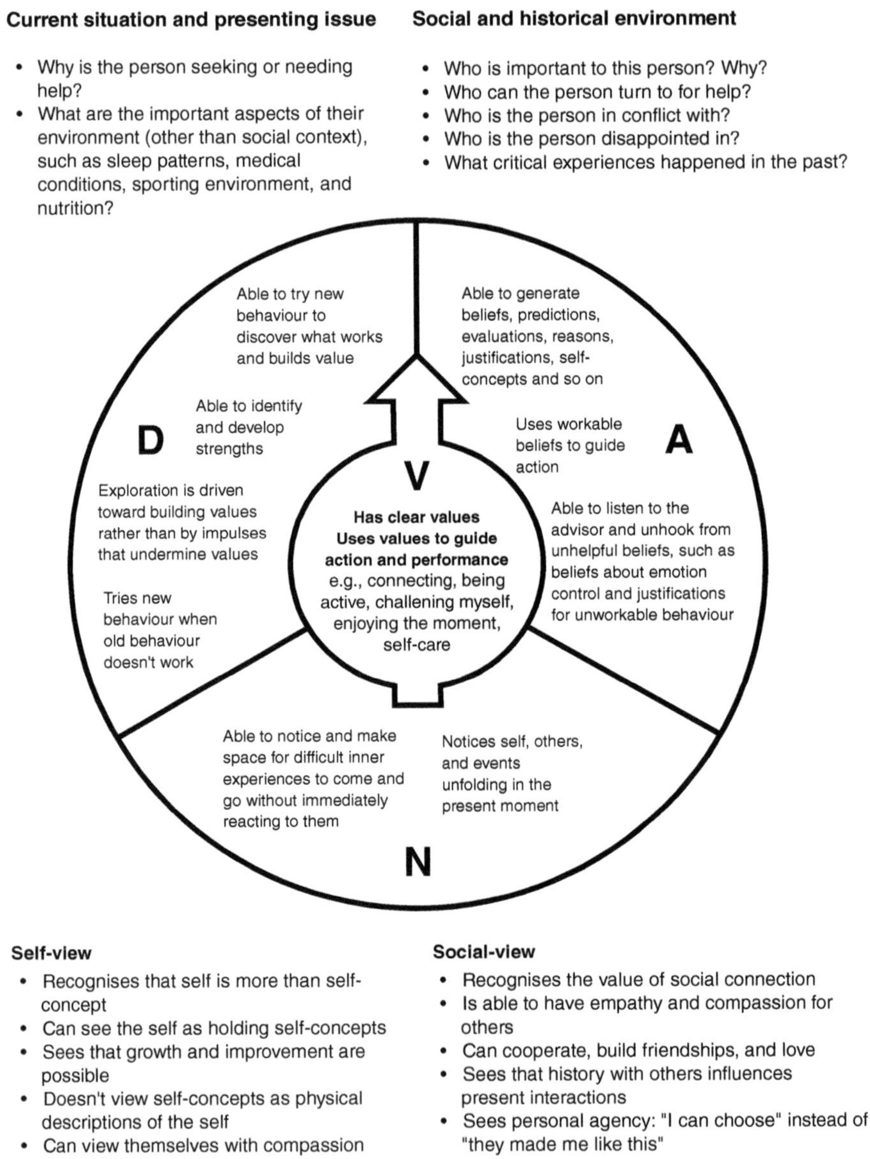

Figure 7.1 DNA-V model adapted from Hayes and Ciarrochi (2015).

framework, DNA-V promotes psychological flexibility – the ability to adapt, persist, or change behaviour in ways that serve long-term well-being (Hayes et al., 2011). The components of DNA-V can be referred to as skills because everyone can develop them. The outer circle of the model is home of "social" and "self", which represent the two perspectives through which the four processes are viewed (Hayes & Ciarrochi, 2020). "Social" and "self" shape how individuals relate to themselves, interact with others, and navigate challenges in their environment (Hayes & Ciarrochi, 2015).

Values (V) – "What Matters to You?"

Values serve as a guiding principle within the DNA-V model, in that advisor, noticer, and discoverer skills all connect to values to create vitality. We use the word vitality in this context to mean having a sense of energy and connection to what you're doing, even when it's hard (Hayes & Ciarrochi, 2015). Values help individuals align their behaviours with what is personally meaningful, fostering a sense of purpose and motivation, whereas vitality involves actions that "bring a sense of energy and embracing life" (Hayes & Ciarrochi, 2020, p. 303). Values work is not new in sport psychology and, of course, is a prominent aspect of approaches such as ACT (Wilson & Murrell, 2004) and existential psychology (Wong, 2010). When using DNA-V, the aim is to help young people to discern the difference between living a life that is values-driven and life-enhancing as opposed to valueless and life-draining. Value and vitality emerge through six key areas that contribute to overall well-being: connecting with others, challenging oneself and learning, embracing the moment, giving to others, being physically active, and caring for oneself (Hayes & Ciarrochi, 2015). Within sport, this can mean choosing courage, effort, or connection, even when things become difficult.

Importantly, we do not assume that young people have fixed, clearly formed values. Instead, we recognise that valuing is an ongoing process that develops gradually. As a practitioner, our role is to shape and nurture the athlete's values through conversation, experience, reflection, and linking words to actions. For the young person, their values are not fixed, and they may struggle to talk about what matters to them. When discussing values with adolescents, we're often met with answers like "I don't know" or "they all seem important". In DNA-V, we don't expect the young person to have all the answers and recognise that they instead require support to safely explore what their values may be. Rather than being fixed to certain values, we openly explore value and vitality, helping them understand what brings them meaning, energy, and purpose. So don't be surprised if the young athlete you're working with doesn't have clear values! We can support them through indirect values conversations and building positive therapeutic relationships. In time, our conversations may increasingly orient the young person towards a wider repertoire of values activities, such as storytelling, reflection, and real-life experiences in and outside of sport (Hayes & Ciarrochi, 2020).

Instead of asking "define your values" or "select your top three core values", a gentler approach to exploring values through conversation might mean asking questions like "what matters most to you about your sport?" or "If sport disappeared from your life tomorrow, what would you miss the most?" These questions help the athlete to reflect on what it is they care about, and when discomfort shows up, those difficult feelings are messengers, signalling something important is at stake, pointing us towards what really matters.

Values Activity – The Value Coin

This activity is adapted from Hayes (2023).

A successful way of exploring values with an athlete was through the Values Coin metaphor. Discussing a situation in their sport where the athlete experienced discomfort (e.g., freezing before a boxing match or complaining after a ref's decision in football). I ask the athlete to pause, reflect, and notice what feelings or thoughts show up:

Psychologist: "Let's think back to a difficult situation in your sport where you felt discomfort. Maybe some frustration, anger, or annoyance showed up for you?"

Athlete: "Hmm . . . well last week I was playing against my brother in practice, and we were playing a point-based drill and coach gave my brother the point instead of me. I was really annoyed".

Psychologist: "That sounds tough. Can you describe the discomfort that showed up inside of you at the time?

Athlete: "I was annoyed. I thought it was unfair. I felt like my coach likes my brother more than me. I tried hard to show her that I was better, but even when I clearly won the point, she still gave it to him".

Psychologist: "Thank you for sharing that with me. It's understandable that you would feel frustrated in that moment. If it is ok with you to explore this further, can I show you something called the Values Coin which may help you make sense of this discomfort and why this mattered so much?"

[The practitioner can draw or use a real coin for illustrative purposes.]

Psychologist: "The coin has two sides. On one side of the coin is this discomfort you described. On the other side of the coin, is something important to us. If that feeling of annoyance, unfairness and sadness could speak, what might it be telling us about what matters most to you?"

Athlete: "That I just wanted it to be fair. I wanted my coach to notice me and praise me for once instead of my brother".

Psychologist: "That makes sense, so it was more than just the point. It was about feeling that you weren't recognised or valued in that moment by your coach?

Athlete: "Yea, exactly! She always backs him".

Psychologist: "So it sounds like what matters to you was being seen and valued, especially by your coach?"

Athlete: "Yeah, exactly".

Psychologist: "That makes a lot of sense. All these things you mentioned, sound like the other side of the Values Coin. It sounds like being recognised by people close to you and being treated fairly are really important to you?"

Athlete: "Yes, actually that does sound like me".

While this kind of reflection can help athletes identify what matters to them, it's also important to remember that values aren't fixed, especially for young people. What matters to them may shift over time as they try new experiences or face new challenges. That's why it can be helpful to revisit these conversations regularly, using questions like:

- *"When do you feel most like 'yourself' during sport?"*
- *"What's your favourite part of being an athlete?"*
- *"If no one was watching, would you still play? Why?"*

These questions don't assume a final answer but instead support ongoing values discovery, a core aim of DNA-V practice.

After this exercise with the athlete, there is no right place to go next. From our experience, it may be useful to continue exploring values in more depth through other activities, step into the noticer, or explore vitality.

Noticer (N) – "What You Notice Inside and Outside of You"

The noticer actively brings our mind's attention to the world around us and within us (Gillard et al., 2021). Specifically, Hayes and Ciarrochi (2015) describe noticer behaviour as having five key facets, which allow us to: tune in to our bodies, detect sensations, identify and label emotions, map out how our actions affect others, and tune into the world and what it has to offer. Importantly, "Noticer" is not simply a different name for "Being Present" in an ACT model. The noticer accounts for how young people have used noticing skills in their developmental life history. However, there are several similarities to ACT. For example, a skilled noticer will be able to tune into their bodily sensations and accept that such feelings and sensations are part of the human condition (Neumann et al., 2010). The skilled noticer does not try to control their feelings but be aware of them, label them, and accept them. This allows the young person to slow down, and rather than reacting, they can pause, breathe, and look around. This can help them to have more time to notice whether their advisor is being helpful or unhelpful and decide on their course of action from there.

One way to engage with the five facets of the noticer is through mindfulness practice, which includes observing experience; describing experience; acting with awareness; being non-judging of inner experience; and non-reactivity to inner experience (Baer et al., 2006). Drawing on the sport performance literature, we know that mindfulness skills are associated with increased flow, psychological skills, performance, and reduced performance anxiety (Noetel et al., 2019). There are specific mindfulness programmes for sport, such as Mindfulness Sport Performance Enhancement (Kaufman et al., 2009) and Mindfulness Acceptance Commitment (MAC; Moore, 2009). The mindfulness activities within such models may be of benefit to integrate with DNA-V, if you believe the exercises are developmentally appropriate. However, DNA-V emphasises that you do not need to engage with formal, sit-down meditation practice to develop noticer skills. Hayes and Ciarrochi (2015) outline three steps to developing noticer skills. These steps can be remembered as "Normalise AND Allow", and we will provide a description of this below with some tips that we've picked up from our own practice.

Noticer Activity – Normalise "AND" Allow

This activity is from Hayes and Ciarrochi (2015).

Step 1: Normalise

- Be aware that all feelings are normal
- Being aware that no feelings need to be controlled, removed, changed, or downregulated
- Being aware that all feelings pass and move on in their own time, often quite quickly

To normalise the feelings the athlete is experiencing, it can be useful to discuss emotions as a valuable source of information or a signpost to what we need. In westernised society, we are often taught to see emotions as weak or the enemy, and in sporting culture, this is emphasised with a narrative to be tough and unshakable, and, as a result, can lead to avoidance of this vital information source. Within sport, it can be useful to discuss with athletes the amount of energy they are using to fight or push away their emotions, which can instead be put into their performance. To use an ACT term, by dropping the struggle, we have more space to fully engage with performance.

Step 2: Practice AND

A = Aware: being aware of physical sensations in the body (e.g., awareness of your breath moving in and out of your body and scanning the body and noticing sensations)

N = Name: naming the physical sensations in the body and where they are located (internally or spoken aloud)

D = Describe: describing the inner experiences as feeling states, or emotions

In this step, when working with athletes who might be struggling to access labels or sensations of emotions, we may spend more time exploring these experiences in different ways. A few ideas include using an emotions wheel to help build vocabulary for emotions and understanding of emotional granularity, using a "gingerbread man" to map bodily sensations, and activities where the athlete will draw the shape, size, colour, and texture of the emotion.

Step 3: Allow

- Allowing feelings and whatever is there in the present moment
- Allowing judgements about feelings and not reacting to them
- Extend "notice AND allow" skills with daily mindfulness practice

Here, you may find it useful to draw on acceptance and willingness metaphors from ACT. You may also find "the willingness question" useful here: "Are you willing to allow this feeling in order to compete in your sport (valued activity)?"

When extending mindfulness practice, this might be informal mindfulness for the athlete that is general (e.g., brushing teeth mindfully) or sport-specific (e.g., bouncing a tennis ball mindfully) or formal mindfulness meditation. For formal mindfulness meditation, consider age-appropriate resources and apps. For example, we often use the smilingmind or headspace apps due to their age-specific meditations.

This noticer activity can be done formally or informally in a one-to-one with an athlete, or the athlete can go through these steps internally on their own before a performance. For young people, it is also important that their parents and/or coaches are able to reinforce the same messages as in DNA-V. This activity can also be taught to coaches, who can use "Normalise AND Allow" to reflect with athletes after a drill, or even during halftime, or after a match.

Advisor (A) – "What You Tell Yourself"

The Advisor is a metaphor for our internal voice that provides guidance, reasoning, and self-reflection as well as judgement, evaluation, predications, and rules (Hayes & Ciarrochi, 2015). Though our advisors will differ in intensity and frequency, DNA-V assumes that we all have an advisor! You might be able to hear yours now. Try stopping for two minutes and closing your eyes; you might be able to hear your advisor in action. When playing sport, you may also have an active advisor! For example, we might hear our advisor saying, "what a terrible shot, don't do that again" or "why are you bothering, you can't win this". While the "advice" the advisor gives us can be beneficial in decision-making and keeping us safe in certain contexts (e.g., don't touch the fire, you'll burn yourself), the advisor can contribute to self-criticism and negative thinking patterns. DNA-V encourages individuals to develop a balanced relationship with their inner advisor, recognising when its influence is helpful and when it may be unhelpful.

DNA-V aims to develop flexible advisor behaviour, including normalising and accepting predictive thinking (e.g., what if I make a mistake and what if they don't like me). Of course, an athlete questioning themselves on whether they will win might be helpful in motivating them to train harder and perform better, but it will be unhelpful if it cultivates fear and performance anxiety. DNA-V, therefore, will support the athlete to create flexible rules and allow the athlete to decide whether their advisor is being helpful or unhelpful and empower them to choose whether they want to listen or not. Practically, when developing advisor skills, we will help the athlete to increase their awareness of the advisor, see that their advisor is not in control of their behaviour, create flexible rules, and shift between the advisor and noticer. You can also integrate ACT defusion skills when working with DNA-V to create space and awareness of the advisor.

Advisor Activity – Don't Pick It Up!

This activity is adapted from Hayes and Ciarrochi (2020).

Don't pick it up is an activity that helps the athlete to experience that they don't have to listen to the advisor. Note that you can change this to be sport-specific if you like, for example, you could change picking up your phone to kicking a ball, etc. Feel free to get creative!

Psychologist: Is it OK if we do a quick activity to explore your advisor a bit more?

Athlete: Ok . . . !

Psychologist: You're going to need an object for this activity, do you have your phone or a pen?

Athlete: Yes, I've got my phone.

Psychologist: OK great. So, I want you say over and over to yourself that you cannot pick up your phone. Tell yourself that it is impossible to pick up your phone. Keep repeating this to yourself now for 30 seconds, I'll tell you when to stop.

athlete silently repeats phrase to themselves

Psychologist: OK, now pick up your phone.

athlete looks at psychologist questioningly, but picks up their phone.

Psychologist: Tell me what you noticed then, you might even find it useful to step into your noticer like we practiced last week to see what's showing up for you right now.

Athlete: Well, first, I thought that I couldn't pick it up and I was kind of questioning it. But then I realised I could, so . . . I did. I noticed some confusion and, strangely, some uncertainty about whether I could pick it up which seems a bit silly!

Psychologist: Isn't it interesting how just saying something to ourselves can make us uncertain about our abilities! That voice telling you not to pick it up, that's your advisor and they can be very good at telling us what to do (or not to do)! What you just proved is that you don't have to listen to your advisor. Someone who hears their advisor, considers, and then acts is a sign of someone with helpful advisor skills and is exactly what you did here with your phone. But, choosing what to do in sport can be tough, right? To help us with that, we need to tune into the discoverer and our values.

Discoverer (D) – "What You Do, What Action You Take"

The discoverer promotes exploration and experimentation and encourages individuals to engage in new behaviours, test different approaches to problem-solving, and adapt based on outcomes. In short, the discoverer is when the young person engages in trial and error experiences (Hayes & Ciarrochi, 2020). The discoverer is underpinned by evolutionary theory, where principles of variation, selection by consequences, and retention can explain how environments shape our development and the behaviours we engage with or avoid. In a sporting context, for example, an athlete might experiment with new techniques during training (variation). Some of these are positively reinforced, such as a skill that leads to praise from a coach or improved performance, while others are not (selection). Over time, the athlete is more likely to repeat the skill that has worked in the past (retention). A failure to thrive and grow can be seen as a failure in variation (Hayes & Ciarrochi, 2015). For example, you might be working with a young athlete who shows no variation in their behaviour because they are so fearful of making a mistake and not being selected for the team. This fear may come along with an active inner narrative (i.e., advisor) and lead to the athlete standing back in matches and not wanting to get involved. By avoiding making mistakes, this reinforces the behaviour to stand back and not get involved. Working with this athlete on developing DNA-V skills, we can help the athlete to develop more flexible thinking and behaviours. Here, the discoverer skill allows the athlete to build a repertoire of behaviours to test, which is key for development, where young people are constantly learning about the physical world, adapting their behaviours, and engaging in risk-taking, which is essential to positive development (Duell & Steinberg, 2019; Parsons et al., 1997). Encouraging exploration of discoverer behaviours can lead to the development of helpful rules from the athlete's advisor (e.g., when I try my best, coach appreciates me; putting in effort is important), as well as unhelpful rules (e.g., when I make a mistake coach shouts at me; I shouldn't make mistakes).

We might track behaviours (old and new) with the athlete to explore workability, for example, "is standing back in matches and not getting involved working for you?" and "does this behaviour bring you vitality or bring you towards your values?". Tracking is a skill whereby we encourage athletes to select a behaviour based on autonomy and strengths, and it is essential to track behaviours within a specific context (Hayes & Ciarrochi, 2020). For example, you might get the athlete to track: the situation/context, what they did (behaviour), what happened next (consequence), and did it work/did it help your performance or well-being in the long run (workability).

Discoverer Activity – Something New

This activity is adapted from Hayes (2023)

This activity introduces the athlete to the discoverer through trying something new. This engages the experimental and trial-and-error aspects of the discoverer, engaging the athlete in an experiential discovery. Following the introduction of the advisor through this activity, you can start to explore what the athlete's discoverer behaviours look like based on the strengths, their values, and what gives them vitality.

Psychologist: Today I want you to do something new that you've never done in a psychology session before . . . are you willing to do try this with me?

Athlete: Yeah, that sounds . . . interesting! What are we going to do?

Psychologist: Well, that's for you to decide, can you think of something we can do here today that you've never done before? It could be to do with your sport or something completely random!

Athlete: Hmm, it's a bit strange, but how about . . . using our tennis rackets as broomsticks and flying around the room?

Psychologist: This is a great idea, shall we do it together?

Athlete: Yes!!

The psychologist and athlete fly around on the tennis rackets like broomsticks

Psychologist: OK! How was that, what did you notice inside and outside?

Athlete: I was quite excited to start with because it was new! But I did feel a bit nervous knowing that I was going to look silly and was a bit worried what I would look like doing it. But now that we've finished, I thought it was quite funny, and I enjoyed doing it.

Psychologist: OK, so you had a mixture of excitement and nerves but did it anyway and afterwards, you felt good about it?

Athlete: Yeah, I felt happy afterwards, like I wanted to keep smiling but I did keep thinking that I shouldn't do it, it's too silly!

Psychologist: Do you remember when we spoke about the advisor last week? Sometimes, our advisor may be nervous to try something new; it might seem uncertain or scary to your advisor because you have no evidence from past experience to refer to. As we get older, we get stuck in the same behaviours, the same responses, the same pattern of play in a tennis match, but it can be useful to try new behaviours, new patterns. Your discoverer is what helps you to try different behaviours to give you different results or new experiences, just like we did here today!

DNA-v Case Formulation with an Athlete

With your understanding of the components of DNA-V, we want you to practice viewing an athlete case with a DNA-V lens. To bring this to life, we have provided a case example linking to the four DNA-V processes before mapping this onto a case formulation. Before doing this, we want to highlight that within the DNA-V skills, we will talk to clients about "helpful" and "unhelpful" behaviours which are associated with these skills. To ensure the anonymity of the clients whilst still providing you with examples from our practice, we will merge various clients into one example, providing examples of various points in the sport psychology consultancy process.

Jermain's Case

Jermain is a 15-year-old footballer who attended an elite football academy. It was coming towards the end of the season, where he would be given news of being retained and accepted into the scholars' programme or released for good. During training, his abilities and work ethic were evident and often praised by coaches, but on match day, he hesitated on the ball, made rushed or "poor" decisions, and made mistakes that only reinforced his fear – that he wasn't "good enough". When asking Jermain about how he felt when this happened, he struggled to label his feelings and kept saying, "I'm not sure, it's just a weird feeling", and that he "didn't like it". His inner voice would show up telling him things like "I am not good enough" or "I am bad at this, why am I even trying", and "I am rubbish, why would they keep me?" (unhelpful advisor). This internal narrative reinforced to Jermain that he was a failure, and it negatively affected his performance, heightening his fear on the ball (unhelpful discoverer). When asking Jermain what he would change if he could, he said he would "want the ball" more and "actively ask for the ball" (helpful discoverer), but despite knowing what to do, he says he "can't do it on the day" (unhelpful advisor). Jermain says he always worries about what other people think of his performance and thinks he's "so bad" when he loses against teams that he "should easily beat" (unhelpful advisor). Jermain says he has been playing football since he was so young that he doesn't know why he's doing it anymore (valueless). He doesn't want to let his parents down; they've invested so much time and money into his development (unhelpful advisor).

Jermain and I collaboratively worked through a DNA-V case formulation (see Figure 7.2). During the case formulation, Jermain and I identified the advisor as a key area to focus on. Following the completion of the case formulation, I explained to Jermain that he can choose where to begin. Allowing space for the athlete to choose where to begin is important, as this allows for autonomy and their willingness to engage in this process.

Following the intervention, if developing DNA-V skills with Jermain was successful, we would hope that he can be present and notice when his advisor is being unhelpful, providing him with space to engage with helpful

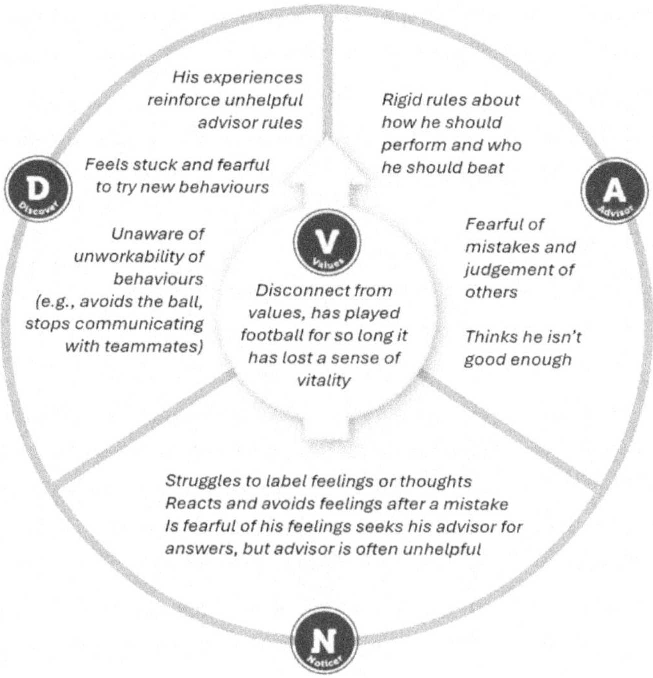

Figure 7.2 Jermain's DNA-V case formulation.

Note: The full case formulation worksheet can be found on the DNA-V international website.

discoverer behaviours during a match. To action a helpful discoverer behaviour, he would have developed skills to understand his values and how these link to his discoverer actions (i.e., does he have some different actions he can take in this scenario to be flexible when faced with discomfort?). Much like in ACT, his advisor would still verbalise unhelpful thoughts, and he will still experience uncomfortable emotions, but he is able to notice them and refocus onto a helpful discoverer behaviour.

Summary and Closing Suggestions

This chapter has outlined the DNA-V model as a practical way to develop psychological flexibility in youth athletes, and we hope that this introduction to the DNA-V model has sparked your interest (and perhaps more questions!). We would like to emphasise that this chapter is a *brief* introduction to what is a nuanced model, with many more resources available online for you to explore. As mentioned at the beginning of this chapter, the resources you will find in sporting contexts will be limited, but exploring the clinical resources for therapists and teachers will greatly benefit you if you decide to explore this model in more depth. For example, exploring the "social" and "self" components of DNA-V in more detail, and exploring more experiential activities and metaphors that align with DNA-V. It is important to use accessible, engaging metaphors and exercises that resonate with young athletes' lived experiences. Flexibility in delivery is key to ensuring the model supports growth in a meaningful and lasting way. Finally, we encourage sport psychologists to engage in reflective practice and supervision when applying DNA-V, and to contribute to the growing research base by documenting and evaluating their work. DNA-V has the potential to not only improve sport performance but to foster well-being, adaptability, and thriving in adolescence and beyond.

References

Baer, R. A., Smith, G. T., Hopkins, J., Krietemeyer, J., & Toney, L. (2006). Using self-report assessment methods to explore facets of mindfulness. *Assessment, 13*(1), 27–45. https://doi.org/10.1177/1073191105283504

Duell, N., & Steinberg, L. (2019). Positive risk taking in adolescence. *Child Development Perspectives, 13*(1), 48–52. https://doi.org/10.1111/cdep.12310

Gillard, D., Reid, A., Bull-Beddows, R., Mohamed-Goush, S., Stanley-Duke, M., & Cook, E. (2021). Universal well-being practices in schools: Framing evidence-informed practice within the five ways to well-being. *Educational Psychology Research and Practice, 7*(1), 1–12.

Hayes, L. (2023). *Helping young people to grow with psychological flexibility* [workshop]. Contextual Consulting. Online.

Hayes, L., & Ciarrochi, J. (2020). Growing up flexibly: DNA-v as a contextual behavioural science approach to working with young people. In *Innovations in acceptance and commitment therapy: Clinical advancements and applications in ACT: New Harbinger Publications, 2020*, 296.

Hayes, L., Ciarrochi, J., & Bailey, A. (2022). *What makes you stronger: How to thrive in the face of uncertainty using acceptance and commitment therapy*. New Harbinger Publications.

Hayes, L., & Ciarrochi, J. V. (2015). *The thriving adolescent: Using acceptance and commitment therapy and positive psychology to help teens manage emotions, achieve goals, and build connection*. New Harbinger Publications.

Hayes, S. C., Strosahl, K. D., & Wilson, K. G. (2011). *Acceptance and commitment therapy: The process and practice of mindful change*. Guilford Press.

Johles, L., Gustafsson, H., Jansson-Fröjmark, M., Classon, C., Hasselqvist, J., & Lundgren, T. (2020). Psychological flexibility among competitive athletes: A psychometric investigation of a new scale. *Frontiers in Sports and Active Living, 2*, 110. https://doi.org/10.3389/fspor.2020.00110

Kaufman, K. A., Glass, C. R., & Arnkoff, D. B. (2009). Evaluation of mindful sport performance enhancement (MSPE): A new approach to promote flow in athletes. *Journal of Clinical Sport Psychology, 3*(4), 334–356. https://doi.org/10.1123/jcsp.3.4.334

Liu, Y., Chen, Y., Liu, Z., Zhang, Y., Wu, M., & Zhu, Z. (2023). The effect of DNA-V model intervention on learning behaviors and stress in Chinese adolescents: A randomized controlled trial. *Journal of Contextual Behavioral Science, 30*, 181–190. https://doi.org/10.1016/j.jcbs.2023.10.005

Moore, Z. E. (2009). Theoretical and empirical developments of the mindfulness-acceptance-commitment (MAC) approach to performance enhancement. *Journal of Clinical Sport Psychology*, *3*(4), 291–302. https://doi.org/10.1123/jcsp.3.4.291

Neumann, A., van Lier, P. A., Gratz, K. L., & Koot, H. M. (2010). Multidimensional assessment of emotion regulation difficulties in adolescents using the difficulties in emotion regulation scale. *Assessment*, *17*(1), 138–149. https://doi.org/10.1177/1073191109349579

Noetel, M., Ciarrochi, J., Van Zanden, B., & Lonsdale, C. (2019). Mindfulness and acceptance approaches to sporting performance enhancement: A systematic review. *International Review of Sport and Exercise Psychology*, *12*(1), 139–175. https://doi.org/10.1080/1750984X.2017.1387803

Parsons, J. T., Siegel, A. W., & Cousins, J. H. (1997). Late adolescent risk-taking: Effects of perceived benefits and perceived risks on behavioral intentions and behavioral change. *Journal of Adolescence*, *20*(4), 381–392. https://doi.org/10.1006/jado.1997.0094

Samuel, V., Constable, C., Harris, E., & Channon, S. (2023). Developing the content of a brief universal acceptance and commitment therapy (ACT) programme for secondary school pupils: InTER-ACT. *Pastoral Care in Education*, *41*(1), 42–62. https://doi.org/10.1080/02643944.2021.1977991

Shao, S., Zhang, Y., Yang, M., Li, C., Zhao, R., Liu, Z., Wu, M., Liu, Y., Zhu, Z., & Cui, L. (2024). The effectiveness of the DNA--V program on reducing anxiety among Chinese adolescents: Outcomes of the face---to---face and web---based versions-. *Journal of School Psychology*, *106*, 101357. https://doi.org/10.1016/j.jsp.2024.101357

Wilson, K. G., & Murrell, A. R. (2004). Values work in acceptance and commitment therapy. In *Mindfulness and acceptance: Expanding the cognitive-behavioral tradition* (pp. 120–151). New York: Guildford Press.

Wong, P. T. (2010). Meaning therapy: An integrative and positive existential psychotherapy. *Journal of Contemporary Psychotherapy*, *40*(2), 85–93. https://doi.org/10.1007/s10879-009-9132-6

8 Stress, Burnout, and Well-Being in Sports Coaching

Luke Barnes and Peter Olusoga

Learning Objectives

1. Recognise how coaching pressures and burnout relate to core ACT concepts, understanding how organisational demands and value-behaviour misalignment reduce psychological flexibility and contribute to burnout
2. Explain how ACT hexaflex processes can be applied to support coaches practice and well-being, with a particular emphasis on values, acceptance, defusion, and committed action to manage stress and maintain a sense of purpose
3. Analyse the application of ACT through the case study of Paul, demonstrating how values clarification and ACT-based skills can reduce burnout symptoms, guide more effective behavioural choices, and promote more sustainable, values-driven coaching

Introduction

Sports coaching, particularly at the highest competitive levels, has been described as a demanding, stressful, and even unsustainable profession, due to the significant challenges often experienced by coaches (Hägglund et al., 2024). The work of coaches is multifaceted, including planning, monitoring, leadership, and management of people and resources (Mallett, 2010). Across all levels of competitive sport, the demands placed on coaches have been steadily increasing, and coaches' experiences of stress have been well-documented (Norris et al., 2017). The impact of job demands and psychological stress on coaches' well-being and mental health outcomes has also received growing attention in the research literature (e.g.,214 Henttä et al., 2024; Pilkington et al., 2022). Although this research has largely focused on burnout (Olusoga et al., 2019), coaches' overall well-being and the sustainability of the profession have become important topics for discussion. Indeed, a recent swell in research attending to the unsustainable nature of sports coaching (e.g., Higham et al., 2024; Kenttä et al., 2024; Simova et al., 2024) has encouraged calls for the prioritisation of coach well-being and the creation of more sustainable work conditions for coaches (Olusoga et al., 2025).

DOI: 10.4324/9781003515203-10

At the individual level, a focus on recovery (Eccles et al., 2023; Higham et al., 2024), exploration and integration of personal values and identity (Simova et al., 2024) and mindfulness, self-awareness, self-compassion, and vulnerability (Hägglund et al., 2024) have all been recently discussed as potentially fruitful intervention strategies. ACT has also been identified as a relevant approach to aid sports coaches (Hill & Oliver, 2019). At their core, ACT approaches aim to increase psychological flexibility; the ability to stay present, accept difficult internal experiences (thoughts, feelings, urges), and still act in line with chosen values. Coaches taking part in group-based ACT interventions have reported improved self-awareness of thoughts and emotions, increased relational effectiveness, encouraging greater needs supportive coaching, and lower perceived levels of burnout (e.g., Tian & Cheng, 2025; Gutman et al., 2025a, 2025b). Quantitative insights from Tian and Cheng (2025) also suggested that a four-week Coach ACT intervention was sufficient to increase coaches' mindfulness and reduce job stress and burnout.

Group-delivered ACT programmes have also demonstrated effectiveness in high-stress occupational and healthcare settings by reducing distress and improving psychological flexibility, outcomes that are also directly relevant for elite coaching environments (O'Brien et al., 2019; Piot et al., 2024; Prudenzi et al., 2021). Within sport, MAC protocols adapted for teams have been shown to enhance emotion regulation, attentional focus, and values-consistent behaviour, mechanisms that are protective against stress and burnout sport performers (Gardner & Moore, 2012; Josefsson et al., 2024). Although widespread coach-focused interventions remain limited, converging evidence supports the application of ACT for sports coaches and multidisciplinary teams (MDTs) (Unruh et al., 2022; Wang et al., 2023)

Case Study

Paul is a 28-year-old coach, who has recently joined a leading, elite soccer academy from a lower-ranked academy. Paul is ambitious to coach at the highest level. He has previously completed a range of soccer coaching qualifications and has a BSc in Sports Coaching. With almost a decade of coaching experience, primarily working with players aged 12–16 previously, Paul has been hired to coach an older age group (17–21 years), which he says is "out of his comfort zone". His job is full-time, and the expectation at the academy is that Paul (alongside other staff) is available seven days a week, with the majority of training and games on evenings and weekends. Paul has recently become a father for the first time, and he wants to spend as much time with his newborn baby and partner as he can. However, the academy is in the middle of pre-season training, and the work demands placed on Paul are intense. As a member of the coaching staff, Paul works alongside a range of other coaches and support staff as part of a MDT. As a follow-up to an MDT meeting, Paul books in with the sport psychology consultant to discuss how he can integrate sport psychology principles with his players as part of his coaching role. He says his goal is to "be the best coach possible" to the players he works with.

Session 1: Intake and Identifying Problems

Establishing rapport, understanding the client's context, and identifying surface-level and underlying issues that may need to be addressed are vital in the initial stages of consultancy (Chow et al., 2022; Sharp et al., 2015). ACT interventions emphasise the importance of open discussion to build this rapport and establish a detailed client context (e.g., Barnes, 2024). Paul presents as highly motivated and eager to learn how to integrate sport psychology principles into his coaching practice. However, beneath his enthusiasm lie several personal and professional stressors. The following dialogue captures the first consultation with Paul, highlighting his presenting issues and potential areas for targeted ACT intervention.

Consultant: Thanks for meeting today, Paul. I appreciate you would like to discuss how you can integrate psychology with some of the stuff you do with players, but before we go into that I'd like to get to know more about you, your role, and how things have been since you joined the academy?

Paul: Honestly, it's been a bit of a whirlwind. The environment here is a step up from what I'm used to. I've always coached younger players, but now I'm responsible for lads who are basically adults. It's a step up and some of them have even played in the first team already. It feels a bit out of my comfort zone to be honest.

Consultant: Thanks for sharing that. What do you think makes it feel out of your comfort zone?

Paul: The maturity of the players, really. They're closer to the first team, so expectations are higher on them, but also on me. They challenge you more, they ask questions, and I sometimes feel like I'm under the microscope. I want to do a good job, but I worry I'm not experienced enough yet.

Consultant: That sounds like a lot of pressure and I understand that you just want to do as well as you can in the role. How are you finding the demands of the role overall?

Paul: Pretty tough. It's full-on. We're expected to be here most days of the week, including evenings and weekends. Pre-season is intense. To be honest, I'm struggling with the balance because I've just become a dad too! I want to be at home with my partner and my little one, but I feel guilty when I'm not giving everything to the academy.

Consultant: Congratulations on becoming a father! That's a huge life change. Sounds like you have lots of competing demands. How does it feel trying to juggle both roles, as a coach and as a dad?

Paul: Right now, it feels like I'm failing a bit at both. When I'm here, I'm distracted thinking about home. When I'm at home, I feel like I should be preparing sessions or watching footage. I'm tired all the time. I find myself being short-tempered, which isn't like me. Sometimes I doubt whether I can handle this level. I keep telling myself I need to "push through", but it's wearing me down.

Consultant: Thanks for being open about that and sharing how you feel. (Pauses) Can I ask a bit more about what made you book this meeting with me today?

Paul: Well, I want to integrate psychology into my coaching. I see it as essential for developing players. I thought maybe if I can learn more, I'll be a better coach. My ultimate goal is to coach at the highest level, and I want every tool possible to help me get there.

Consultant: I can see you're really ambitious and driven. When you say, "be the best coach possible", what does that look like for you in practice?

Paul: For me it's about creating an environment where players feel supported, but also challenged. I want them to trust me, to develop as footballers and as people. I think psychology plays a massive role in that; building resilience, confidence, focus. But I'm not sure how to bring it in day-to-day.

At this stage of the intake process, the consultant has used active listening skills to ascertain Paul's current situation and his thoughts about it. The conversation has highlighted two key themes: Paul's current stressors and his future professional practice aspirations. There are several areas the consultant may wish to explore in more depth, based on Paul's use of language (e.g., "feels like I am failing" and "needing to push through"). However, at this early stage of the consultancy, an overview of Paul's current situation might be more valuable. A vocalised consultant summary is a way of checking Paul's current level of insight into these issues and provides an opportunity for Paul to expand further if he wants to. In turn, the consultant and Paul can collaboratively generate client-centred, ACT-informed next steps for the consultancy work.

Consultant: OK. So, on one hand, you want to learn practical ways to use psychology with your players. On the other, you're navigating new pressures, like a step up in your role, long work hours, and new family responsibilities.

Paul: Yeah, that's right. And it's definitely having an impact. Sometimes I'm not as present as I want to be, and not actually focussed on what I'm doing. If I'm stressed or tired, I know I'm in my head and not giving the players my best. And I don't want to be like that.

Consultant: That's some really useful insight and it seems like you're quite aware of what's going on. What do you feel you need most right now to help you with this?

Paul: Honestly, some guidance. How to manage the stress, how to balance my roles better, and then how to practically apply some of those principles with the players too. If I can get more confident in those areas and managing those pressures myself, I think I'll grow into the job more.

This initial intake conversation with Paul reveals he is both ambitious and driven as a coach, but also vulnerable and fallible as a human being. He has highlighted several issues (transition to coaching older, more demanding players; work–life imbalance, high workload expectations and his new responsibilities as a father, signs of stress and possible burnout, self-reported fatigue, irritability, and self-doubt) but has also mentioned a key developmental goal, centred on integrating sport psychology principles into his coaching practice to enhance both player performance and his own effectiveness.

These insights provide a foundation for the consultancy relationship, with priorities being to connect Paul with his values, as an important process to promote his well-being and alleviate coach burnout. In the aforementioned dialogue, Paul has already started to identify with strong professional **values**, surrounding growth, player development, and excellence despite the intake dialogue not explicitly targeting values or associated **committed action** (e.g., "wanting to be the best coach possible" and to "be the best dad possible"), but admitted feeling pulled away from these priorities by stress and workload demands. Research suggests that connecting with and/or negotiating values is an important process for promoting coach well-being and alleviating burnout (Simova et al., 2024). There are many places one might begin consultancy in ACT; however, due to the existing evidence base and the previous dialogue with Paul, exploring values appears a sensible place to start. The consultancy dialogue, therefore, focuses on increasing Paul's psychological flexibility by first unpacking and articulating his **personal values.**

During the intake dialogue above, Paul also described being **fused with self-doubting thoughts** ("I'm not experienced enough") and experiencing **avoidance** of discomfort by "pushing through" fatigue rather than acknowledging it. He also reported difficulties with **present-moment awareness**, reflecting that he is often distracted during coaching sessions and at home, which undermines his sense of effectiveness and fulfilment in both roles. Therefore, in addition to initial values exploration, the consultancy work will subsequently focus on cultivating **acceptance** strategies to help him open up to stress without being dominated by it, using **cognitive defusion** techniques to understand and reduce the impact of self-critical thoughts, enhancing mindful **present-moment focus** so he can be engaged with both players and family, and supporting **committed action** by clarifying concrete, values-driven behaviours. These ACT processes will provide the framework for integrating psychological skills into Paul's own coaching practice while also supporting his holistic, personal well-being across contexts.

Session 2: Further Values Articulation and Clarification

A central aim of ACT is to help individuals clarify their values (beliefs about what is important in life), which might subsequently be used to guide behaviour. Unlike goals, values are not "achieved" but may be lived out daily, across different contexts, without reaching a specific endpoint or outcome. The *Inner Compass* activity (see Gutman et al., 2025a) might be used to explore and articulate Paul's "True North", a direction of travel that represents alignment with his core values. This activity positions values as the guiding orientation on a compass: each action can either move the client closer to, or further away from their values. The following dialogue demonstrates how the consultant and Paul worked together to uncover and refine the qualities that make up his True North, as well as recognising barriers that pull him away from this.

Consultant: Paul, today I'd like us to work on clarifying your values using an activity called the *Inner Compass.* Think of values as your True North, no matter where you are or what situation you're in, they can guide you back to the direction that matters most. Our task is to work out what your True North is. How does that sound?

Paul: Sounds helpful. I think I've lost sight of what matters with everything going on.

Consultant: Great. So, let's begin by imagining this: if someone close to you, maybe your partner, your players, or even your child when they're older was describing what kind of person you were, what qualities would you want them to notice?

Paul: Hmm . . . I'd want them to say I cared. That I wasn't just focused on myself or results, but that I genuinely supported people.

Consultant: Caring. Tell me more about what that looks like in action, whether at home, at work, or with friends.

Paul: At home, it's being patient and listening. At work, it's checking in with players beyond football – like how they're coping with school or family. With friends, it's making time even when I'm busy.

Consultant: That's powerful. So "caring" seems like a quality that runs across all areas of your life. Does that feel like part of your True North?

Paul: Yes, definitely.

Consultant: Okay, let's keep going. Think about your own growth. When you feel at your best, what direction are you moving in?

Paul: I think it's when I'm learning. I've always pushed myself to get better in everything I do. Coaching courses, in my uni degree, and now at the academy. I like the idea of helping others grow too, not just me. I went on a course a few years ago about having a "Growth Mindset" and that really resonated with me.

Consultant: Would you say "Growth" is another value – both personal growth and helping others develop?

Paul: Yes, that fits. It feels like a reason why I coach in the first place.

Consultant: Great, that's fantastic that you are identifying values that have driven your behaviour and choices as a coach. If we "zoom out" and think about your overall life as Paul again . . . when you're moving toward your best self, what does that look like?

Paul: It's about not letting one part of life take over. Football is huge for me, but I don't want it to drown everything else out. I want space for family, for rest, for health. I see lots of talk on social media about life balance, which is important to have. I don't think I have that balance at the moment and it's something I feel I need.

Consultant: Sounds like "balance" is another compass point for you. Does that feel right?

Paul: Yes. Without balance, everything else slips – I get short-tempered, I lose patience, I feel exhausted.

Consultant: So, let's put this together. From what you've shared, your True North is made up of *Caring, Growth* and *Balance.* Every action you take either moves you closer to or further away from that True North. What kinds of things tend to pull you away from these directions?

Paul: Stress is a big one. When I'm stressed, I'm less caring. Doubts about whether I'm good enough pull me away from growth. Pressure from results makes me compromise on integrity sometimes. And the culture here, full-on, seven days a week, makes it almost impossible to keep balance.

Consultant: That's a very clear picture. The barriers are like storms or detours on the path of where you want to be. Stress, doubt, pressure, organisational culture, that can all push you off course. Our work is not about removing all those barriers, but about noticing them and still choosing to head towards your True North.

Paul: I like that. It feels like even if things get tough, perhaps I don't have to lose sight of where I'm going.

Through the *Inner Compass* activity (Gutman et al., 2025a; see Figure 8.1 for worksheet example), Paul gradually identified three overarching values: *Caring, Growth*, and *Balance.* These values together define his True North, transcending context, applying equally to his coaching, family, and personal life,

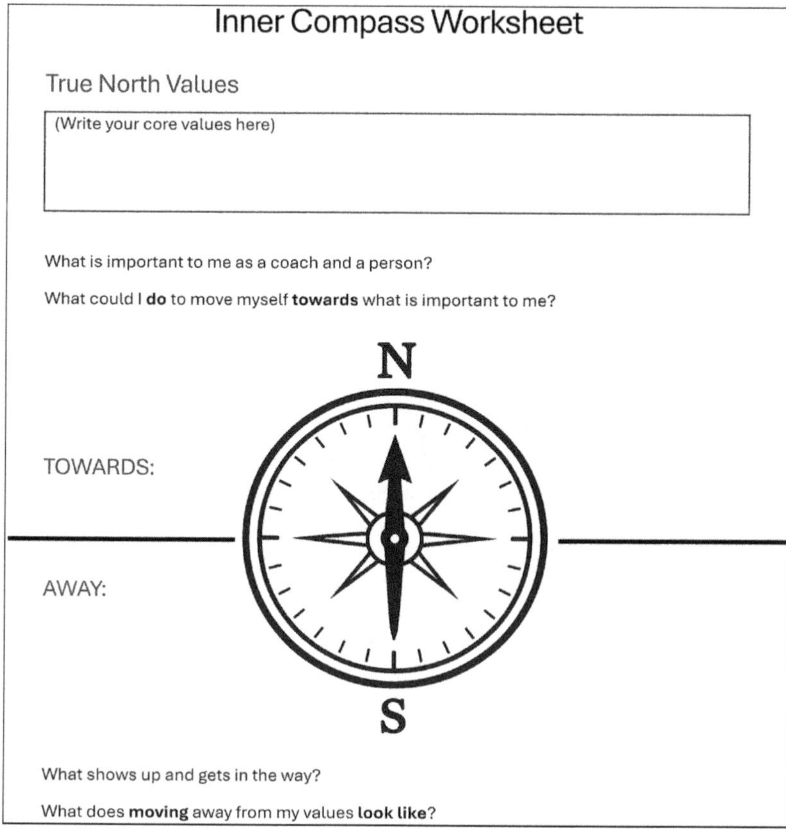

Figure 8.1 Inner compass example worksheet.

offering a consistent guide across settings. Importantly, Paul also recognised barriers such as stress, self-doubt, external pressures, and the demanding academy context, which often pulls him away from acting in line with his values and characterise burnout. From an ACT perspective, this conversation strengthened Paul's **values clarity** and set the foundation for committed action. This compass metaphor now provides Paul with both clarity and motivation to ensure his behaviours align more closely with what truly matters in the face of stressors and burnout.

Session 3: Cognitive Defusion and Acceptance

The consultant now encourages Paul to reflect further on what gets in the way of living his values in daily life. Such barriers often take the form of internal thoughts and emotions that may lead individuals away from committed action.

Individuals may initially struggle to identify these internal thoughts and feelings, as they may feel like vague sensations of worry, discomfort, or anxiety rather than clearly defined words or images (Hayes et al., 2006). In this session, the consultant allows space to help Paul build awareness of his thoughts before introducing the *leaves on a stream* metaphor to support articulation and cognitive defusion. In addition, the *struggle switch* activity is then used to normalise acceptance of difficult internal experiences (see Hayes, 2025 for activities).

Consultant: Paul, last time we mapped out your values – your True North. Do you remember them?

Paul: Yeah . . . caring, growth, balance.

Consultant: Exactly. Those values give us a direction to travel towards. Today I'd like us to look at what makes it hard for you to stay on that path. Often it can be the mind that gets in the way, the thoughts and feelings that show up. Could you tell me about a time recently when you felt pulled away from one of those values?

Paul: (pauses, thinking) Um . . . I'm not sure. I just feel stressed a lot at the moment!

Consultant: That's okay. Stress is a signal something's happening and it can be tricky to unpack sometimes. Let's take one example. Can you think of a moment this week where you felt that stress strongly?

Paul: (hesitant) At training, with the older players on Tuesday. I came away feeling frustrated at the end of the session.

Consultant: Okay. Let's slow down a moment and lean into it. In that moment, when frustration was there after the session, what was your mind saying to you?

Paul: (long pause) I don't know . . . I just felt like it wasn't going well.

Consultant: OK, that's a start. When you say, "not going well", how did your mind interpret that? What story was it telling you?

Paul: (sighs) Maybe . . . that I wasn't handling it properly.

Consultant: And if your mind says, "I'm not handling it properly", what does that suggest about you as a coach or a person?

Paul: (after a pause) It's like it's saying . . . "You're not good enough".

Consultant: There we go. That's clearer. That sounds like a really strong thought, which can be uncomfortable to have. Does that thought show up often?

Paul: (nods slowly) Yeah. More than I'd like to admit.

Consultant: Thank you for naming that. Thoughts like "I'm not good enough" can really pull us away from our values. What happens in your behaviour when that thought is around?

Paul: I get stricter. I tighten up, shout more, try to prove myself. Which . . . goes against caring.

Consultant: Right. That thought makes it harder to live your value of caring. Let's see if there are others. Are there times you feel pulled away from balance or growth too?

Paul: (quietly) Yeah. When I'm at home with my wife and baby, sometimes I just sit there, but my mind keeps going.

Consultant: Where does your mind go?

Paul: To work. It tells me . . . (struggles to put words together) that I should be doing more. That I'm slacking if I'm not thinking about football.

Consultant: A thought like "I should be doing more" keeps you from being present at home?

Paul: Exactly. It makes me restless, and I can't be present with my wife and baby and loads of negative things just come into my head, out of nowhere.

Consultant: That feels important. When you say these negative things come into your head, what is your mind saying to you?

Paul: It might sound stupid, but at home it might be things like "what if I drop the baby?" I hate those. I push those thoughts away straight away (Pauses). Then, at work sometimes I get random flashes that enter my head, like in training the other day I kept thinking "what if they laugh at you?" as I was delivering a serious team talk.

Consultant: I really appreciate you sharing that, Paul. I know it's not easy to experience those thoughts and sometimes the mind throws up thoughts suddenly, almost out of nowhere. Those are what we call intrusive thoughts – sudden, unwanted, and often the opposite of what you value. Everyone gets them, but they feel disturbing because they clash with what matters to you. How do you usually react when they come up?

Paul: I fight them. Tell myself not to think like that. But then they just come back stronger and they are harder to get rid of.

Consultant: That makes sense. It makes sense to want to struggle with them, right? But actually, the harder we struggle, the more they stick.

This session slowed the process of self-awareness, allowing Paul to gradually articulate his specific recurring thoughts (*"I'm not good enough" and "I should be doing more"*) and intrusive flashes (*"what if they laugh at you" and "what if I drop the baby"*), after initial difficulty in naming them. Through careful questioning, Paul recognised how these thoughts disrupted his values of caring and balance, and how his attempts to suppress them intensified their impact. Once challenging thoughts have been identified by Paul, this provides an opportunity for the consultant to help Paul defuse from these thoughts, creating distance between himself and the thoughts he is experiencing.

Consultant: I would like us to try something a bit different now we have identified those challenging thoughts. An experiential exercise as a way of relating to those thoughts that takes some of their power away. How does that sound?

Paul: Yeah . . . I'd like to give it a go.

Consultant: Okay. Close your eyes if you're comfortable. Imagine you're sitting beside a calm stream, with leaves drifting by. Each time a thought comes – "I'm not good enough", "I should be doing more", even "what if I drop the baby" – gently place it on a leaf and let it float past. You don't have to push it away or hold onto it. Just watch it drift slowly past, one by one.
(Long pause as Paul imagines the exercise.)

Paul: I can see it. They keep coming, but . . . I don't feel like I have to grab them. They just pass.

Consultant: Exactly. You're recognising thoughts as passing events of the mind, rather than truths. You can let them float, even the intrusive ones. You are not your thoughts.

Paul: That feels lighter. I don't have to fight, it's like a bit of lightbulb moment.

With the *leaves on a stream* defusion exercise, Paul experienced thoughts as passing events rather than binding truths. The consultant now introduces the *struggle switch* metaphor, which helps Paul foster further acceptance of his internal experiences. This process also aims to strengthen his present-moment awareness, equipping him with greater psychological flexibility to stay aligned with his values in the moment, despite intrusive or self-critical thoughts.

Consultant: Imagine you have a switch in your brain. When it's on, you're fighting your thoughts and feelings, telling yourself they shouldn't be there. When it's off, the thoughts are still there, but without the extra struggle.

Paul: So . . . when I push them away, I'm flipping the switch on?

Consultant: Exactly. But if you could let the switch stay off – what might that mean for you?.

Paul: (after a pause) Maybe I'd be able to pay more attention to the important stuff? That actually makes sense. I don't have to win against the thoughts. I just have to keep moving toward my values, even if the thoughts come along. The thoughts will happen regardless, but I can choose what I do with them and how I behave.

Consultant: Beautifully put, Paul. That acceptance is really important. Accepting the presence of difficult thoughts and feelings, while still choosing to act in line with your True North values.

Session 4: Committed Action and Choice Point

While values provide Paul with a True North, the day-to-day challenge is whether his actions take him *towards* or *away* from those values. In this session, the consultant guides Paul through a *choice point* exercise (see Hayes, 2025), unpacking the specific contexts of his life and coaching role, and helping him link his values to clear, tangible committed actions in service of his long-term goals. Each moment presents a fork in the road, where actions can either take Paul *towards* his values (True North) or *away* from them. The consultant would encourage Paul to explore specific situations in both his coaching and personal life, identifying "away moves" driven by old thought patterns and "toward moves" that expressed his values in action. The consultant provides space to help Paul clarify not only what those actions look like, but also what they build towards in terms of his long-term goals as a coach, father, and partner.

Consultant: Paul, last time we worked on letting thoughts float by, rather than fighting them. How has that been for you this week?

Paul: It's been different. The thoughts still come, but I've caught myself noticing them more. Sometimes I can just let them go.

Consultant: That's great progress. Today, let's build on that. Right now, you're starting to free yourself up from that struggle against thoughts and feelings. The other side of what we're doing here is starting to think about actually moving toward your values with the choices you make. Have you heard of the choice point before?

Paul: Vaguely, but I'm not sure what it is to be honest.

Consultant: Picture every situation as a fork in the road. One path takes you toward your True North values, the other pulls you away. We can't control the thoughts that pop up, but we can choose our direction. Let's walk through some real-life examples in line with your specific values of caring, growth and balance. Let's begin with *caring.* Think back to a recent time where you felt yourself slipping into stress or frustration. Perhaps that example you shared last session about that training session. What was happening?

Paul: It was with the older group. A couple of players weren't following what I asked. My first instinct was to clamp down, raise my voice, and show I was in charge, even though I didn't feel confident in doing that.

Consultant: Okay. And how did the players react in that moment?

Paul: I shouted at them, I probably snapped a bit to be honest. They went quiet, heads down, looking away. I could tell they were disengaging, but at the time I thought, "At least they have stopped messing about".

Consultant: That sounds like an away move, moving away from caring. If you check in with your values, what's the cost of responding like that?

Paul: It damages trust. I say I value caring, but in those moments, I didn't exactly show it. Players see me as strict and reactive instead of supportive. Long-term, they probably wouldn't open up to me if they needed to and may be worried about me snapping again, or feeling that I don't care about them or their development.

Consultant: That's an important insight. Now let's flip that on its head and look at the *toward move*. Same scenario, the training session with players not listening. What would caring look like as an action?

Paul: (pauses) I'd stop, breathe, lower my tone. Maybe pull the main leadership players or age group captain aside and explain clearly what I wanted. Remind them why it matters but also give them a chance to feedback and have their own say, make them feel they have some autonomy and feel more connected with me as a coach. I'd still set boundaries, but without shutting them down.

Consultant: And what outcome does that create for you if you show these behaviours consistently do you think?

Paul: Over time, it builds that trust up. It might take a while, but players will know I care about them, not just the performance. That kind of connection could mean they're willing to work harder for me and actually listen more. And if I want to be a coach known for developing people, not just winning games, that's essential. It also helps me stand out as someone who players respect enough to confide in, which is what I've admired in the coaches I looked up to when I was younger.

This section of the session may offer opportunity to pause and then move onto other values that represent Paul's True North. Dialogue between consultant and Paul below address another of Paul's values, balance. The dialogue focusses on "towards moves" and alignment with long term goals as a means of alleviating burnout.

Consultant: Let's move to *balance*. Picture an evening at home with your partner and baby. One thought you mentioned in a previous session was "I should be doing more at work", and that is there quite a lot. What usually happens when the thought "I should be doing more" shows up?

Paul: Honestly? I grab my phone. I check emails or write down drills. My partner notices straight away, she goes quiet, which makes me feel guilty. But my brain says, "If you don't do this now, you'll fall behind". I'm stuck between feeling guilty and inadequate.

Consultant: So that's the *away move* from *balance.* You're physically home but mentally back at work. What's the impact of that pattern?

Paul: I'm not present. My baby grows up while I'm staring at a screen. My partner ends up carrying more of the load, and I can feel the distance it creates.

Consultant: And if you were to choose the *toward move*, towards balance, what would that look like in practice?

Paul: (Pauses) I'd put the phone in another room. I'd pick up my baby, maybe do bedtime, changing, feeding, settling down. Or just sit with my partner and actually talk about her day, connecting with them.

Consultant: And if you did that consistently, what outcome would it create long-term?

Paul: My baby would actually *know* me as a present dad. I wouldn't miss those early moments everyone says fly by. My partner would feel supported, like she's not doing this alone. Balance at home means that when I'm older, I can look back and say I didn't sacrifice my family for football. That's something I really don't want to regret. I want to feel connected and fulfilled across my different life areas.

Through the choice point exercise, Paul unpacked in detail how different values can be expressed through specific, realistic actions in daily life. He recognised that in moments of frustration, living with *caring* means breathing, lowering his voice, and guiding players constructively, actions that build long-term trust and respect. For *balance*, Paul identified concrete behaviours such as putting away his phone and actively engaging with his partner and baby, ensuring his long-term identity as a present and supportive father. By connecting these *toward moves* to his long-term vision, Paul experienced how daily decisions at each "fork in the road" build the legacy he wants to leave, as a coach respected for his humility and professionalism, and as a father remembered for his presence and care.

The case of Paul represents one potential way of using ACT to address coach burnout, using personal values development as a key anchor and starting point. The consultancy work used the ACT hexaflex as an iterative, underpinning model to promote client self-awareness, openness, and engagement with values and committed action (Hayes et al., 2006). Here, we have focused on getting the client to reconnect with values, work through defusion and acceptance exercises, and think about "away" and "toward" moves that might be helpful for him, not only in sport but also in his life away from the sporting arena. Focusing holistically on the coach as a whole person, rather than just a sports performer, is an important consideration in coach well-being and managing workplace stress. It is important to note that while this "intervention" focuses on the individual coach, sports organisations also have a responsibility to cultivate environments that allow for sustainable well-being (Konttä et al., 2024). The responsibility for managing burnout should not lie with the individual coach, but there are several ACT-based strategies that the coach can still apply to their practices and everyday life. Of course, there are many other applications of the ACT model and directions that a consultant might take, working flexibly to develop awareness, openness, and engagement with values across individual and organisational contexts.

References

Barnes, L. T. (2024). Promoting values-informed development in an elite dual-career endurance athlete. *Case Studies in Sport and Performance Psychology*, *8*(1), 66–75. https://doi.org/10.1123/cssep.2024-0004

Chow, G. M., Garinger, L. M., Freeman, J., Ward, S. K., & Bird, M. D. (2022). "It's about going from good to great": Expert approaches to conducting a first sport psychology session. *Journal of Clinical Sport Psychology*, *18*(1), 14–36. https://doi.org/10.1123/jcsp.2021-0107

Eccles, D. W., Gretton, T. W., Harris, N., & Wolf, S. A. (2023). "Switching the mind off completely"– Understanding the psychology of rest in coaches. *Psychology of Sport and Exercise*, *69*, 102479. https://doi.org/10.1016/j.psychsport.2023.102479

Gardner, F. L., & Moore, Z. E. (2012). Mindfulness and acceptance models in sport psychology: A decade of basic and applied scientific advancements. *Canadian Psychology/Psychologie Canadienne*, *53*(4), 309–318. https://psycnet.apa.org/doi/10.1037/a0030220

Gutman, T., Lev-Arey, D., Erez, T., & Tarrasch, R. (2025a). Coach assist: Assessing youth basketball coaches' feedback on participation in an acceptance and commitment therapy-based intervention incorporating self-determination theory principles. *International Sport Coaching Journal*, *1*, 1–9. https://doi.org/10.1123/iscj.2024-0058

Gutman, T., Lev-Arey, D., Gottlieb, A., & Tarrasch, R. (2025b). Integrating the mindfulness-acceptance-commitment framework with self-determination theory principles to promote need-supportive sport coaching. *Psychology of Sport and Exercise*, *80*, 102893. https://doi.org/10.1016/j.psychsport.2025.102893

Hägglund, K., Kenttä, G., Bentzen M., Thelwell, R., & Wagstaff, C. R. D. (2024). Mindful self-reflection as a strategy to support sustainable high-performance coaching: A mixed method study. *Journal of Applied Sport Psychology*, *36*(6), 974–996. https://doi.org/10.1080/10413200.2024.2353288

Hayes, S. C. (2025). *Get out of your mind and into your life: The new acceptance and commitment therapy*. Oakland, CA: New Harbinger Publications.

Hayes, S. C., Luoma, J. B., Bond, F. W., Masuda, A., & Lillis, J. (2006). Acceptance and commitment therapy: Model, processes and outcomes. *Behaviour Research and Therapy*, *44*(1), 1–25. https://doi.org/10.1016/j.brat.2005.06.006

Higham, A. J., Newman, J. A., Rumbold, J. L., & Stone, J. A. (2024). You wouldn't let your phone run out of battery: An interpretative phenomenological analysis of male professional football coaches' well-being. *Qualitative Research in Sport, Exercise and Health*, *16*(2), 213–227. https://doi.org/10.1080/2159676X.2023.2260377

Hill, J., & Oliver, J. (2019). *Acceptance and commitment coaching: Distinctive features*. London: Routledge.

Josefsson, T., Gustafsson, H., Robinson, P., Cedenblad, M., Sievert, E., & Ivarsson, A. (2024). Examining the effects of the mindfulness-acceptance-commitment (MAC) programme on sport-specific dispositional mindfulness, sport anxiety, and experiential acceptance in martial arts. *Scandinavian Journal of Sport and Exercise Psychology*, *6*, 19–26. https://doi.org/10.7146/sjsep.v6i.140996

Telnttä, G., Dieffenbach, K., Bentzen, M., Thompson, M., Côté, J., Mallett, C., & Olusoga, P. (2024). Position paper: Rationale for a focused attention on mental health of high-performance sports coaches. *International Sport Coaching Journal, 11*(3), 457–465. https://doi.org/10.1123/iscj.2022-0123

Mallett, C. J. (2010). High performance coaches' careers and communities. In J. Lyle & C. Cushion (Eds.), *Sports coaching: Professionalism and practice* (pp. 119–133). London: Elsevier.

Norris, L. A., Didymus, F. F., & Kaiseler, M. (2017). Stressors, coping, and well-being among sports coaches: A systematic review. *Psychology of Sport and Exercise, 33*, 93–112. https://doi.org/10.1016/j.psychsport.2017.08.005

O'Brien, W. H., Singh, R., Horan, K., Moeller, M. T., Wasson, R., & Jex, S. M. (2019). Group-based acceptance and commitment therapy for nurses and nurse aides working in long-term care residential settings. *The Journal of Alternative and Complementary Medicine, 25*(7), 753–761. https://doi.org/10.1089/acm.2019.0087

Olusoga, P., Bentzen, M., & Kentta, G. (2019). Coach burnout: A scoping review. *International Sport Coaching Journal, 6*(1), 42–62. https://doi.org/10.1123/iscj.2017-0094

Olusoga, P., Hägglund, K., Aronsson, M., Bartnes, H., Bentzen, M., Breslin, G., . . . & Kenttä, G. (2025). Sustainable high-performance coaching: Recommendations from an international expert round-table summit. *Journal of Sport Psychology in Action*, 1–14. https://doi.org/10.1080/21520704.2025.2548827

Pilkington, V., Rice, S. M., Walton, C. C., Gwyther, K., Olive, L., Butterworth, M., . . . & Purcell, R. (2022). Prevalence and correlates of mental health symptoms and well-being among elite sport coaches and high-performance support staff. *Sports Medicine – Open, 8*(1), 89. https://doi.org/10.1186/s40798-022-00479-y

Piot, F., Taylor, G., & Grégoire, S. (2024). A group intervention based on acceptance and commitment therapy for improving psychological well-being at work: A randomized controlled trial. *Canadian Journal of Behavioural Science/Revue canadienne des sciences du comportement*. https://psycnet.apa.org/doi/10.1037/cbs0000438

Prudenzi, A., Graham, C. D., Clancy, F., Hill, D., O'Driscoll, R., Day, F., & O'Connor, D. B. (2021). Group-based acceptance and commitment therapy interventions for improving general distress and work-related distress in healthcare professionals: A systematic review and meta-analysis. *Journal of Affective Disorders, 295*, 192–202. https://doi.org/10.1016/j.jad.2021.07.084

Sharp, L. A., Hodge, K., & Danish, S. (2015). Ultimately it comes down to the relationship: Experienced consultants' views of effective sport psychology consulting. *The Sport Psychologist, 29*(4), 358–370. https://doi.org/10.1123/tsp.2014-0130

Simova, M., Olusoga, P., & Brown, C. J. (2024). Understanding well-being in high-performance coaches: A constructivist grounded theory approach. *International Sport Coaching Journal, 12*(2), 217–227. https://doi.org/10.1123/iscj.2023-0009

Tian, Q., & Cheng, L. (2025). Effects of four-week mindfulness training on job pressure, burnout, and coping strategies in sports coaches: A randomised controlled trial. *WORK: A Journal of Prevention, Assessment & Rehabilitation, 81*(2), 2631–2639. https://doi.org/10.1177/10519815251317310

Unruh, I., Neubert, M., Wilhelm, M., & Euteneuer, F. (2022). ACT in the workplace: A meta-analytic examination of randomized controlled trials. *Journal of Contextual Behavioral Science, 26*, 114–124. https://doi.org/10.1016/j.jcbs.2022.09.003

Wang, Y., Lei, S. M., & Fan, J. (2023). Effects of mindfulness-based interventions on promoting athletic performance and related factors among athletes: A systematic review and meta-analysis of randomized controlled trial. *International Journal of Environmental Research and Public Health, 20*(3), 2038. https://doi.org/10.3390/ijerph20032038

9 ACT to Address Trauma in Sport

Aura Goldman and Misia Gervis

Learning Objectives

1. Explain key mechanisms of trauma, recognising how psychological, physiological, and contextual factors interact to shape traumatic responses
2. Analyse how sport and exercise environments can initiate, reinforce, or exacerbate trauma, with particular attention to power dynamics, performance pressures, and cultural norms
3. Evaluate the application of TFACT with case study examples, demonstrating how trauma-informed principles can guide ethical, supportive, and effective applied practice

What Is Trauma?

Trauma is not an event; trauma is the embodied response to the event (van der Kolk, 1994; Kozlowska et al., 2015). Trauma results from an event, series of events, or set of circumstances in which there is actual or threatened physical or psychological harm to the self or others (Saunders et al., 2023). For an event to create the grounds for traumatisation, it must be consciously or unconsciously perceived as life-threatening and/or beyond our capacity to deal with (Ehlers & Clark, 2000). Therefore, it is essential to acknowledge that two people can experience exactly the same event, such as a cycling accident, and one may be unaffected, while the other is traumatised (Kessler et al., 2017). Whether a person is traumatised by an event is mediated by age (with younger people being more susceptible), temperament (with more sensitive people being more vulnerable), and past experiences (Levine, 2010). Further, trauma can be categorised as acute (e.g., high-impact injury), chronic (e.g., long-term coach-athlete abuse), or developmental (i.e., acquired in childhood) (Ross et al., 2021).

In order to understand how trauma manifests, it is critical that we consider the brain, the nervous system, and the physiology of trauma. With respect to the brain, there are three regions that are particularly influential in a trauma response: the thalamus, the amygdala, and the medial prefrontal cortex. First,

DOI: 10.4324/9781003515203-11

the thalamus filters and rapidly routes signals of threat from the external and internal worlds towards cortical and subcortical threat circuits such as the amygdala (Shin & Liberzon, 2010; Yoshii, 2021). Second, the amygdala integrates these inputs and orchestrates defensive responding, sounding the metaphorical alarm and signalling danger (Marek et al., 2013; Shin & Liberzon, 2010). Third, regions of the medial prefrontal cortex help to determine whether the threat is "real" and present (Milad & Quirk, 2012; Liberzon & Abelson, 2016). Activation of these neurological circuits engages the sympathetic nervous system and the fight-flight-freeze-flop defence cascade (Kozlowska et al., 2015). In a traumatised brain, altered thalamic processing, heightened amygdala reactivity, and reduced prefrontal regulation bias the system towards hyperarousal and persistent threat anticipation (Yoshii, 2021). This results in the metaphorical alarm constantly sounding, even when there is no danger.

The role of the sympathetic nervous system in trauma can be further explained by the use of the Polyvagal Theory (Porges, 2011, 2023). Central to this theory is the role of the autonomic nervous system (ANS) and the parasympathetic vagus nerve. The vagus nerve is the tenth cranial nerve that runs from the brainstem at the base of the skull, down through the heart, lungs, diaphragm, and stomach. The vagus nerve regulates our experience of the world in terms of safety and danger, and has two branches: the dorsal branch and the ventral branch. In evolutionary terms of mammalian development, the most ancient part of the ANS is the dorsal vagal complex, which is represented at the bottom of Deb Dana's (2018) Polyvagal ladder (see Figure 9.1), followed by the sympathetic nervous system, and the most "recent" development to the ANS, the ventral vagal complex, sits at the top of the ladder. The conceptualisation of the ladder reminds us that in order to move from dorsal to ventral, we must pass through the sympathetic.

When there is no threat present, real or perceived, then the ventral vagal branch is dominant. When there is a threat present, perceived or otherwise, then the sympathetic nervous system takes over to protect us. Typically, active defence (fight or flight) is recruited first. If the person is able to complete their defensive response, then traumatisation becomes less likely (Van der Kolk, 2014). However, when escape or counter-aggression is blocked, and the threat is appraised as inescapable, defensive control often shifts from sympathetic mobilisation to parasympathetically mediated immobilisation (freeze and flop). This shift is adaptive at the systems level for survival as it reduces movement and detectability and downregulates metabolic demand via vagal-brainstem pathways, whilst behaviourally presenting as marked motor inhibition and "shut-down" – think of a mouse "playing dead" in the presence of a cat in order to survive (Beissner et al., 2013; Kozlowska et al., 2015). When this happens, this is trauma and is evidenced in a dysregulated nervous system, which manifests as a range of responses, such as: addiction, perfectionism, dissociation, compartmentalisation,

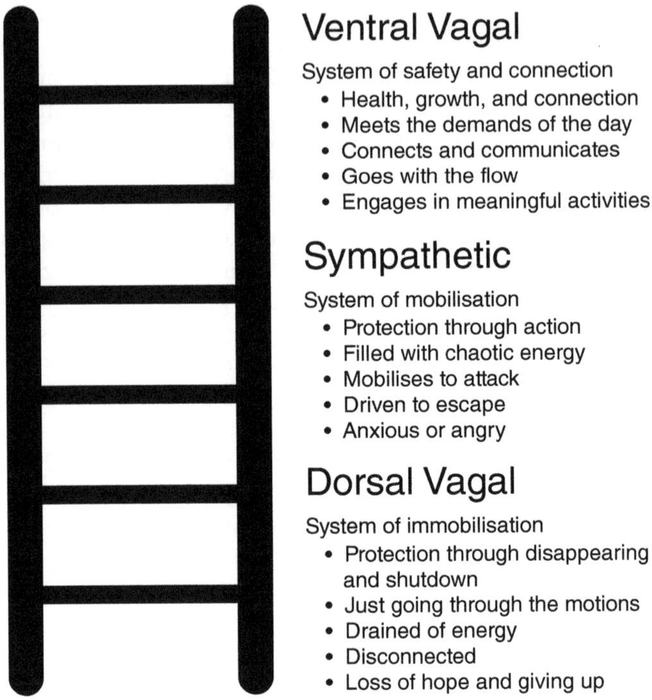

Figure 9.1 The Polyvagal ladder (diagram adapted from Dana, 2021).

anxiety, aggression and anger, depression, sleep disturbance, eating disorders, obsessive-compulsive disorder (e.g., Aron et al., 2019; Levine, 1997). These "dysfunctional behaviours" represent versions of self-regulation and attempts to soothe and protect the nervous system – they are the person's solution to the problem, not the problem itself.

Whilst we have explored the nervous system from the individual perspective, it is important to understand that humans are social animals with interconnected and co-regulating nervous systems. For example, if a lion were stalking a herd of zebras, and one zebra picks up on the threat and becomes alarmed, this will quickly spread to other members of the herd through co-regulation, who will then respond appropriately by fleeing. In sport, this may appear as an anxious coach in the dressing room, whose cues up-regulate the squad's nervous systems, so jitters spread. It is through this biological survival mechanism that we seek and receive comfort and reassurance from others who have the capacity to make us feel safe and secure. For example, an upset or overwhelmed child will seek comfort from someone who makes them feel safe. However, if a child grows up never experiencing the feeling of safety or security (i.e., their caregivers were unable to provide helpful co-regulation), they are at a markedly increased risk of altered autonomic and stress-system regulation, heightened threat sensitivity, and emotion-regulation difficulties (Feldman, 2017; McLaughlin et al., 2015).

The impact of experiencing trauma in childhood has been shown to have devastating long-term effects on mental health and well-being, the development of the nervous system, and the ability to regulate the nervous system. In the literature, these are referred to as adverse childhood experiences (ACEs) and include such experiences as: physical abuse, sexual abuse, substance abuse by carers, mental illness of carers, witnessing violence, and criminal behaviour in the household. In Felitti et al.'s (1998) landmark study, it was found that when a person had experienced four or more ACEs, there was a significant increase in health risks in adulthood, such as alcoholism, drug abuse, suicidality, cancer, heart disease, obesity, and depression, and a significant decrease in life expectancy with six or more ACEs.

Recognising ACEs is imperative in understanding the earliest years of a child's development. Mary Ainsworth and John Bowlby's seminal theory of attachment refers to patterns of communication and interaction within relationships that are established in the first years of life (Ainsworth & Bowlby, 1991). The four attachment styles are: secure, and the three insecure attachment styles: anxious, avoidant, and disorganised. The impact of ACEs can be exacerbated by insecure attachment; likewise, insecure attachment can impact the experience of ACEs, making them more traumatic (Papandrea, 2022).

In summary, when seeking to understand trauma, it is critical to consider these three theoretical aspects: the Polyvagal Theory and the physiology of trauma, ACEs, and attachment theory. It is only by exploring through all these lenses that we can begin to realise a complete understanding of a person's experience of trauma.

Trauma in Sport

Sport is the initiator and/or the incubator of trauma, but not inevitably. By this, we mean that athletes and staff (including coaches, managers, physios, sport scientists, and psychologists) may have had an experience in sport that initiates a trauma response (Aron et al., 2019). Likewise, athletes and staff may enter sport with pre-existing trauma, such as an ACE, that is then incubated by the sport environment. Risk is contingent on context, power dynamics, and prior vulnerability (Tuakli-Wosornu et al., 2024; Mountjoy et al., 2025). Maltreatment has been documented across organised sport, including community and youth settings, with higher prevalence typically observed in high-performance/elite pathways (Gervis et al., 2025; Vertommen et al., 2016; Willson et al., 2022). Conversely, in psychologically safe, well-safeguarded, supportive environments, sport can help – participation is linked to psychological and social benefits, and physical activity can reduce post-traumatic symptoms (Eime et al., 2013; Rosenbaum et al., 2015).

Moreover, trauma in sport is not as rare as might be imagined. Indeed, recent research suggests that as many as one in eight elite athletes suffer from post-traumatic stress disorder (PTSD) symptomology (Aron et al., 2019; Lynch, 2021). The sporting context is undoubtedly a catalyst for traumatic experiences, but this is often unacknowledged, normalised, expected, and/or silenced (Day, 2018). Certainly, sporting organisations are frontline organisations that perpetuate uncertainty, leaving people vulnerable to constantly experiencing threat, which has implications for the ANS (Gervis et al., 2019). For example, periods of transition and instability, deselection, poor performance, or loss can become the foundation for chronic trauma.

Whilst sport has the potential to offer positive, cathartic, and supportive experiences, it is critical that we name the range of commonly occurring experiences in sport, particularly in elite and professional sport, that can be traumatising. These include, but are not limited to: abusive coach relationships, harsh training environments, injury, and public scrutiny and discrimination.

Participation in sport begins at an early age, and in early maturation sports, such as gymnastics, diving, and swimming, children may be spending more time with their coaches than their parents (Gervis & Dunn, 2004). This makes the coach an important attachment figure for the athlete (Davis et al., 2021). When the coach has an insecure attachment style, they are unable to create safety for their athletes, which can be problematic and increase the risk of child maltreatment, abuse, and trauma (Lo et al., 2019). There has been extensive research that has shown that when the coach-athlete relationship is abusive, this must be considered an ACE (Gaedicke et al., 2021; Kavanagh et al., 2017; Kerr et al., 2020). This abuse tends to be operationalised to secure obedience and takes the form of practices that use isolation (e.g., culture of silence and retribution), intimidation (i.e., physical, emotional, and sexual abuse), and body regulation (e.g., coaches engaging in public weight management) (Smits et al., 2017).

Sport has a reputation that in order to get to the top, you have to train hard and be "tough", both physically and mentally (Owusu-Sekyere & Gervis, 2016). Whilst this is not necessarily untrue, the methods through which this tends to be achieved can be an invitation to create training environments that are harsh, insensitive, and uncompromising (Owusu-Sekyere & Gervis, 2016). Indeed, Owusu-Sekyere and Gervis (2016) note that "It is possible that this could occur with or without an intention to do harm, and may result in coaches creating training environments that may be regarded as negative, unfavourable, morally and ethically questionable, or simply abusive" (p. 7). This means that in the quest to create tough and resilient athletes, coaches may be inadvertently traumatising them. In practice, whether such environments precipitate trauma reflects a transaction between athlete-level factors (e.g., age, temperament/sensitivity, and prior adversity) and contextual conditions (coaching practice, power dynamics, and organisational culture), with the primary duty of care residing in the latter (Ehlers & Clark, 2000; Ozer et al., 2003; Mountjoy et al., 2025).

When an athlete is subjected to excessively harsh training, their nervous systems can become dysregulated in three main ways: first, chronic sympathetic activation, evident in an increased and prolonged stress response (e.g., after forced physical exertion as punishment, such as continuous laps until the point of collapse; Lowrance et al., 2016); second, parasympathetic suppression and a reduced ability to shift into a recovery state (e.g., children training for many hours without any breaks; Lehmann et al., 1993); and third, burnout, if excessive training continues, where the athlete's nervous system shifts into autonomic shutdown, which will, of course, result in performance decrements (Roberts & Karatsoreos, 2021).

Injuries are perhaps the most obvious and most commonly experienced example of trauma for athletes, which can be acute, chronic, or vicarious. Acute injuries would include such things as a cyclist crashing at 50 mph, a fighter breaking their leg, or a horse rider falling from their horse and experiencing a concussion. These injuries are too much, too soon, too fast, and can overwhelm the ANS and leave the athletes with incomplete defensive responses, which contribute to trauma and PTSD symptomology (Bateman & Morgan, 2019; Payne et al., 2015). Chronic injuries are those that are ever-present and never seem to be fully recovered from. In sport, there are countless athletes who experience this type of injury, and in some instances, it is the catalyst for retirement. When an athlete has a chronic injury, the body's natural response is to rest, whereby both the ventral and dorsal vagal complexes are active and facilitate healing (Porges, 2023). However, if the athlete experiences overwhelm and subsequent dorsal vagal dominance without sufficient ventral vagal input, they will not heal (Porges, 2023). This is when mental health issues such as depression, addiction, misuse of medication, and suicidal ideation can arise (Gervis et al., 2022). Vicarious injuries occur when witnessing a traumatic injury. For example, footballer Fabrice Muamba had a heart attack in 2012, nearly died on the pitch, and had to receive life-saving medical attention. Another example would be ice hockey player Adam Johnson, whose carotid artery was severed during a game in 2024, and he died. Such events are traumatising for all involved.

The challenge for every athlete who competes is the potential for public scrutiny of their performance. This is true whether you are competing in the school sports day, or the World Cup final – the people watching create the emotional climate for the sport and often feel entitled to criticise and abuse athletes, which can lead to traumatisation (e.g., an athlete whose sense of safety is compromised through racist abuse). This scrutiny comes in many forms, from social media, the media, to spectators, the team, and friends and family. Indeed, social media has created new avenues through which to abuse athletes physically, sexually, emotionally, and discriminatorily (Kavanagh et al., 2020). This has been found to have many negative psychological, behavioural, and performance-based impacts; indeed, "The existence of virtual maltreatment and its potential to cause harm, is irrefutable" (Parry et al., 2015, p. 10). Likewise, the "traditional" media has also been found to negatively impact athlete mental health (Faustin et al., 2022). It is worth further expanding on the potentially traumatising impact of discrimination in all forms (e.g., racism, sexism, homophobia, and ableism) on athletes, which often emerges through the vehicle of public scrutiny. Discrimination is a form of victimisation that can traumatise and often manifests in sport through seemingly innocuous daily microaggressions as well as blatantly discriminatory language (e.g., Brittain & Beacom, 2016; Carter & Olusoga, 2023; Goldman & Gervis, 2021; Symons et al., 2017).

It is the view of the authors that trauma in sport is currently overlooked and misunderstood by the majority of professionals working in sport, including sport psychologists who may mistakenly believe that they have no responsibilities beyond performance. Trauma-related harms in sport are frequently under-recognised and inconsistently managed, evidenced by high maltreatment prevalence across youth and elite settings and by documented training/role gaps among sport staff, including sport psychologists (Mountjoy et al., 2025; Vertommen et al., 2016; Newman et al., 2024). As a psychologist in sport, you will be dealing with trauma all the time, even if you don't understand that that's what you're looking at (Aron et al., 2019). Often, there is a tendency in sport to blame the "problematic" behaviour (e.g., an athlete who is addicted to painkillers) and not go beneath the behavioural response, to the trauma which drives the behaviour (Roberts et al., 2020). It is important to overcome our natural reluctance to confront trauma and recognise that these behaviours are protective, not problematic; the problem is, inevitably, the trauma. Further, it is important to remember that if you have grown up in sport, the things you recognise as "normal" may not be (Muhonen et al., 2024).

Trauma Through an ACT Lens

TFACT states that trauma has three core clusters of symptoms that are present regardless of how the trauma presents (e.g., PTSD, chronic pain, depression, and perfectionism). Each of these symptom clusters is described below, and readers are reminded that these symptoms will present themselves differently in every individual.

1. Re-experiencing refers to the athlete literally re-experiencing the event as if it is happening in the present. This can come in the form of flashbacks, night terrors, and/or rumination on the past.
2. Hyper- and hypoarousal refer to how the nervous system responds to the re-experiencing. Hyperarousal is characterised by either a "fight" response, expressed as aggression, anger, and irritation, or a "flight" response, which presents as avoidance, anxiety, and fear. Hypoarousal is characterised as a "freeze" or "flop" response, expressed as lethargy, disengagement, dissociation, and shutdown.
3. Psychological rigidity refers to inflexible attention, experiential avoidance, fusion, and remoteness from values and unworkable action.

Further, TFACT has a compassion-based, exposure-centred approach to working with trauma. Compassion is of central importance within the ACT framework and refers to the acknowledgement of pain with kindness. Compassion creates embodied and psychological safety, not only within the client–practitioner relationship but also within the client themselves, which will impact how they respond to their internal experiences. This is particularly challenging for many within the sport environment, who often begin with judgement, and view compassion as a vehicle for weakness (Backman et al., 2024). Exposure in TFACT refers to organised contact with the repertoire-narrowing stimuli (i.e., triggers) in order to develop emotional, cognitive, and behavioural flexibility. Exposure must be paced and gradual in order not to provoke re-traumatisation, and the interrogation is not of the trauma itself (e.g., the career-ending injury), but of the symptoms as they emerge (e.g., the numbness). It is incredibly important to exercise due caution when working with exposure, as too much, too soon, too fast, can re-traumatise and further damage the athlete.

The three therapeutic strands a TFACT practitioner will employ are: living in the present (i.e., be present), healing the past (i.e., open up), and building the future (i.e., do what matters). Figure 9.2 illustrates this approach. At the core is Harris's (2009) original triflex, around which are some of the trauma responses that clients may present with. Finally, the three therapeutic strands are aligned

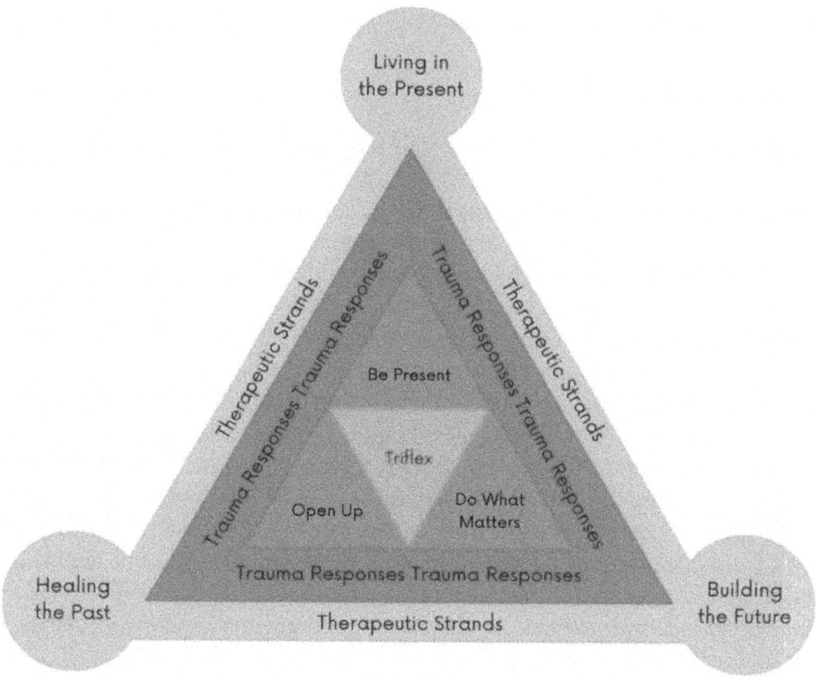

Figure 9.2 The TFACT Triflex (adapted from Harris, 2009).

with their corresponding triflex process and further illustrate how any of the therapeutic strands can be used to work with any trauma presentation. Whilst a skilled TFACT practitioner will be able to move between the three strands, in the presence of overwhelm, it is essential to return to the present, for example, by "dropping anchor" (Harris, 2009), in order to establish safety (Walton et al., 2024).

We cannot make someone else feel safe if we are not safe ourselves. Felt safety depends on neuroception of safety cues; when our own system broadcasts threat, others' physiology entrains accordingly, undermining safety (Porges, 2022). Within the client–practitioner relationship, we are constantly co-regulating with our client, such that the practitioner is the "other" that is regulated and regulating. In order to be able to do this, we must know and understand our own nervous systems, specifically to recognise when we might be entering threat or shutdown states. If this happens, then we are no longer able to create safety for our clients, which will diminish the therapeutic process. As on an airplane, fit your own oxygen mask first – only then can you help others. When we are regulated, we can provide the safety needed to work with a client who may be overwhelmed.

The term "overwhelm" seems to suggest an exaggerated response; however, overwhelm can show up in small but significant ways which practitioners have to be able to notice and recognise. Overwhelm can look like distractibility (e.g., unable to remain focused), disengagement (e.g., withdrawing from the activity), disconnection (e.g., withdrawing from the relationship), and dissociation (e.g., checking out or shutting down). These strategies are natural survival responses that protect from pain, harm, and horror.

TFACT in Practice

Any practitioner who wants to work with trauma using ACT processes needs to understand the following basic principles. Build a therapeutic alliance by checking that you have the capacities, capabilities, and training necessary to create the kind of relationship that will facilitate the nature of this work. This is achieved through compassion, respect, and appropriate playfulness, which lead to radical equality within the relationship. Continually checking in and gaining informed consent is also critical to this process – do not assume that having asked once, it remains the same. Be explicit to the client that they can always say "no" and that you will respect their boundaries; "no" is a complete answer, and you are not entitled to interrogate it. It can be helpful to establish a non-verbal "safety signal" so that the athlete can communicate their overwhelm. This empowers the client, helps the therapist attune to the needs of the client (especially for clients who struggle to verbally express their experiences), and facilitates the establishment of the client–practitioner relationship as a team – a concept that will be familiar and reassuring to most athletes. As in all ACT sessions, it is critical to agree on behavioural goals at the start of the therapeutic process, to clarify the focus and intention of the work.

In order to demonstrate the application of TFACT, we will consider two case studies. For each one, a functional analysis of the case will be presented, followed by some suggestions for how a sport psychologist might intervene using TFACT. For reference, functional analysis is composed of three elements: Antecedents, Behaviour (both public and private), and Reinforcing Consequences.

Case 1

Grace is a U16 academy footballer who is also in the national team. She loves playing and feels this is the only thing that she is "any good at". Her behavioural goal is not to get sent off.

Antecedents:

- Grace's parents divorced when she was five years old.
- Her mother has long been emotionally unavailable as she suffers from depression.
- Grace has experienced racist micro-aggressions at school and on the football pitch.
- She has an ACE score of 3 and a disorganised attachment style, evident in her distrust of adults and their ability to meet her needs.

Behaviour:

- She has a tendency to lose her temper on the pitch and get red-carded.
- Grace is regularly sent out at school for fighting.
- She has recently injured herself by becoming so angry that she kicked the goal post and fractured her foot.
- Grace is fearful of being kicked out of the academy, who have threatened her with expulsion due to her "bad behaviour".
- In sessions, Grace frequently disconnects.

Reinforcing consequences:

- Expressing her fear through anger provides relief, cathartic release, and a sense of control.
- Coaches constantly question her behaviour and commitment to the sport, which reinforces her distrust of adults.
- Coaches threatening expulsion and meeting anger with anger reinforces her "fight" responses.
- The racism present in her environment and Grace's mother's emotional unavailability reinforce a lack of safety.

Using the TFACT Triflex (see Figure 9.1), a sport psychologist might consider the following strategies:

Living in the Present: To create the safety needed for this work and address the disconnection showing up in sessions, it is essential that Grace is able to "come into the present moment". Whilst she is disconnected, no meaningful work can happen. A core skill that might be introduced to Grace to facilitate this would be "dropping anchor" (Harris, 2009). A helpful way of teaching this skill so that it also facilitates co-regulation is to practice it together. Every time the psychologist notices that Grace has disconnected, they can return to this skill. Grace would also be encouraged to drop anchor when she is playing if she notices that she's starting to feel angry or overwhelmed. The sport psychologist could also prompt her to drop anchor if they notice her behaviour change in a game.

Healing the Past: Helping Grace to understand that her anger is a protector against the difficulties that she experiences externally, and the fear that she experiences internally is important. This perspective shift is a powerful mechanism for healing through normalisation, kindness, and validation. It also permits the psychologist to begin to access the fear underneath the anger and work with it through, for example, a compassionate hand (Harris, 2009). This facilitates acceptance by acknowledging, allowing, and accommodating her difficult experiences. It also teaches her a method of self-soothing and self-regulation in the absence of a co-regulatory adult.

Building the Future: Given that Grace's behavioural goal is to no longer be sent off, the sport psychologist might work with establishing values-driven committed actions around on-pitch behaviour. Moreover, any time the sport psychologist sees Grace enacting her values on the pitch, they can notice and reinforce these behaviours.

Case 2

Timothy is a 21-year-old swimmer who competes for his university and has competed at national age-group championships. He has been swimming competitively since he was seven and regularly trains over 20 hours per week. Timothy's behavioural goal is to be able to express his needs to his coach, especially when he is feeling fatigued.

Antecedents:

- Timothy's father is controlling and coercive, dictating his training and competition regimes.
- His mother enabled his father and did not protect him.

- When he was ten years old, his coach emotionally abused him through body shaming.
- He has an ACE score of 2 and an avoidant attachment style.

Behaviour:

- Timothy is very compliant and polite and will work hard to meet all training demands and expectations, often to the point of over-training, exhaustion, and injury as a strategy to avoid conflict.
- Following a poor performance, he will double-down on his efforts, believing that he didn't work hard enough.
- His mind can be harsh and self-critical, and he constantly wrestles with feelings of not being good enough, which manifests as perfectionism.
- Whilst he feels emotionally numb, this is hidden behind a mask of compliance and disordered eating behaviours.
- He often dissociates in therapy.
- He struggles to make friends, avoiding revealing anything of himself, and using training as an excuse to withdraw.

Reinforcing consequences:

- Timothy is often labelled as the "perfect athlete" due to his compliance and perfectionism, which reinforces his belief that "if the grown-ups are happy, then I am safe".
- His perfectionism provides him with a false sense of self and voice.
- If Timothy performs well, he receives the approval he seeks from his father, but if he performs poorly, he receives vitriol.
- Coaches praise him when he is leaner.

Using the TFACT Triflex (see Figure 9.1), a sport psychologist might consider the following strategies:

Living in the present: For Timothy, this therapeutic strand is about acknowledging, allowing, and accommodating his internal experiences, without shutting them down or dissociating from them. This could be facilitated by Harris's (2009) unwanted visitor metaphor, which facilitates an expansive understanding of acceptance, as well as the compassionate hand, which seeks to facilitate self-care and kindness in moments of adversity.

Healing the past: It will be important for Timothy to address his relationship with his parents and his coach. Often, children who have been abused believe that it was their fault, and if only they had been "better" or "more perfect", then it might not have happened. Providing Timothy with a safe, co-regulating space to be heard, without judgement, creates a reparative relationship in which his autonomy and voice might be restored.

Building the future: Whilst initially Timothy had sport-related goals, they quickly became relational. The sport psychologist could help Timothy to find his voice and facilitate a conversation between him and his coach. In this way, the psychologist protects Timothy and provides safety whilst also enabling him to express his needs.

Conclusions

In the author's experience, the majority of sport psychologists have come from sport in some capacity, whether as an athlete or coach. Being embedded in a sport culture can normalise abnormal behaviours and practices, and therefore, practitioners can be complicit in the perpetuation of traumatisation in sport. Given that sport psychologists rarely work in a vacuum, they are also exposed to the voices of coaches, physiotherapists, and sport scientists, who will inevitably colour perceptions of the athlete. For example, Grace is likely to have been spoken about in derogatory terms such as "you can't trust her – she'll let people down" or "she's a liability". We must check our assumptions and look beyond and beneath the narratives and pre-conceived notions that can propagate in sport, and that you can inadvertently bring into therapy. Rather than condemning the behaviour, we need to ask better questions: where is the trauma?

It should be self-evident that using TFACT is highly skilled and complex work. In order to be competent for this work, it requires many hours of continuing training, ongoing supervision (including post-qualification), and personal therapy – you cannot do the work if you have not done the work. It is time for us to use the language of trauma, which many within sport, to date, have been reluctant to engage with. This diminishes the experiences of athletes and staff and removes the responsibility of those in sport to change its current practices. If we continue to silo our understanding of trauma into neat, behavioural, symptom-based categories, we will never address the systemic nature of this issue. The problem is not the athlete or staff member's perfectionism, depression, or addiction – these are merely protective symptoms of the problem: trauma.

Overall, TFACT is a helpful way of working with trauma. It targets the core sequelae of trauma (e.g., rigid avoidance, narrowed attention, and threat-dominated meaning-making) by cultivating psychological flexibility and present-moment anchoring to create more nervous system regulation; acceptance and defusion to tolerate and disentangle from overwhelming internal cues (i.e., exposure done gently and on purpose); self-as-context to widen perspective beyond the trauma story; and values-guided, consent-led action to restore agency, choice, and connection. Because these processes are transdiagnostic, they allow for the navigation of complex and changing arousal states, allow titrated progress without re-traumatisation, and sit well with a trauma-informed stance (co-regulation, safety, clarity, autonomy). In short, TFACT gives practitioners a principled way to meet complexity, working with, not against, the nervous system, whilst helping athletes build lives that are bigger than their trauma.

References

Ainsworth, M. S., & Bowlby, J. (1991). An ethological approach to personality development. *American Psychologist*, *46*(4), 333.

Aron, C. M., Harvey, S., Hainline, B., Hitchcock, M. E., & Reardon, C. L. (2019). Posttraumatic stress disorder (PTSD) and other trauma-related mental disorders in elite athletes: A narrative review. *British Journal of Sports Medicine*, *53*(12), 779–784.

Backman, E., Hejl, C., Henriksen, K., & Zettler, I. (2024). Compassion matters in elite sports environments: Insights from high-performance coaches. *Psychology of Sport and Exercise*, *75*, 102718.

Bateman, A., & Morgan, K. A. (2019). The postinjury psychological sequelae of high-level Jamaican athletes: Exploration of a posttraumatic stress disorder – Self-efficacy conceptualization. *Journal of Sport Rehabilitation*, *28*(2), 144–152.

Beissner, F., Meissner, K., Bär, K. J., & Napadow, V. (2013). The autonomic brain: An activation likelihood estimation meta-analysis for central processing of autonomic function. *Journal of Neuroscience*, *33*(25), 10503–10511.

Brittain, I., & Beacom, A. (2016). Leveraging the London 2012 Paralympic Games: What legacy for disabled people? *Journal of Sport and Social Issues*, *40*(6), 499–521.

Carter, L., & Olusoga, P. (2023). Prologue. *Journal of Applied Sport Psychology*, *35*(1), 1–4.

Dana, D. (2018). *The Polyvagal theory in therapy: Engaging the rhythm of regulation (Norton series on interpersonal neurobiology)*. WW Norton & Company.

Dana, D. (2021). *Anchored: How to befriend your nervous system using polyvagal theory*. Boulder, CO: Sounds True / St. Martin's Essentials.

Davis, L., Brown, D. J., Arnold, R., & Gustafsson, H. (2021). Thriving through relationships in sport: The role of the parent – Athlete and coach – Athlete attachment relationship. *Frontiers in Psychology*, *12*, 694599.

Day, M. (2018). Researching trauma in the context of sport. In *Sport, mental illness, and sociology* (pp. 63–77). Emerald Publishing Limited.

Ehlers, A., & Clark, D. M. (2000). A cognitive model of posttraumatic stress disorder. *Behaviour Research and Therapy*, *38*(4), 319–345.

Eime, R. M., Young, J. A., Harvey, J. T., Charity, M. J., & Payne, W. R. (2013). A systematic review of the psychological and social benefits of participation in sport for children and adolescents: Informing development of a conceptual model of health through sport. *International Journal of Behavioral Nutrition and Physical Activity*, *10*(1), 98.

Faustin, M., Burton, M., Callender, S., Watkins, R., & Chang, C. (2022). Effect of media on the mental health of elite athletes. *British Journal of Sports Medicine*, *56*(3), 123–124.

Feldman, R. (2017). The neurobiology of human attachments. *Trends in Cognitive Sciences*, *21*(2), 80–99.

Felitti, V. J., Anda, R. F., Nordenberg, D., Williamson, D. F., Spitz, A. M., Edwards, V., Koss, M. P., & Marks, J. S. (1998). Relationship of childhood abuse and household dysfunction to many of the leading causes of death in adults. The Adverse Childhood Experiences (ACE) Study. *American Journal of Preventive Medicine*, *14*(4), 245–258.

Gaedicke, S., Schäfer, A., Hoffmann, B., Ohlert, J., Allroggen, M., Hartmann-Tews, I., & Rulofs, B. (2021). Sexual violence and the coach-athlete relationship-a scoping review from sport sociological and sport psychological perspectives. *Frontiers in Sports and Active Living*, *3*, 643707.

Gervis, L., Baker, L., & Imoedemhe, O. (2019). Hidden in plain sight – Mental health challenges in football clubs. *Football Medicine & Performance*, *30*, 24–27.

Gervis, M., Baker-Power, L., Goldman, A., & Mackenzie, J. (2025). A collaborative rapid response to abuse in UK gymnastics using group focused acceptance and commitment therapy-based program. *Journal of Clinical Sport Psychology*, *1*(aop), 1–13.

Gervis, M., & Dunn, N. (2004). The emotional abuse of elite child athletes by their coaches. *Child Abuse Review: Journal of the British Association for the Study and Prevention of Child Abuse and Neglect*, *13*(3), 215–223.

Gervis, M., Pickford, H., Nygård, H., & Goldman, A. (2022). The prevalence and impact of debilitative psychological and behavioral responses to long-term injury in athletes. *Journal of Clinical Sport Psychology*, *17*(3), 249–270.

Goldman, A., & Gervis, M. (2021). "Women are cancer, you shouldn't be working in sport": Sport psychologists' lived experiences of sexism in sport. *The Sport Psychologist*, *35*(2), 85–96.

Harris, R. (2009). *ACT made simple: An easy-to-read primer on acceptance and commitment therapy*. New Harbinger Publications.

Kavanagh, E., Brown, L., & Jones, I. (2017). Elite athletes' experience of coping with emotional abuse in the coach – Athlete relationship. *Journal of Applied Sport Psychology*, *29*(4), 402–417.

Kavanagh, E., Jones, I., & Sheppard-Marks, L. (2020). Towards typologies of virtual maltreatment: Sport, digital cultures & dark leisure. In *Re-thinking leisure in a digital age* (pp. 75–88). Routledge.

Kerr, G., Willson, E., & Stirling, A. (2020). "It was the worst time in my life": The effects of emotionally abusive coaching on female Canadian national team athletes. *Women in Sport and Physical Activity Journal*, *28*(1), 81–89.

Kessler, R. C., Aguilar-Gaxiola, S., Alonso, J., Benjet, C., Bromet, E. J., Cardoso, G., . . . & Koenen, K. C. (2017). Trauma and PTSD in the WHO world mental health surveys. *European Journal of Psychotraumatology*, *8*(sup5), 1353383.

Kozlowska, K., Walker, P., McLean, L., & Carrive, P. (2015). Fear and the defense cascade: Clinical implications and management. *Harvard Review of Psychiatry*, *23*(4), 263–287.

Lehmann, M., Foster, C., & Keul, J. (1993). Overtraining in endurance athletes: A brief review. *Medicine & Science in Sports & Exercise*, *25*(7), 854–862. https://doi.org/10.1249/00005768-199307000-00015

Levine, P. A. (1997). *Waking the tiger: Healing trauma: The innate capacity to transform overwhelming experiences*. North Atlantic Books.

Levine, P. A. (2010). *In an unspoken voice: How the body releases trauma and restores goodness*. North Atlantic Books.

Liberzon, I., & Abelson, J. L. (2016). Context processing and the neurobiology of post-traumatic stress disorder. *Neuron*, *92*(1), 14–30.

Lo, C. K., Chan, K. L., & Ip, P. (2019). Insecure adult attachment and child maltreatment: A meta-analysis. *Trauma, Violence, & Abuse*, *20*(5), 706–719.

Lowrance, S. A., Ionadi, A., McKay, E., Douglas, X., & Johnson, J. D. (2016). Sympathetic nervous system contributes to enhanced corticosterone levels following chronic stress. *Psychoneuroendocrinology*, *68*, 163–170.

Lynch, J. H. (2021). Posttraumatic stress disorder in elite athletes. *Current Sports Medicine Reports*, *20*(12), 645–650.

Marek, R., Strobel, C., Bredy, T. W., & Sah, P. (2013). The amygdala and medial prefrontal cortex: Partners in the fear circuit. *The Journal of Physiology*, *591*(10), 2381–2391.

McLaughlin, K. A., Peverill, M., Gold, A. L., Alves, S., & Sheridan, M. A. (2015). Child maltreatment and neural systems underlying emotion regulation. *Journal of the American Academy of Child & Adolescent Psychiatry*, *54*(9), 753–762.

Milad, M. R., & Quirk, G. J. (2012). Fear extinction as a model for translational neuroscience: Ten years of progress. *Annual Review of Psychology*, *63*(1), 129–151.
Mountjoy, M., Sloan, S., Ali-Zada, M., Bindra, A., Blauwet, C., Budgett, R., Burrows, K., Currie, A., Engebretsen, L., & Erdener, U. (2025). International Olympic Committee consensus-driven guidelines for athlete mental health support at sporting events. *British Journal of Sports Medicine*, *59*(21), 1459–1470.
Muhonen, J., Stirling, A., & Kokkonen, M. (2024). Athletic identity affects prevalence and disclosure of emotional abuse in Finnish athletes. *Frontiers in Sports and Active Living*, *6*, 1406949.
Newman, J. A., Lickess, A., & Higham, A. J. (2024). Fighting the system: Psychology consultants' experiences of working with cases of maltreatment in sport. *Journal of Applied Sport Psychology*, *36*(2), 210–230.
Owusu-Sekyere, F., & Gervis, M. (2016). In the pursuit of mental toughness: Is creating mentally tough players a disguise for emotional abuse? *International Journal of Coaching Science*, *10*(1).
Ozer, E. J., Best, S. R., Lipsey, T. L., & Weiss, D. S. (2003). Predictors of posttraumatic stress disorder and symptoms in adults: A meta-analysis. *Psychological Bulletin*, *129*(1), 52.
Papandrea, C. C. (2022). *A study of the relationship between adverse childhood experiences, attachment, and trauma-related growth*. College of Saint Elizabeth.
Parry, K. D., Kavanagh, E., & Jones, I. (2015). Adoration and abuse: The impact of virtual maltreatment on athletes. *The Conversation*, *14*.
Payne, P., Levine, P. A., & Crane-Godreau, M. A. (2015). Somatic experiencing: Using interoception and proprioception as core elements of trauma therapy. *Frontiers in Psychology*, *6*, 124489.
Porges, S. W. (2011). *The polyvagal theory: Neurophysiological foundations of emotions, attachment, communication, and self-regulation (Norton series on interpersonal neurobiology)*. WW Norton & Company.
Porges, S. W. (2022). Polyvagal theory: A science of safety. *Frontiers in Integrative Neuroscience*, *16*, 871227.
Porges, S. W. (2023). The vagal paradox: A polyvagal solution. *Comprehensive Psychoneuroendocrinology*, *16*, 100200.
Roberts, B. L., & Karatsoreos, I. N. (2021). Brain – Body responses to chronic stress: A brief review. *Faculty Reviews*, *10*, 83.
Roberts, V., Sojo, V., & Grant, F. (2020). Organisational factors and non-accidental violence in sport: A systematic review. *Sport Management Review*, *23*(1), 8–27.
Rosenbaum, S., Vancampfort, D., Steel, Z., Newby, J., Ward, P. B., & Stubbs, B. (2015). Physical activity in the treatment of post-traumatic stress disorder: A systematic review and meta-analysis. *Psychiatry Research*, *230*(2), 130–136.
Ross, S. L., Sharma-Patel, K., Brown, E. J., Huntt, J. S., & Chaplin, W. F. (2021). Complex trauma and trauma-focused cognitive-behavioral therapy: How do trauma chronicity and PTSD presentation affect treatment outcome? *Child Abuse & Neglect*, *111*, 104734.
Saunders, K. R., McGuinness, E., Barnett, P., Foye, U., Sears, J., Carlisle, S., . . . & Trevillion, K. (2023). A scoping review of trauma informed approaches in acute, crisis, emergency, and residential mental health care. *BMC Psychiatry*, *23*(1), 567.
Shin, L. M., & Liberzon, I. (2010). The neurocircuitry of fear, stress, and anxiety disorders. *Neuropsychopharmacology*, *35*(1), 169–191.
Smits, F., Jacobs, F., & Knoppers, A. (2017). 'Everything revolves around gymnastics': Athletes and parents make sense of elite youth sport. *Sport in Society*, *20*(1), 66–83. https://doi.org/10.1080/17430437.2015.1124564

Symons, C. M., O'Sullivan, G. A., & Polman, R. (2017). The impacts of discriminatory experiences on lesbian, gay and bisexual people in sport. *Annals of Leisure Research, 20*(4), 467–489.

Tuakli-Wosornu, Y. A., Burrows, K., Fasting, K., Hartill, M., Hodge, K., Kaufman, K., . . . & Rhind, D. J. (2024). IOC consensus statement: Interpersonal violence and safeguarding in sport. *British Journal of Sports Medicine, 58*(22), 1322–1344.

Van der Kolk, B. (2014). *The body keeps the score: Brain, mind, and body in the healing of trauma*. New York: Viking.

Van der Kolk, B. A. (1994). The body keeps the score: Memory and the evolving psychobiology of posttraumatic stress. *Harvard Review of Psychiatry, 1*(5), 253–265.

Vertommen, T., Schipper-van Veldhoven, N., Wouters, K., Kampen, J. K., Brackenridge, C. H., Rhind, D. J., . . . & Van Den Eede, F. (2016). Interpersonal violence against children in sport in the Netherlands and Belgium. *Child Abuse & Neglect, 51*, 223–236.

Walton, C. C., Purcell, R., Pilkington, V., Hall, K., Kenttä, G., Vella, S., & Rice, S. M. (2024). Psychological safety for mental health in elite sport: A theoretically informed model. *Sports Medicine, 54*(3), 557–564.

Willson, E., Kerr, G., Stirling, A., & Buono, S. (2022). Prevalence of maltreatment among Canadian national team athletes. *Journal of Interpersonal Violence, 37*(21–22), NP19857–NP19879.

Yoshii, T. (2021). The role of the thalamus in post-traumatic stress disorder. *International Journal of Molecular Sciences, 22*(4), 1730.

10 Team ACT at the Olympic Games

Peter Haberl and MeiLan Haberl

Learning Objectives

1. Analyse how applied sport psychology practice integrates within the performance environment of the Olympic Games, considering the unique organisational, cultural, and pressure-driven demands of the setting.
2. Explain how applied sport psychologists collaborate with coaches and teams to clarify shared values, translate these into daily behaviours, and cultivate psychological flexibility that supports both well-being and performance.
3. Evaluate the nature of athletes' psychological work – and the sport psychologist's role in supporting it – within the high-stakes crucible of performance, highlighting how psychological skills are enacted and adapted under pressure.

Introduction

On 8 August 2024, while in Paris at the 2024 Olympic Games, I[1] received a congratulatory text from a trusted colleague and close friend, Dr Cristina Fink. She texted:

> *Well done Peter! So excited to see you there!*

She included a picture of the US Women's Rugby 7's team celebrating their first-ever Olympic medal, bronze, in the sold-out Stade De France stadium.

I replied to her message:

> Thank you. What a wild ride and ending. Never been so integrated with a team, never done so much work in the three years leading into the games, never done so much work in the week leading into the Games and never done so much work in the three hours between the semi-final and bronze medal game, sport psych heaven!

DOI: 10.4324/9781003515203-12

Winning the bronze medal – particularly in an upset over the gold medal favourite, Team Australia – certainly did feel heavenly, but the medal outcome was *not* the reason that my past years of work with the US Women's Rugby 7's team were "sport psychology heaven".

"Heaven" for an applied sport psychologist is *not* about athletes claiming an elite prize, or presenting a few slide shows a year to a group of highly receptive and confident players, or sitting in a comfortably cultivated, pristine office space waiting for the arrival of a client with a problem to solve. For me, at least, "heaven" is captured in the sheer depth and breadth of the work we – the players and staff of the US Women's Rugby 7's team – had engaged in since Tokyo 2020, work captained by Head Coach Emilie Bydwell. She had a clear vision. A vision that included preparing the team psychologically for exactly the kind of unbelievable moment that occurred in the last 30 seconds of the bronze medal game in Paris. A vision that aimed for the team to be psychologically flexible under pressure, open and aware of unpleasant thoughts and feelings, able to be fully present, focused on the moment and taking committed actions, guided by values, no matter what the score was.

In this chapter, I will present the saga of the psychological journey and preparation of US Women's Rugby 7's for the 2024 Paris Olympic Games as a case study: one that displays what that work with a team sport looks like when a practitioner works from an Acceptance and Commitment Training lens[2], and the depth of work that is made possible through a fully integrated approach to applied sport psychology. To do so, this chapter is split into three parts:

1. Awareness, Approaches, and Looking in the Mirror→ framing the role of applied sport psychology at the Olympic Games, different models of integration, and background on the circumstances of Rugby 7's.
2. Committing to Digging Mindful Trenches→ describing the key factors, practices, and preparation implemented by the team to prepare for the Paris 2024 Games.
3. Last Trainings and the Eye of the Hurricane→ a play-by-play of the culmination of all this work, and a snapshot at the adaptations required of applied sport psychology from an ACT perspective at the Games.

Awareness, Approaches, and Looking in the Mirror

Let's return, for a moment, to the text that my colleague, Dr Fink, sent: *so excited to see you there!* As much as this is a happy sentiment, it also signifies the significant challenges faced by sport psychology and performance practitioners in gaining *accreditation* to access their Olympic athletes at the Olympic Games. Physical sport psychology presence at the Games is still an exception, rather than a rule. Accreditation is essentially a passport in the Olympic Games universe and a very limited resource because it is based on the size of a participating country's delegation.

In Paris, my accreditation with USA Rugby allowed me not only to have access to the team at the competition venue, but also to have access to the Olympic village and transportation system at all hours. The logistical challenges of acquiring accreditation, the accessibility barrier it presents to practitioners, their athletes, and their work bring up a key question:

Does sport psychology have a role and a place in such an intense setting?

To put it simply, should a sport psychologist working with a team at the Olympic Games also *be* at the Olympic Games? And if so, what is the sport psychologist doing there?

These are perennial questions for applied sport psychology and have been discussed for a long time in our literature (e.g., Haberl & Peterson, 2006; Birrer et al., 2012; Elsborg et al., 2015). Beyond the literature, working with a number of team sports "on site" at ten Olympic Games has certainly given me a lot of time and experience to attempt to formulate an opinion on this topic. And, if you will permit me to (temporarily) answer a question with a metaphorical question, I will try to provide another understanding of sport psychology at the Olympic Games. My question:

Do you need a mirror in the morning?

The answer is . . . no! You don't *need* a mirror in the morning. So equally: no, you don't *need* a sport psychologist at the Olympic Games. But both can be extremely valuable tools, in life and in performance.

Why am I comparing the function of a mirror to that of a psychologist? For most of us, it is actually quite helpful to have a mirror in the morning, even if it isn't an absolute need! It can be really helpful to "see yourself" as you are, reflected in your mirror, before you head out the door. Otherwise, you may be caught unaware of the consequences of how you "look". That brief moment of literal reflection provides you with an opportunity to be aware of yourself, your surroundings, and glean valuable information about what actions you might choose to take (changing your hairstyle, cleaning your face, simply taking a deep breath before you head out to work) that can have an impact throughout your day. Similarly, the role a sport psychologist plays at the Games is as a facilitator of awareness, attention, and adaptation, helping their athletes and their teams be conscious of what thoughts and feelings are present in the inevitable emotional storm of the Olympics. Like a mirror, a sport psychologist can give a performer the tools to reflect on, and "see", their own mind at work. And when athletes understand how their minds work, they can more skilfully learn to work with them.

This ability to "see yourself" is especially important in a high-pressure environment such as the Olympic Games. Seeing yourself only really works when you have practiced seeing yourself and <u>accepting</u> what you see, from a perspective unclouded by pressure, before you take meaningful action. Seeing yourself, and seeing how you fit into the context that surrounds you in a given moment, matters for performance – particularly when your team knows that not medalling will most likely result in drastic funding cuts, threatening the program itself. This is the position that Team USA's Women's Rugby 7's Team found ourselves in, coming into the Paris 2024 Olympic Games.

Rugby 7's, Walsh's Approaches to Mental Skills Work, and Introducing the Engine Room Success Profile

A brief history of the Rugby 7's program, up to that point: Rugby 7's, not to be confused with Rugby 15's, was added to the Olympic program in 2016. Each game lasts 14 minutes with two seven-minute halves. Teams consist of 12 players (with two alternates). Seven players from each team are on the field at any given time, hence the sport's name. The US Women's 7's program finished fifth in the 2016 Rio Olympics, losing in the quarterfinals and coming just short of the podium competitions. Despite higher hopes for Tokyo 2020, the team finished a disappointing 6th place – even after winning all three pool games, including an upset over gold medal favourite Team Australia. The quarterfinal, this time against Great Britain, bested the team once again. With COVID delaying the Tokyo Games until 2021, the next Olympic cycle leading into Paris was now compressed into three years, rather than the usual complete four; then-head coach Chris Brown resigned that fall; against the backdrop of these challenges and the previous failures to medal, repeating history in 2024 would likely lead to severe budget cuts and a further drop in the performance capabilities of the program.

In my then function as a United States Olympic & Paralympic Committee (USOPC) sport psychologist assigned to summer team sports, I had worked with Women's Rugby 7's under multiple different head coaches: first, from 2012 to 2015 (with coach Ric Suggit), then again right before and during the 2016 Games (with coach Richie Walker, who became head coach shortly before those Games), and then from 2018 to the Tokyo Games (with coach Chris Brown.) Coaches are often the main stakeholders mediating the extent of a sport psychologist practitioner's engagement with athletes in a team setting. To understand the different – and often fluctuating – levels of engagement possible for an SPP working with different coaches, even while collaborating with the same team, we will investigate how NZL mental skills coach Aaron Walsh (2024a) conceptualises and describes five approaches to mental skills work in elite sports:

- No program
- The minimalist approach
- The deficit approach

- The skill approach
- The integrated approach

Let's break down these approaches:

"No program" doesn't mean sport psychology isn't considered important. Rather, it means that an organisation, oversight body, or coach doesn't know where to start in bringing in this kind of work, so they do not actively engage it.

The Minimalist Approach is characterised by a mental skills provider making just a couple of appearances with a team in a year, maybe doing a few talks or a workshop, but with no further integration.

The Deficit Approach is where the work is focused on players who are struggling with their performance – a struggle is attributed to "mental issues", thus the need to see a sport psychologist to "fix" the athlete. Historically, the deficit approach has been the most common for providers in this space.

The Skill Approach is characterised by an understanding that *everyone* needs to work on their mental skills, and the focus of work is on providing tools and helping athletes/performers grow in their ability to use those tools, with a lot of one-on-one work and accessibility.

Walsh considers the Integrated Approach as the optimal approach and "the most immersed model", driven by a clear strategy. The organisation/administrators/staff/athletes all agree that mental skills are considered crucial for performance, and this buy-in is reflected in the financial resources allocated and time commitment made for this approach. The provider is fully integrated for everyday access to the athletes and staff, has continuous and consistent engagement with the team as a whole in ongoing workshops/mental skills sessions/allotted time for psychological tool building, and even travels with the team as a member of its permanent support staff.

While my initial engagement with Women's Rugby 7's, back in 2012, may have started from a deficit approach, the work quickly moved to a skill approach over the following years. However, it did not advance to an integrated approach (and realise that approach's full potential) until Emilie Bydwell became the team's interim head coach in fall 2021. We first started working together in 2012–2013, when Emilie was still herself an athlete on the Rugby 7's team. Then, again, we were colleagues when she was an assistant coach on the 2016 team and continued working together as she transitioned to being the High Performance Director in 2018. As she assumed the role of Head Coach after Tokyo, Coach Bydwell developed and had each of her staff members complete a self-reflection exercise titled "the Engine Room Success Profile".[3] Throughout the rest of this chapter, I will refer to the guideposts crystallised by the Engine Room Success Profile to demonstrate the goals and execution of my work with Rugby 7's – the "mirror" reflecting itself, as it were. The Profile lists the Team Values and the Critical Success Factors that apply to the team as a whole, and poses a number of crucial questions that guide the work of the respective staff member (not unlike the sport psychology canvas for soccer academies – see Feddersen et al., 2025). Specifically, the profile addressed the staff members:

- Role
- Purpose
- Area of accountability
- What success looks like
- What the position needs to be successful
- What actions will the respective staff person take to support the team in reaching its goals

While medalling at the Paris Olympics was our desired outcome goal, the shared "Critical Success Factors" we developed served as guideposts to judge our success. Or, as conceptualised in the Walsh framework (2024b) – our vision of what success would look like:

- *Execute on a clearly defined game model that delivers an effective and adaptive team that plays to their potential under pressure, winning today and tomorrow.*
- *Develop the culture and mental flexibility required to deliver a resilient and united team under pressure.*
- *Employ a training philosophy that drives standards, connects physical demands with the game model, and promotes adaptive behaviours.*

This second Critical Success Factor – *develop the culture and mental flexibility required to deliver a resilient and united team under pressure* – directly encompasses the role of sport psychology at the Olympic Games, and my purpose with this team: contribute to building a team that is psychologically flexible and resilient[4].

ACT and Psychological Flexibility at the Olympic Games

Why would we place such an emphasis on psychological flexibility, rather than, say, a more traditional sport psychology concept, such as mental toughness (see Gucciardi, 2017)?

As someone who practices from an ACT perspective, emphasising flexibility, adaptability, and resilience reflects where I am housed philosophically in sport psychology. In viewing performance through an ACT lens, I regard "toughness" as an unhelpful concept at the Olympic Games. Trying to acquire and instil "toughness" is, to use ACT language, a concept that sets a trap for experiential avoidance. In my experience, athletes associate mental toughness with unwavering, impenetrable, and inflexible confidence and an absolute absence of negative and unpleasant emotions. From my perspective, this conceptualisation of "toughness", and subsequent attempts to pursue it, fails to understand the psychological reality of the Olympic Games. Negative, unpleasant, and uncomfortable emotions are almost unavoidable at the Olympic Games, especially if you compete for a medal. If the outcome means the world to you, and the outcome is uncertain, anxiety, fear, pressure, and worry are likely to arise in intensities and frequencies beyond your control.

Rather than emphasising the impossibility of emotional control and being "tough" in such an exceptionally intense performance environment, an ACT perspective encourages athletes to accept whatever emotional experience – however positive, negative, or neutral – emerges at the Games without attempting to change it. Instead, it turns their attention to working skilfully with what arises. As I have written elsewhere, to me, this attention is the currency of performance at the Olympic Games (Haberl, 2016). This experiential perspective is backed up empirically by the latest neuroscience research as summarised in Jha (2021) and exemplified by a Delphi study (Albertella et al., 2023), in which the perspectives of dozens of performance experts were analysed in order to consolidate a consensus on crucial components of performance in high-stakes environments. Ultimately, Albertella et al. (2023) argue that attention is the key cognitive driver of performance under pressure. Thus, the mental preparation that USA Rugby 7's engaged in order to perform under pressure at the Olympic Games centred on mindfully training their awareness and ability to take charge of their attention, in order to flexibly adapt to the circumstances that arose.

Being psychologically flexible means understanding that the mind works as a thought- and emotion-producing factory. It means developing an awareness of those thoughts and feelings as they show up in the individual mind and the team as a whole, without preference or judgement (being open). It means engaging the ability to contact the present moment (being present) regardless of the appearance of all kinds of mind states. And it means taking actions guided by values (doing what matters). While we might not be able to control the output of feelings and thoughts from the factory of the mind, we can potentially control our attention and our subsequent actions on the field of play.

Back in Tokyo, at the 2020/1 Olympic, USA Rugby 7's did not respond to what the Games offered up with flexibility. Rather, there was a sense of mental rigidity. When we faced Team Great Britain in the quarterfinal, the team had just won all three pool play games. In scrimmages a month earlier, we had won all four games against GB; combined with winning the pool, there was a sense of confidence and excitement to play Team Great Britain again.

Team Great Britain did not care about Team USA's pleasantly confident state of mind, winning the quarterfinal 21–12. Confidence, as a state of mind, and as all states of mind, comes and goes; confidence is impermanent. Previous successes and the pleasant states of mind they can elicit, such as confidence, are not guarantees in the actual moment of performance. Pleasant states of mind can lead to underestimating the challenging task ahead.

So, how can an integrated approach help take a team from a point of rigidity and fragile confidence into one that has developed, as we put it in the second critical success factor, *the culture and mental flexibility required to deliver a resilient and united team under pressure*?

Committing to Digging Mindful Trenches

Key Components of Success, Actionable Steps, Social Meditation, and the Mind Gym

In my Engine Room Success Profile, I defined what success – within my "area of accountability" as the sport psychology provider – would look like for USA Rugby 7's:

- The athletes would regularly engage in the training of psychological flexibility, alone or with their teammates, and in the process strengthen their resilience and focus in competition and practice
- Athletes would be clear about their individual values and the team values and would be able to use them to guide committed action.
- Athletes would have an understanding of how the mind works as a thought- and emotion-producing factory, and with that understanding, more skilfully work with their thoughts and feelings in competition and training while taking charge of their attention.

With this picture of success in mind, I completed the next item on the Profile ("what the position needs to be successful") to provide actionable frameworks to support these goals:

- Regular communication with the head coach
- Attend key competitions and work with the team
- Weekly time with the team to practice attention, awareness, and attitudes of mind and work on communication and psychological flexibility
- Individual working relationship with the players

The head coach of a team sport is the key stakeholder in an integrated sport psychology approach. For Walsh (2024a), a lack of support from key stakeholders is one of four major obstacles to the integration of mental skills into elite sports. The other obstacles are as follows: (2) the siloing of mental skills work, (3) the failure to understand the key performance demands of the environment (in our case, the Olympic Games), and (4) presenting information in a way that is too complicated, even irrelevant, to the needs of the athletes. Eliminating the first obstacle, I had the benefit of a long and trusting relationship with Coach Bydwell, following our years of work together from her playing career to her administrative roles. We continued to build this relationship through the first item mentioned earlier – regular communication. Not only was there full support from this "key stakeholder", she is actually the one who pushed for the full integration of sport psychology with the team's training, consolidating my position with the rest of the coaching staff so that the work was not siloed (Walsh's second obstacle.) As for addressing the third obstacle of comprehending key demands: after nine Olympic Games with team sports, I felt I had a good understanding of the performance demands of the environment as well as a practical framework that (although often challenging presuppositions about toughness and confidence, as above) had been refined to be relatable and accessible to the athletes (Haberl, 2022).

However, to employ this framework and my understanding to support the team, I would need to be present in some form myself (as indicated by the latter three items). While I was not embedded full-time physically with the team at their base in San Diego, I travelled with 7's to the majority of their competitions throughout the year. In particular, during the Olympic qualification year, I joined the team for six out of the seven tour stops (by the time the seventh stop rolled around, we had already qualified for the Games). Each trip on the road was a week-long affair, during which the team was somewhat literally a captive audience while we engaged in the item of "practic[ing] attention, awareness and attitudes of mind and work on communication and psychological flexibility". When I was not physically present with the team, we held a weekly Zoom session, during which the work continued. Furthermore, I made myself available for individual meetings with players and staff on an appointment basis. I also designed the mental skills training sessions that Emilie dubbed "Mind Gym", which she then executed on the ground with the team. Emilie and I would speak multiple times a week to plan and implement these sessions as the team's needs evolved. Emilie also wanted to focus on actively developing the team's leaders, so we held weekly meetings with the leadership group. These meetings charged and supported players with leadership responsibilities in taking intentional, active steps towards bringing out the best in their teammates, bolstering our values-based approach and culture, and creating a system of open communication between players and staff.

The next element on the Engine Room Success Profile summarises these items as action steps I committed to taking throughout the three years leading up to Paris:

- Offer innovative group mental training approaches/program off the pitch in the mind gym
- Connect those training approaches to the work on the pitch
- Be available for optional weekly 1 v 1 sessions to deepen the practice and development of psychological flexibility
- Offer a confidential listening ear to the athletes and coaches

- Assist and collaborate with the coaching staff and the players in building a cohesive team that lives its values and is super resilient on and off the field
- Be open to input

The innovative group mental training approaches I offered in the Mind Gym are based on an evolution of traditional mindfulness training developed by two Dharma teachers, Vince Horn and Kenneth Folk (Gleig, 2019). I have trained with Vince Horn since about 2015, first in traditional mindfulness approaches; then, Horn introduced social meditation, an approach he had learned from Folk and then further refined. Unlike typical solo mindfulness meditation, in social meditation, participants practice together and aloud[5].

Repeated mindfulness practice trains attention and awareness (Kabat-Zinn, 1994), which has also been observed in corresponding neuroscience research (again, see Jha, 2021). Folk and Horn (Gleig, 2019) stress that attention and awareness don't need to be practiced in isolation and/or silence, but can be integrated into the community. The aim of this pedagogical innovation is to enhance the quality of (social practice leads to less mind wandering) and motivation to practice (it is more fun to practice with others). In addition to these benefits, social meditation offers a unique avenue for a team to develop increased awareness, acceptance of emotional states, and command of their attention *together*. Psychological flexibility, the ability to adapt to a changing, pressurised performance environment, is not simply ascertained by using the *mirror* to reflect with awareness, it requires repetitive practice to strengthen and exercises to develop the ability to repeatedly guide attention back to the next action; this is what Kabat-Zinn calls the work of digging mindful trenches, and why Coach Bydwell referred to these sessions as a Mind "Gym" where the team would practice and practice and practice building mental muscles in tandem.

Beyond the weekly team sport psychology sessions and the Mind Gym practice sessions, which were mandatory, the athletes could also choose to work individually on their mental skills in one-on-one sessions with the sport psychologist, or online over zoom. Just like with the team sessions, the focus for the individual sessions was on strengthening the "muscle" of psychological flexibility and to actively train the mind to prepare for the pressure of performing at the Olympic Games.

In the years between Tokyo and Paris, USA Rugby 7's would engage in three to four Mind Gym practices a week, ranging from 5 to 20 minutes. Different exercises would develop awareness, attention, and attitudes of mind – overarching principles that connected to and derived from the team's core values.

Connecting to Values, Elevating the Highwomen Story

Coach Bydwell is a very values-driven coach (in alignment with the ACT model's integration of values as a guiding compass) and wanted the team to revisit their values after the 2021/22 season. Beyond simply defining a set of core values for the team – Love, Work Ethic, Courage, Resilience, and Selflessness – which were incorporated into the Engine Room Success Profile, Emilie contextualised these values within a concrete narrative.

To this end, she found inspiration in a country song – the self-titled "Highwomen" by American country superband "the Highwomen".[6] The song is about four unnamed women from periods of social upheaval and/or facing great adversity (revolution in Nicaragua, the Salem Witch Trials, and the Civil Rights Movement), employing archetypes and "untold stories" of female strengths. This song provided a sense of shared identity that the players resonated with. The "Highwomen" in the song display the team's core values, as well as serving as both a reflection and an acknowledgment of the team's diversity, and presenting that diversity not as a dividing principle, but a source of individual strengths braided into an even stronger collective.

Connecting to historical archetypes also allowed us an opportunity to honour the work of those who came before. Practically, we approached/realised these connections by asking players to choose and present "highwomen" from history and "highwomen" from their own family backgrounds to the rest of the team, actively engaging their contributions in a process of sharing stories of resilience, courage, selflessness, work ethic, and love that would connect these values and the team's journey to a greater purpose[7] and story. In the Mind Gym, we selected practices that also allowed us to actively engage with our values: social meditations following a "may it arise" format (the "it" being a team value, e.g., "may Love arise"), or "multidimensional meditations" (where we explore the value of courage from different "dimensions", such as an aspiration, an inquiry question, an inhabiting[8], etc.). By actively incorporating values into storytelling and the Mind Gym practices, we ensured that values weren't just words on a wall, but active daily guides for the team's committed actions.

Stories and storytelling were further involved in actions taken to prepare and bring the team together, as Coach Bydwell tasked the team to read the book Chop Wood Carry Water: How to Fall in Love with the Process of Becoming Great (Medcalf, 2015). Short chapters and excerpts became discussion and reference points in our team meetings, creating a shared bank of knowledge to draw from to further connect with our values and psychological flexibility.

As I have written elsewhere, at the Olympic Games, attention is the currency of performance (Haberl, 2016, 2022), not the right thoughts and not feelings; hence my tag line, "I don't care how you feel". I do care, but I care that athletes notice what feelings are present, what thoughts are present. So, a yardstick for successfully implementing sport psychology is asking if you, as an athlete, and you, as a team, were able to be in the moment, focused on the here and now, focused on the task at hand, no matter the score. All of the work described above is in preparation for such a moment. Hopefully, it is clear how intensive and intentional this trench digging was built. Commitment took the form of time invested in storytelling, in mindfulness practices individually and as a team, in reading and connecting practice to value-based action, mental training to build mental muscles, and continuous communication in the name of strengthening connections that would weather any storm.

Because the Olympic Games are often a tempest of emotions, changing circumstances, uncertainty, and adaptation – for athletes and staff alike.

Last Trainings and the Eye of the Hurricane

Just Before the 2024 Paris Olympic Games

On 17 July, I joined the team for their pre-Olympic Games acclimatisation camp in Tours, where they practiced with the Irish national team. The focus on the first few days of the camp in Tours was on reviewing the tactical approach to our pool opponents, after which Emilie carved out considerable time to revisit and fine-tune our focus on the psychology of the Olympic Games as we transitioned into the village. As we boarded the bus to Paris on Monday, 22 July, the tranquillity of Tours gave way to the upcoming and unavoidable emotional intensity of what was to come. The tension was palpable. The Opening Ceremony was on 26 July with competition starting on 28 July.

At this juncture, the sport psychology focus was on staying connected with some of our key themes built over the last three years, such as:

- Staying in the moment
- Bringing the wandering mind back to the present moment
- Being open to uncomfortable thoughts and feelings
- Staying connected to our values – especially love

Sport psychology sessions consisted of a mixture of mindfulness practices in the Mind Gym (e.g., gratitude practices, heartfulness practices, equanimity practices, awareness, and attention practices), storytelling, reflections, and small group discussions (which were often done in the form of a mindful conversation). We reflected on such questions as:

What is it like to be in love?
What are the actions of love?
What happens to your attention when you are in love?
What made you fall in love with rugby?
Talk about a time when rugby has broken your heart?
How do we define success/failure here?

Why so many questions/reflections on "Love"? Love was a core value for the team, and "love" also allowed us to discuss "heartbreak" in the form of fear of failure. "What if" thoughts are rather common for Olympic athletes. One such thought is "what if we don't medal?" and "what if we fail?", which comes with a host of unpleasant feelings. The aim of these conversations and meetings was to counterbalance the inevitable magnet pull of the outcome goal of winning a medal, which would draw our athletes' attention away from the present moment, and the understandable and unavoidable desire to feel the "right way". A medal at the Olympic Games is the biggest jackpot, and as research on pressure tells us (Smoulder et al., 2024), the bigger the jackpot, the easier it is for the mind to get distracted. The same goes for wanting positive emotional states. Every athlete wants to feel great at the Olympic Games.

Working with athletes and teams at nine Olympic Games teaches you that positive emotional states are actually the exception, and not the rule, for medal winners, especially as they get closer to the medal event. This makes the ACT perspective of "willingness" (Harris, 2019) very helpful and relevant in this context, as its key question isn't "am I feeling the right way?", but rather, "am I willing to feel whatever shows up?" and then show up by taking actions (guided by my values!)

Being open to unpleasant states and normalising such states was a continuous message in the work we had done over the last three years. Rather than letting that work languish, the closer we got to the actual competition, we kept revisiting and strengthening the "muscles" of awareness, attention (focusing and refocusing on the task at hand), and attitudes of mind (taking values-guided actions). This also meant revisiting what we control and what we don't control when it comes to working with the mind.

Our conversations allowed us to be open to such thoughts and feelings, to (in ACT parlance,) notice, name, and normalise them, to look at them through the lens of purpose and workability (Harris, 2019), and then reconnect with the actions of "love". Philosophically, the action(s) of love invite a willingness to have your heart broken, for only then can you actually fall in love (and experience love). The value of love was also a focus of our team sessions. For example, we had introduced the concept of "Ubuntu" at earlier tour stops, and we revisited this theme in Paris. "Ubuntu" is a word from the Bantu (South African) languages and captures the essence of being human – that we are interconnected, not isolated as human beings – "I am because you are" (Kerr, 2013) – we are in this together, and we will experience it together.

Arriving in Paris

Three days before the start of the competition on 26 July, the team had a chance to visit the Olympic stadium for the first (and only) time prior to the competition. 26 July was a busy day. Again, Emilie carved out time for Mind Gym at the stadium. We went through our process of stepping into awareness, anchoring ourselves in the present moment, and connecting with our values. Besides the stadium visit, it was also the day of the Opening Ceremony. Weeks earlier, we had discussed the costs and benefits of walking or not walking in the Opening Ceremony as a team. While walking would provide a psychological boost, it would also come at considerable physiological costs[9]. Emilie wanted the team to have autonomy over the decision – after said discussion, the athletes decided collectively not to walk in the Opening Ceremony. Instead, the plan was to dress up in the opening ceremony outfits, briefly join the marching athletes in the village, and then stay behind.

We also scheduled the "Jersey Ceremony" for that afternoon. The Jersey Ceremony, where each player receives their game jersey, is a rugby-specific ritual that all teams incorporate into their process. For the Paris Jersey Ceremony, the players' families were invited, and our aim was to connect players, staff, and families with our "ubuntu" theme. To that end, Emilie addressed the players and families in a moving speech, and the team's video analyst, Lauren Barber, had put together a highlight reel of each player and staff member, very much in the spirit of the team value of "love". At the end of the jersey ceremony, there was not a dry eye in the room. There was a sense of deep connection and belonging (a state of being that we had deliberately nurtured in the three-year lead-up to the Games, such as when we used the Ubuntu theme at various tour stops).

From the Quarterfinal to the Bronze Medal Game

Every competition day on tour comes with the "run sheet", which outlines how the day of competition will flow, to the minute, specifying when and where the habitual preparation routines are scheduled. From a psychological perspective, these routines all provide helpful anchors of attention, which, when stepping into awareness, allow the athletes to ground themselves in the present moment, focusing their attention on the respective activities on the schedule, and bringing the thought- and emotion-producing mind back to the present moment every time it inevitably wanders off.

We had trained these routines over the course of the last three years, and they also included collective and individual psychological components. For example, on the second day of competition in Paris, after the last pool game vs France at 3:30 in the afternoon, the run sheet had to be adjusted immediately after that game to include the respective quarterfinal opponent that evening.

After losing our last pool game to France (although by winning our first two games, we were already qualified for the quarterfinal), it was immediately time to get ready for the Quarterfinal. We had returned to the village after the France game at 4:50 pm, the players had nap time and recovery from 5:30 to 7:00 pm. Then it was time to return to the stadium and start the process again. Again – this is the hurricane. A storm in which we would face a familiar opponent.

Just as in Tokyo, we drew Team GB for the quarterfinal. But, in Tokyo, we had won all three pool games, upsetting the top-seed Australia in the process, drawing what felt like an "ideal" opponent in the quarterfinal, and we were full of confidence. As the minutes ticked by and we fell behind, that feeling of confidence disappeared into thin air.

In many ways, the quarterfinal is the most important game of the tournament because it decides if you play for the medals or if you are packing your bags for the flight home. That Tokyo quarterfinal loss was, on some level, not unlike a traumatic experience for the returning players. There was a good chance some of those feelings and memories of the loss would return now that we faced GB again.

One way we had prepared for this over the last few seasons was, perhaps counterintuitively, to deliberately use a historical frame. Most people are familiar with the phrase "history repeats itself". What people are less familiar with, however, is the perspective of actual historians on the phrase. World-renowned historians such as Marcy Shore (Snyder, 2022) and Timothy Snyder (Snyder, 2017) argue that history does not repeat at all, but rather that history "instructs". We can be "instructed" by what happened in the past, reminding us that we can take actions, as individuals and as teams, that shape and impact what happens next. We wanted the team to be *aware* of this mental trap of believing in inevitable repetition, and then, from that perspective of awareness, be open to those memories and those unpleasant thoughts and feelings. Then, with that openness, step into the present moment, and come back to the actions we wanted to take.

The feeling in the locker room in Paris was very different from Tokyo. Gone was the sense of confidence. Instead, there was an openness to the uncertainty and unavoidable anxiety present: the fear of losing again! Having trained that openness allowed the players to notice, name, and normalise the feeling states and skilfully meet them. For the mind gym practice, we chose to do two rounds of an "equanimity" practice as well as a "mindful touch" practice. The intention here was to foster and prime for a sense of connection and a sense of being composed while under stress. GB scored first, leading 7:0, a scoreline that easily could have triggered a spiralling of the mind. Instead of freezing, instead of history repeating itself, the team stayed composed and remained focused on Emilie's game plan, slowly taking control of the game, and in the end winning 17:7.

History had instructed. Resilience and flexibility emerged.

Improvising Quiet in the Storm: A Chair Lift Consult

The quarterfinal had started at 9:30 pm. We returned to the village at about 11:15 pm. On the way back, on the bus, a player visited with me, engaging in what former colleague Sean McCann has referred to as the "chair lift consult" (McCann, 2000), which describes an impromptu informal sport psychology meeting in any setting other than a formal office. Basically, all sport psychology meetings at the Olympic Games fall into the "chairlift" consult type. Since there is no "office" for the sport psychologist, every space becomes an "office".

The player wanted to debrief her performance through a psychological lens to prepare for the next day, as she was not happy with her defensive play. In and of itself, this is nothing unusual (e.g., I had met with 12 of the 14 athletes – the 12 Olympians plus the two alternates – in the week leading into the Games). What makes it worthwhile mentioning here in this context is that this meeting was on the bus back to the village. Conversations such as this one on the bus are a normal occurrence on tour during the lead-up to the Olympic Games, where accreditation is less of an issue[10]. Again, however, accreditation is a potentially highly significant hurdle for a provider.

Coach Bydwell decided she wanted to have the sport psychologist at the Games, and continue with the same integrated service approach during the Olympic Competition as the team did during their regular 7's season competition for the last three years. This meant that I *did* have the access to provide a chairlift consult to athletes in the Olympic village and at all hours[11]. Furthermore, Emilie's commitment and desire for full integration didn't waver at all when my employment situation changed. After 25 years of being employed at the US Olympic Committee, I found myself in private practice starting in February of 2023. This change meant the NGB now needed to fund the sport psychology program rather than getting it for free from the USOPC. To my knowledge, three NGBs, the United States, Australia, and Great Britain, had sport psychology staff on the ground in Paris with their teams. Other teams had sport psychology involvement as well, but did not bring their consultants to the Games (e.g., New Zealand, Ireland, Canada, and France), thus not working from an integrated perspective. For Walsh (2024a), one hallmark of the integrated sport psychology approach is to put financial resources in place. USA Rugby, committed to the integrated approach, put those resources into play.

However, as aforementioned, the continuation of those resources was at stake, depending on how the team performed – something all members of the team were acutely aware of.

On Day 3, the next morning, we had a late start. I got a text from one of the athletes asking to meet first thing in the morning. The athlete shared she had a very hard time going to sleep the night before, saying she probably didn't fall asleep until 3:00 am, still so wound up from the later quarterfinal game. Her aim was to rest some more, and we agreed on doing a body scan practice. In my experience, a body scan practice is often very relaxing to the point of putting one to sleep. Making relaxation a goal may seem contradictory for somebody who claims "I don't care how you feel", in order to communicate that there is no need to change how you feel in this performance space. ACT argues that you can act calmly in a challenging environment without feeling calm (Harris, 2019). Here, though, in the village, we were not in a "challenging" environment; we were not in competition, so recovery and rest were the goal. The body scan practice proved effective, the athlete fell asleep, and got more recovery in. Mission accomplished.

After breakfast (at 10:00) and treatments, next up was Mind Gym and Hand Eye Coordination at 12:40. This occurred in the 10 minutes prior to leaving for the stadium at 1:00, for our semifinal game vs NZL. Despite a strong first half, we ended up losing – a loss that was immediately followed by prep for the bronze medal match, the second and last chance to compete for a medal.

In these moments, I make an effort to step into awareness myself: What does my mind offer up? I was aware that the expectation in my mind was that, should we lose to NZL, who was the clear favourite, we would most likely face Canada in the bronze medal match. The mind offered up that this was a 50/50 situation. Not bad odds.

But, as we finished our debrief, we learned that Canada had produced a stunning upset against the number 1 team in the world, Australia. Now our bronze medal opponent was Australia, *the* favourite. My mind certainly didn't offer up a 50/50 scenario, as we hadn't beaten Australia in over a year. Being in the locker room with the team and reading the room, the Canadian upset of Australia had brought forth a lot of unpleasant emotions for players and staff.

It was time to remind us of our steps to psychological flexibility: acknowledge the doubt that emerged, make room for it, ground ourselves in the present moment, and reconnect with our values. The framework guided not just my interaction with the team at the end of the debrief, but also the next Mind Gym practice in the only 75-minute recovery time between the semi-final and the bronze medal game. The same framework also guided the chair-lift consults with three players in that time window, who thought out a short conversation or individual practice time (individual Mind Gyms), and two conversations with the coaching staff – just like we would during the regular season, albeit in a far more compressed time and space. Here again, history instructed. Now we would see how preparation, values, awareness, and resilience fared on the pitch.

Making History

As I said in the text to my colleague at the start of this chapter: *What a wild ride and ending.*

Australia had just scored their second try in the bronze medal match in the second and final half of the game. This put them at 12:7 over Team USA. By the time Australia recuperated from that try and was ready to put the ball back into play, there were only 29 seconds left on the clock.

What was left was the possibility of one last play, but only if we could get possession first. Australia decided to kick deep into US territory, into the "red zone", with the aim of throttling the US team at their tryline – which put Team USA on the back foot: no room for error, and the daunting task of getting the ball down the entire length of the field. After a crazy bounce, we got our hands on the ball. And then successfully moved the ball down the line to player Alex

"Spiff" Sedrick. Spiff made the catch only meters from the US try(goal) line. All of Australia's players were spread before her, in a line intended to force her back.

In a stunning split-second turn, Spiff broke not one, but two tackles from a pair of the best tacklers in the world. Running free, she sprinted the full length of the field, scoring under the posts.

Now the game was tied up at 12 all. Making – or not making – the conversion for two more points would seal the victory as time had expired. There was only one problem now: due to tactical substitutions made by the coaching staff earlier in the game, there were no more specialist kickers on the field. However, practice, practice, and more practice for whatever the Games offered up had prepared Spiff for just a scenario. She *had* practiced a few conversions during warm-up with the coaches, but those didn't go too well. Does history repeat?

It didn't matter. Spiff, under time pressure, locked in, kicked her own conversion, and secured the USA's first ever medal in Rugby 7s.

Did We Achieve Our Vision?

Starting with the end in mind, our team's vision of sport psychology for Women's Rugby 7's was to develop a psychologically flexible team, united and resilient under pressure. Given how complex and multifactorial performance at the Olympic Games is (Gould et al., 1998), it is important to be careful with reading too much into single performance indicators, and perhaps more sensible to look at such indicators as pieces of a psychological and physiological puzzle.

Through that lens, the dramatic outcome of this game and that heart-stopping final play by Spiff Sedrick can be looked at as one such puzzle piece. Sedrick, in a podcast (Goff, 2024), spoke about the communication from the captains on the field during the game, reminding the team to simply focus on the next play: another puzzle piece, part of an assemblage that may depict an image of psychological flexibility in practice. A few other puzzle pieces come in the form of comments athletes made to the media immediately after the conclusion of the game. Again, caution is necessary to not read too much into such comments, but it is intriguing how the players talk about staying in the moment, how they reference working with doubt and being guided by team values in response to various reporter questions, and their "willingness" to have their hearts broken[12]:

Q: How much doubt was there, after they took that lead late how did you guys regroup and do this?

Stephanie Rovetti: There is always doubt. I mean we deal with doubt every single day, every single moment it is about bringing us back, you know, making eye-contact with each other, you know we've been in so many ups and downs this year, I think it's just like prepared us for these moments and just like not losing faith, keeping in the moment and no matter the doubt, no matter the excitement, confidence, whatever, like we're in the moment, we're connecting with each other and we are just doing what's in front of us

Q: What just happened?

Alena Olsen: We surprised ourselves. We knew we could do it. Moment by moment we took it and all our values shine through; we just defied the odds, I guess.

I never thought that I would get a bronze medal . . . the doubt that creeps into your head in every moment in a competition like this is so strong, you don't want to put yourself out there, but we put ourselves out there for a heartbreak and that is the only way you can also get joy like this, get success like this if you also put your heart out there to be broken.

Q: When you fell behind late, how concerned were you that this might not happen

Alena Olsen: . . . there was still time (a minute and 30 on the clock) and so you are just holding on to the next moment there is always a chance, there is always a chance until the seconds are out.

Q: What are your emotions

Alev Kelter: There is no words to describe it, this one is for anybody who has ever fell short of their dreams and still pushed through . . . our values as a team, are courage, selflessness, resilience, work ethic and love and I think you saw every ounce of that today and I'm so proud of these girls, I am so unbelievably proud . . .

The positive outcome, no doubt, can lead to an attributional bias. However, as stated in the beginning of the chapter, what made the work sport psychology *heaven* wasn't the outcome, but the level of integration led by Emilie Bydwell's vision, developed and dug into over the course of three years, a week, three hours, 75 minutes, and the awareness, dedication, and commitment to training by the US Women's Rugby 7's team.

Notes

1 Whenever we use "I", it refers to the first author.

2 I refer to it as Acceptance and Commitment training rather than Acceptance and Commitment therapy (Hayes et al., 1999; Harris, 2019) – as you will see in this chapter, that is a much more appropriate description as indeed the focus is on training the mind rather than providing therapy. The focus of training is on developing the relevant mental skills, as an individual and also as a team, in order to perform to potential in the Olympic environment.

3 The metaphor refers to the fact that the staff works in the shadows (in the background) so to speak to keep the ship running.

4 In Bydwell's model, my areas of accountability were as follows:
   - Sport psychology
   - Psychological flexibility
   - Resilience
5 We are currently working on a conceptual article to introduce social meditation/multiplayer meditation to our field. For a more detailed description of these practices, see The Purpose, Origins, & Evolution of Social Meditation.
6 Here is a link to the song: The Highwomen – Highwomen (Live Performance).
7 This YouTube clip does a wonderful job capturing the Highwomen concept: The Highwomen – USA Rugby (EHR).
8 Here is an example of such a multidimensional practice Multidimensional Meditation on Loving Awareness.
9 Athletes who participated in the Opening Ceremony (with the boat trip on the Seine) returned well after midnight.
10 Still even on tour – teams are limited in the number of staff a sport can bring, forcing the NGB to make difficult decisions – so on tour, in order to bring the sport psychologist, the team decided to have the video analyst work remotely and for the strength and conditioning coach to double up as team manager.
11 Another access option is a day pass, which is a tedious process where you need to surrender your passport at 9:00 am in the morning and then you can be in the village until 9:00 pm (but you can't leave). Then there is also a P credential – a personal coach credential – which gives you venue access but no access to the village or the transportation system, making access limited and difficult. There is a third and new accreditation from the International Olympic Committee (IOC) – the Welfare Officer – whose focus is on athlete mental health and not on performance.
12 The comments can be found here: Joyful women's Rugby 7s players celebrate bronze at Paris Olympics.

References

Albertella, L., Kirkham, R., Adler, A. B., Crampton, J., Drummond, S. P., Fogarty, G. J., . . . Yücel, M. (2023). Building a transdisciplinary expert consensus on the cognitive drivers of performance under pressure: An international multi-panel Delphi study. *Frontiers in Psychology, 13*, 1017675.

Birrer, D., Wetzel, J., Schmid, J., & Morgan, G. (2012). Analysis of sport psychology consultancy at three Olympic Games: Facts and figures. *Psychology of Sport and Exercise, 13*(5), 702–710.

Elsborg, P., Diment, G. M., & Elbe, A. M. (2015). Sport psychology consultants' perceptions of their challenges at the London 2012 Olympic Games. *The Sport Psychologist, 29*(2), 183–195.

Feddersen, N. B., Champ, F., & Littlewood, M. A. (2025). The sport psychology canvas: Designing, adapting, and documenting sport psychology provisions in men's football academies in England. *Journal of Applied Sport Psychology*, 1–22.

Gleig, A. (2019). *American dharma. Buddhism beyond modernity*. New Haven, CT: Yale University Press.

Goff, A. (2024, August 22). *RuggaMatrix America – GoffRugbyReport RMA 24–7: Spiff Sedrick, Emilie Bydwell, and the Bronze Medal* [audio podcast]. www.goffrugbyreport.com/news/rma-sedrick-and-bydwell-and-game#:~:text=Spiff%20Sedrick%20grounds%20it.,interview%20as%20we've%20had.

Gould, D., Guinan, D., Greenleaf, C., Medbery, R., Strickland, M., Lauer, L., et al. (1998). *Positive and negative factors influencing U.S. Olympic athlete and coaches: Atlanta*

Games assessment. US Olympic Committee Sport Science and Technology Final Grant Report, Colorado Springs, Colorado.

Gucciardi, D. F. (2017). Mental toughness: Progress and prospects. *Current Opinion in Psychology, 16*, 17–23.

Haberl, P. (2016). Mindfulness and the Olympic Athlete – A personal journey. *Mindfulness and Performance*, 211–234.

Haberl, P. (2022). Expert approaches to sport psychology. In M. W. Aoyagi & A. Poczwardowski (Eds.), *Expert approaches to sport psychology. Applied theories of performance excellence* (new and updated ed.). Morgantown, WV: Fitness Information Technology.

Haberl, P., & Peterson, K. (2006). Olympic-size ethical dilemmas: Issues and challenges for sport psychology consultants on the road and at the Olympic games. *Ethics & Behavior, 16*, 25e40. https://doi.org/10.1207/s15327019eb16014

Harris, R. (2019). *ACT made simple. An easy-to-read primer on acceptance and commitment therapy*. London: New Harbinger Publications.

Hayes, S. C., Strosahl, K. D., & Wilson, K. G. (1999). *Acceptance and commitment therapy: An experiential approach to behavior change*. New York, NY: Guilford Press.

Jha, A. P. (2021). *Peak mind. Find your focus. Own your attention. Invest 12 minutes a day*. New York, NY: HarperCollins e-books.

Kabat-Zinn, J. (1994). *Wherever you go, there you are. Mindfulness meditation for everyday life*. Hyperion: New York.

Kerr, J. (2013). *Legacy. 15 Lessons in leadership. What the all blacks can teach us about the business of life*. London: Constable.

McCann, S. C. (2000). Doing sport psychology at the really big show. In M. B. Andersen (Ed.), *Doing sport psychology* (pp. 209–222). Champaign, IL: Human Kinetics.

Medcalf, J. (2015). *Chop wood, carry water*. How to Fall in Love with Process of Becoming Great.

Smoulder, A. L., Marino, P. J., Oby, E. R., Snyder, S. E., Miyata, H., Pavlovsky, N. P., . . . & Batista, A. P. (2024). A neural basis of choking under pressure. *Neuron, 112*(20), 3424–3433.

Snyder, T. (2017). *On Tyranny. 20 Lessons from the 20th century*. New York, NY: Tim Duggan Books.

Snyder, T. (2022). *The making of modern Ukraine. Episode 20 (November 28, 2022): Maidan and Self-Understanding with guest lecturer Marci Shore* [audio podcast]. https://yalepodcasts.blubrry.net/2022/11/28/20-maidan-and-self-understanding-with-guest-lecturer-marci-shore/

Walsh, A. (2024a). *Why the upswell in demand for mental skills is not being translated into effective work*. Leaders Performance Institute. Retrieved October 30, 2024, from https://leadersinsport.com/performance-institute/articles/why-the-upswell-in-demand-for-mental-skills-is-not-being-translated-into-effective-work/

Walsh, A. (2024b). *Your team's mental performance program will only be effective with a clear strategy*. Here's What you Should Do Leaders Performance Institute. https://leadersinsport.com/performance-institute/articles/your-teams-mental-performance-program-will-only-be-effective-with-a-clear-strategy-heres-what-you-should-do/

11 Navigating Disruption

Applying ACT to Injury Rehabilitation and Transitions in Sport

Rebekah-Danielle Brockbank and Samuel Wood

Learning Outcomes

1. Review the psychological impact of injury and the key factors influencing rehabilitation and career transition
2. Apply the ACT hexaflex model in supporting injured athletes through rehabilitation and transition, using an applied case study

Introduction

Athletic careers are rarely linear. They rise, twist, and sometimes pivot in unpredictable ways. From the thrill of progressing through sport to the uncertainty of setbacks, change is woven into the fabric of athletic life. These moments of change – whether planned or sudden – can shape not only an athlete's performance but also their identity, well-being, and future (Park et al., 2012). Some transitions are eagerly anticipated: earning a professional contract or making a national team. Others arrive uninvited and unwelcome: injury, deselection, or the end of a career before an athlete feels ready. Researchers describe these moments as "critical incidents" – points in time when an athlete's sense of control and purpose can be disrupted, sometimes profoundly (Ivarsson & Gledhill, 2024).

What makes these transitions so powerful isn't just what happens externally, but how athletes make sense of them internally. Studies suggest that the voluntariness of a transition – the degree to which it's chosen or forced – can profoundly shape how athletes cope, recover, and reorient their lives beyond sport (Arvinen-Barrow et al., 2017; Gledhill & Forsdyke, 2021). Yet despite decades of research, one question remains underexplored: How can sport psychologists help athletes not just survive these transitions, but grow through them?

Sport performance practitioners (SPPs) often find themselves helping athletes navigate the emotional turbulence that accompanies injury and identity change (Brewer, 2009; Park et al., 2012). Increasingly, one approach that has begun to capture attention in this field is ACT. Unlike traditional performance enhancement methods, ACT invites athletes to engage with discomfort, clarify their

DOI: 10.4324/9781003515203-13

values, and build psychological flexibility – the ability to stay grounded and purposeful even when life doesn't go according to plan. Although ACT's evidence base in sport psychology is still developing (Wood & Turner, 2025a, 2025b), early findings suggest it holds promise for helping athletes navigate the emotional complexity of injury, transition, and career evolution. This chapter aims to bring these ideas to life through a case study from the first author's applied practice. Specifically, this chapter will:

1. Explore how injury impacts athletes – physically, psychologically, and professionally – and highlight factors influencing rehabilitation and career transition.
2. Detail the application of ACT in supporting athletes through injury and transition.
3. Present a case study illustrating the use of ACT with an injured athlete in recovery.
4. Discuss the ethical and practical considerations for SPPs moving forward.

In short, this chapter is about more than coping with change – it's about redefining it. If transitions are inevitable in sport, perhaps the real question is not how to avoid them, but how to move through them with purpose, resilience, and integrity.

Injury Rehabilitation in Sport: A Psychological Perspective

While athletes, their coaches, and other team members take preventative measures to avoid injury, injury is often "part and parcel" of the athletic endeavour (Arvinen-Barrow et al., 2014). UK Sport data suggests that 67% of interruptions to training are due to injury (Battle Against Injury and Illness, 2012). Moreover, Edouard et al. (2024) found 90% of their 7870 athletes in a French athletic study reported injury. Given these statistics, it seems inevitable that, at some point in their careers, SPPs will need to support athletes through injury or injury-associated transitions. However, not all injuries are equal. Some injuries can carry detrimental consequences to athletes' success and careers, in turn, affecting livelihoods, quality of life, and well-being. In short, injuries can affect contextual and psychological aspects of athletes' lives, not just physical capabilities (Arvinen-Barrow et al., 2014; Martin et al., 2025; Santi & Pietrantoni, 2013). It is important that practitioners understand such emotional responses to injury as they "affect subsequent behaviour and self-regulatory capacity during rehabilitation" (Arvinen-Barrow et al., 2014, p. 770). Despite the ever-growing importance and acceptance of the role of sport psychologists in sport (Moran, 2013) and rehabilitation processes (Weiß et al., 2024), the specifics of the psychological responses to injury and rehabilitation are comparatively underexamined in sport psychology literature (Espinozaa & Cho, 2024). Common injuries, such as ACL ruptures, do have extensive research around the psychological factors affecting athletes (see Lai et al., 2018 for a review). Though Martin et al. (2025) note that there is no exact model outlining athlete responses to ACL injuries, there is evidence to suggest athletes report higher levels of depression with ACL injuries compared to concussion (Mainwaring et al., 2010). However, if no exact model for athlete response has been found for a highly prevalent injury like those affecting the ACL, it stems to reason that there is even less clarity around responses for other injuries, their rehabilitation, and athlete adherence.

With the interest of increasing athletes' adherence to rehabilitation protocols, there are several models within sport psychology literature (see Santi & Pietrantoni, 2013) that provide practitioners with information on athlete experiences and how to develop adaptive coping strategies. Such models include stress and coping, social cognitive, and self-determination theories (for an overview, see Espinoza & Cho, 2024) and the biopsychosocial model of injury rehabilitation by Brewer (2009). The biopsychosocial model details how the psychological response of an athlete is a combination of the individual social characteristics of the athlete with the physiological characteristics of the injury, with rehabilitation success being dependent on the psychological factors such as cognitive appraisal, emotion, and behavioural response (for a detailed review, see Brewer, 2009). However, to help increase athlete adherence to rehabilitation, understanding the stages athletes may go through during rehabilitation is essential.

In the initial stages of injury, athletes may experience a range of responses, from worry, fear, confusion, and denial (Smith et al., 1990) to anxiety, depression, shock, and frustration (Arvinen-Barrow et al., 2014; Espinoza & Cho, 2024). Athletes might experience self-doubt (Arvinen-Barrow et al., 2014), a "sense of failure" and altered athletic identity due to a disconnect from their sport (Smith, 1996), and lower self-esteem and self-worth (Brewer, 2009; Smith et al., 1990). Modelling the individual nature of emotional responses, O'Connor et al. (2005) proposed a more flexible, affective cycle of injury model, presented as a series of sequential, predictable, and staged responses, similar to Kübler-Ross's (1969) stages of grief, but this did not hold up in sport literature (see Brewer, 2009). The affective cycle, including denial, distress, and determined coping, based on athletes' cognitive appraisals (as seen in the biospychosoical model, Brewer, 2009), leads to different psychological responses based on the individual circumstances of their injury (Clement et al., 2015) and available social support (Arvinen-Barrow et al., 2024; Brewer, 2007). For example, Lyon-Monk et al.'s (2025) findings support a bi-directional relationship between injury and mental ill-health, demonstrating a 10% increase in the likelihood of a mental ill-health episode with subsequent injuries. Thus, first injury compared to second injury can give rise to different appraisals and anxieties. In other words, psychological responses are individual and situationally influenced, with heightened responses found in athletes at higher levels of competition (Arvinen-Barrow et al., 2014; Espinozaa & Cho, 2024).

These psychological responses are pivotal in shaping recovery trajectory (Espinozaa & Cho, 2024). As expected, adherence to rehabilitation protocols is important for successful recovery (Brewer, 2009, 2019). Yet adherence rates are often affected by psychological factors. For example, low self-esteem may limit the motivation needed to engage in rehabilitation protocols (Arvinen-Barrow et al., 2014). Self-doubt and a sense of failure can lead athletes to negatively approach their rehabilitation (Espinozaa & Cho, 2024). Psychological distress due to loss of athletic identity and isolation from teammates may influence adherence to rehabilitation protocols (Williams et al., 2001). Of note, strategies aimed at increasing psychological skills such as goal setting and imagery have been found vital to the rehabilitation process (Arvinen-Barrow et al., 2014; Espinoza & Cho, 2024; Hooi & Wah, 2018; Santi & Pietrantoni, 2013).

Career Transition in Sport: Loss, Identity, and Adaptation

For many athletes, injury is supposed to be temporary – a setback on the road to competition. But sometimes, that injury draws a line in the sand between the life they have known and the one they never planned for. When recovery no longer leads to a return to sport, athletes can find themselves facing forced retirement from competitive sport (Brewer, 2009; Gledhill & Forsdyke, 2021). Unsurprisingly, research has long focused on these involuntary, injury-related transitions (Park et al., 2012). Yet how athletes navigate this turning point – whether they see it as an ending or a beginning – depends on far more than physical healing. Our identity is best thought of as a multidimensional, enduring, and dynamic way in which we see ourselves (Lally, 2007). Therefore, how an athlete experiences their forced retirement following injury hinges on how deeply their sense of self is tied to their athletic identity. An athlete's identity – captured in thoughts like "I am an athlete" – shapes how that individual perceives themselves and their experience (Northoff et al., 2006) and can become a dominant lens through which other life events are viewed. For instance, an athlete may be a partner, parent, or student, yet if their athletic identity outweighs the rest, other aspects of self may receive less attention or value (Lally, 2007). In this way, self-worth can become tied to athletic success. Stoltenburg et al. (2012) found that athletes with strong athletic identities struggled more with retirement than those who maintained role diversity or a balanced sense of self (Fuller, 2014; Lally, 2007). When retirement is involuntary – especially due to injury – the loss extends beyond the sport itself. Athletes often experience a loss of identity and diminished sense of self. Such transitions can evoke powerful negative emotions, including frustration, disappointment, devastation, loss of control, and reduced self-esteem, alongside difficulties coping with everyday stressors (Arvinen-Barrow et al., 2017; Gledhill & Forsdyke, 2021; Mannes et al., 2019; Park et al., 2012; Stoltenburg et al., 2012). The perceived lack of control brought about by career-ending injuries also risks increased anxiety (Park et al., 2012).

While considering athletes' psychological reactions to career transitions in sport, we must also consider how these reactions affect the adaptation to life beyond sport. It has been found that athletes who do not engage in effective post-career planning prior to retirement are more likely to experience a lower quality transition out of sport (Carapinheira et al., 2018). This finding is unsurprising, considering some elite athletes may struggle to adapt to life and careers out of sport. Starting at the bottom of a new career may seem like a step down from the glory of professional sport (Brewer, 2009), or desired jobs may be unattainable due to the lack of experience outside of sport (Park et al., 2012). Adapting to new identities can also be challenging. Therefore, programmes that support athletes in developing a non-athletic identity or encourage a redefinition of self during their athletic careers will provide athletes with the opportunity for smoother transitions (Smith & McManus, 2008). This can include promoting the value in getting involved in other activities, such as educational endeavours and building social support networks (Kerr & Dacyshyn, 2000; Stoltenburg et al., 2012). Overall, the factors contributing to negative career transition experiences suggest four strategies to improve retirement experiences: planning, provision of social support, athlete involvement in the decision-making process, and physical activity (Gledhill & Forsdyke, 2021). Some of these strategies are explored during the application of ACT in the applied case study during the rest of this chapter.

Application of ACT to Injury and Career Transition: A Case Study

From an ACT perspective, psychological inflexibility is associated with depression and anxiety (Bond et al., 2011; Doorley et al., 2020; Mooney, 2022), which have been negatively linked to injury rehabilitation success. Consequently, it is important to maintain psychological flexibility in injury rehabilitation (Bond et al., 2011; Mooney, 2022) and respond to the associated transitions in ways that "facilitate valued goal pursuit" (Doorley et al., 2020, p. 2). Therefore, from an ACT perspective, SPPs should look to promote psychological flexibility to help injured athletes cope with the different circumstances they may encounter in their rehabilitation. In addition, it is important to increase the injured athlete's non-judgemental awareness and acceptance of unhelpful cognitions while committing to living life guided by values and goals (Hayes et al., 1999). SPPs can focus ACT interventions for injury rehabilitation and potential transitions out of sport through the ACT hexaflex model (Hayes et al., 1999): a flexible model with no correct place to start (Wood & Turner, 2025a). The following section will cover the application of ACT using the hexaflex model for injury and career transition. It will discuss how ACT can be applied to achieve recommendations laid out in sport psychology literature through an applied case study.

Context

This case study[1] is from the first author's applied experiences as a Trainee Sport Psychologist on the British Psychological Society's Qualification in Sport and Exercise Psychology – a work-based, professional training programme – while supervised by the second author. The client is Joanne, a 21-year-old ex-national swimmer and current professional netball player. Joanne has two anatomical abnormalities in her knee called trochlea dysplasia and patella alta, which have resulted in numerous dislocations of her knee. Due to her high-intensity sports, she has undergone two previous knee surgeries, including an MPFL reconstruction and lateral release. However, neither surgery was successful, and Joanne, at the time of consultation, was awaiting a third surgery in which she had consented to several highly invasive procedures.

Since her first injury, her ability to train with her team has been limited. The recurrence of the injury has also resulted in her no longer having support through her teams. This resulted in the removal of sport science support, including sport psychology. Joanne's physio recommended she reach out for sport psychology support. As such, the sport psychology support provided aimed to support Joanne through the psychology of pre-injury rehabilitation prior to her third surgery and transition in sport.

Needs Analysis and Case Formulation

An initial meeting was scheduled with Joanne. The initial session was used to gather background information and begin establishing a client–athlete relationship, a key determinant of success within psychology (Xu et al., 2025). Background information included information regarding family relationships, social support, athletic history, and key life events adapted from the Sport Client Intake Protocol (Taylor & Schneider, 1992). Although a plethora of information was gathered during the discovery session, only details relevant to the current problem will be disclosed.

Joanne was experiencing worry about her upcoming surgery, the negative implications of which were particularly potent after two previous surgeries. Joanne also expressed viewing her previous surgeries as "failures" and therefore was questioning whether she was a failure for not completing her rehab effectively, or not being strong enough to not get injured. Additionally, the third injury led Joanne to consider the prospect of whether her knee would support the demands of professional sport. When questioned further, these factors were leading Joanne to ponder the question, "who am I without sport?" Furthermore, Joanne expressed that during her first two surgeries, she had the support of her teammates and access to physiotherapy through her Super League team. However, this was not the case after her third injury: she was let go from the team, and thus, social support was reduced. According to the biopsychosocial model (Brewer, 2009), the reduction in social support could impact individual social characteristics and thus affect Joanne's adherence to her rehabilitation (Arvinen-Barrow et al., 2024; Williams et al., 2001). The integrated model of response to injury and rehabilitation (Kamphoff et al., 2013) suggests that athletes may experience a range of emotions, cognitions, and behaviours, which are all influenced by one another. This model aligns with Joanne's circumstances as she spoke of heightened negative emotional responses to her injury, in part due to previous injuries and current social isolation (due to being dropped from her team), which were, in turn, impacting her personal relationships: for example, tension between her partner, short temper, and increased panic attacks. Joanne also talked of fear or reinjury (Clement et al., 2015) and the effect this was having on her outlook for her rehabilitation post-surgery. Joanne's initial goals for consultation primarily included being "pain free", increasing mental strength, and being in a positive place post-surgery for return to sport. It was discussed with Joanne that pain management could be examined through mindfulness and meditation, but being "pain free" may be beyond the scope of sport psychology intervention (Taylor & Taylor, 1998). These initial goals were revisited and changed regularly throughout the sessions as Joanne felt more comfortable exploring her identity and feelings towards her surgeries.

Taking the work of Lally (2007), it could be postulated that because Joanne's "life revolved around sport from a young age", she had limited opportunities to explore and develop other parts of her identity. Thus, her athletic image overpowered other images of herself (e.g., daughter, sister, and student). These factors suggested the intervention should examine personal attributes and identity beyond the athlete, as well as help Joanne navigate unhelpful thoughts of failure. In addition, in line with the biopsychosocial and integrated models, it appeared that Joanne would benefit from targeting emotional, cognitive, and behavioural responses to social, personal, and biological changes. Taking an ACT approach, the aim of the intervention was to help Joanne increase her psychological flexibility to changing cirumstances. Providing Joanne with techniques (i.e. through mindfulness and present moment awareness) to manage her anxiety about her upcoming surgery (Bond et al., 2011; Doorley et al., 2020; Mooney, 2022) and work on committed action aimed to increase her adherence to her upcoming rehabiitation exercises. Exploring identity through values would allow Joanne a chance to understand herself and consider other images of herself that were previously overpowered by her athletic identity. Finally, ACT could help Joanne cognitively defuse from her unhelpful thoughts about her unsuccessful surgeries to help her adhere to her rehabilitation and pre-habilitation for her upcoming surgery.

Table 11.1 Outline of ACT sessions

Session	*Session focus*
1	Fusion with self-concept and committed action
2	Cognitive fusion and defusion
3	Exploring values
4	Present moment awareness
5	Acceptance
6–8	Committed action

Planning, Delivery, Monitoring, and Evaluation of Intervention

To include Joanne in the consultation process, time was taken to explain the ACT hexaflex and the aims of the intervention. This not only created a shared language that could be used throughout sessions, but also gave Joanne some feeling of control (Park et al., 2012). The intervention was delivered over six sessions, with two additional sessions leading up to the surgery. The hexaflex model promotes psychological flexibility and has no correct or strict starting point (Wood & Turner, 2025a). Therefore, based on Joanne's frequent mentions of struggling to determine her identity away from sport, the self-as-concept seemed a natural starting point. A flexible session outline was created to explore on each of the hexaflex processes. This is outlined in Table 11.1.

The following section will detail each session with Joanne. We do not propose that all innervations for similar cases follow this same outline, but feel this structure proved fruitful in this case.

Session 1: Fusion with Self-Concept and Committed Action

To explore these values across Joanne's athlete- and non-athlete-self, Joanne visually drew her perceptions of herself. This identified Joanne's fusion with self-concept. Joanne focused almost entirely with her career as an athlete, which limited exploration of her identity outside of sport (Lally, 2007). Visually drawing her perceptions of self allowed Joanne to see the disparity between identities. Joanne could easily link her attributes to her actions as an athlete but struggled to see how to live up to these attributes in everyday situations outside her athletic identity (similar to the discussion raised in Session 3). A task was given to think of an event in the past week and discuss how she may have upheld her attributes or, as she saw them at the time, values during that situation. One key event that resonated with Joanne and had added to her emotional week was providing CPR to a cardiac arrest. We discussed how Joanne's actions and behaviours in the situation may have been value-driven; assessing value-consistent behaviours has been the primary measure for assessing value within ACT (Barney et al., 2019). For example, Joanne demonstrated "being someone who can make a difference" by showing empathy to the patient's family by staying with them and reassuring them when the ambulance arrived and being "determined" and "good under pressure" by trusting in herself to handle the needs of the situation.

Retrospectively assessing the situation was helpful for Joanne to see how she could live her values or demonstrate those attributes outside of the sport. Joanne commented that her thoughts after the event were "[Joanne] did that". Further discussion prompted Joanne to see how she might live her values in other areas of her life. Additionally, encourageing Joanne to assess her values in the present moment rather than retrospectively was important. Barney et al. (2019) suggest that ACT is multifaceted and interrelated; therefore, examining values in context with other processes within ACT, such as defusion and self-as-context, is essential to fully encompass an individual's experience of the quality of value work.

Session 2: Cognitive Fusion and Defusion

Whilst exploring self-as-context, Joanne discussed several dysfunctional thoughts (not uncommon for athletes experiencing change; Smith, 1996). For example, she was unable to see herself as dedicated if it did not apply to dedication in training. Joanne explained that on a shopping trip, she began to overthink the purchase of a hoodie with the term "comeback" written on it. Prior to her last surgery, Joanne was confident she would make a comeback to Netball and would excel in gaining contracts. However, she got reinjured. That quote initiated thoughts of "What if I don't come back?" and "I'll look like a fool if I wear this hoodie". This reaction demonstrated Joanne's different appraisal between her first and second injury (Brewer, 2007; Lyon-Monk et al., 2025) and heightened psychological response of self-doubt (Arvinen-Barrow et al., 2014). Joanne's anxiety was also fuelled by thoughts that her "body has failed" and therefore she "was a failure". This is a common psychological response to injury (Smith, 1996). Additionally, Joanna lacked cognitive flexibility in changing plans and was focused on the pain she would have post-surgery. These thoughts escalated her frustration, resulting in outbursts of anger or thoughts that she was "unworthy" of relationships because she was unsuccessful with recovery. Joanne was fusing with these cognitions, responding to her thoughts as if they were absolute truths (or literal; Assaz et al., 2023), which further risked feelings of anxiety, depression, and isolation (Wood & Turner, 2025a).

These thoughts could negatively impact her rehabilitation. For example, if she only viewed herself as dedicated when playing sport, how could she be dedicated to her rehabilitation? The negative thoughts athletes can face during injury and career transition can impact the possibility of recovery, the prospect of returning to sport, re-injury, and mental health outside of sport (Smith, 1996; Stoltenburg et al., 2012). This can lead to feelings of failure, disappointment, or loss, resulting in negative self-talk such as "I am a failure" or "I'm never going to recover" (Arvinen-Barrow et al., 2017; Espinozaa & Cho, 2024; Gledhill & Forsdyke, 2021). Cognitive fusion risked Joanne not adhering to her rehabilitation regime and athlete recovery (Williams et al., 2001).

Cognitive defusion strategies aim to disrupt verbal processes, helping Joanne experience thoughts as internal events, and nonjudgementally (Hayes et al., 1999). Mahoney and Hanrahan (2011) found that the cognitive defusion skills taught to athletes in brief ACT interventions increased acceptance and commitment to rehabilitation. Wood and Turner (2025a) detail four routes to achieving cognitive defusion: shifting focus, increasing workability, creating distance, and separating thoughts from the thinker. For Joanne, three to four exercises were practised during the session and in subsequent sessions, allowing Joanne the autonomy to experiment and determine which methods worked best for her in certain moments.

To distance Joanne from her thoughts (Harris, 2019; Wood & Turner, 2025a), it was suggested that Joanne imagine the thoughts as shapes and colours. Joanne was instructed to change the shape, size, colour, font, and move the shape to emphasise the arbitrariness of the thought and Joanne's control over it (Assaz et al., 2023). Joanne also struggled with negative thoughts about her knee. She found it helped to imagine her injured knee as Nemo's injured fin, thanking it for trying its best when she felt negativity and frustration. She was then able to "thank" her brain for reminding her how her knee was trying, despite the injury, and that being negative wasn't helpful.

Cognitive defusion was revisited during sessions, particularly as Joanne recapped her week, detailing the success of some methods, the difficulties with others, and raising any questions she had regarding her thoughts. A large part of this process was enabling Joanne to become confident in using the methods and adapting them to suit her needs. Planning and organisation were key attributes of Joanne's management strategies. Therefore, throughout the process, a clear structure (e.g., when to use cognitive defusion strategies) was useful. In later sessions, Joanne noted that she would often give herself three attempts to defuse negative thoughts. With each attempt, she would become more frustrated that it "wasn't working", and she had "failed" because the strategy did not work the first time. Discussions often focused on encouragement and reminding Joanne that things take time.

Session 3: Exploring Values

Exploring values was beneficial in aiding Joanne's creation of broader identities. Problems can arise when the athlete's thoughts and behaviours around their values are rigid (e.g., assigning specific behaviours to values) or when values are based

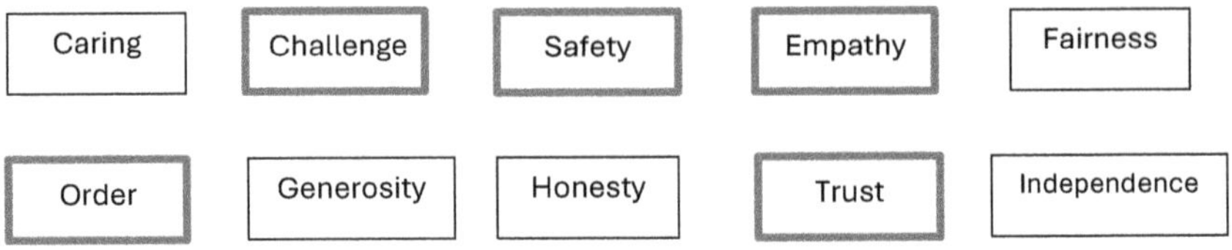

Figure 11.1 Joanne's top values.

around the conceptualised self (as seen in Session 1), leading to psychological inflexibility (Mahoney & Hanrahan, 2011). Therefore, identifying values independent from the contextualised self allows individuals to adhere to consistent behaviours and become psychologically flexible in changing situations. Additionally, Mahoney and Hanrahan (2011) posited that emotion-driven behaviours can negatively impact injury rehabilitation. For example, an injured athlete who is anxious about returning to sport and who values commitment may struggle to attend physiotherapy sessions and comply with prescribed exercises. Therefore, value-driven behaviours can be more beneficial for successful rehabilitation. Joanne shared that her recent behaviours were emotion-driven, but she wished them to be more value-driven. Joanne completed the Harris (2010) values task. Her top ten values can be seen in Figure 11.1, with her top five values highlighted with a bold outline.

Extending the values task, Joanne provided examples of when she upheld or demonstrated those values outside of sport. This task allowed Joanne to identify attributes about her identity as a person, without sport being a dominant focus. Joanne began to see that the values she demonstrated as an athlete could also be part of her identity and personality away from the netball court, without being tied to her as an athlete. This exercise was revisited throughout the sessions to draw Joanne back to the concept of her identity away from sport and build confidence that being separate from sport could be fulfilling.

Session 4: Present Moment Awareness

Joanne's fourth session concentrated on present moment awareness. Injury can be a stressful time for athletes as they experience a range of emotions and uncertainty. Therefore, these sessions aimed to provide Joanne with tools to allow her to focus on the present, handle stress, and maintain emotional regulation. Relaxation and mindfulness techniques have been found to be effective here (see Raugh et al., 2025), especially in increasing psychological flexibility (see Bond et al., 2011) post-acute injury. Furthermore, for athletes with ACL injuries, mindfulness techniques have been found to increase knee strength and decrease pain and anxiety post-operation (Cupal & Brewer, 2001). Relaxation techniques such as Progressive Muscle Relaxation (PMR; Meyers et al., 1996) have also been found to improve cognitive state anxiety (Battaglini et al., 2022), reduce sleep disturbance (Khokhar et al., 2024), and alleviate fear of reinjury after an ACL surgery (Zia et al., 2021). PMR is an alternative technique that follows similar patterns to traditional grounding techniques found in ACT, such as the 5–5–5 technique or drop anchor based on the ACE model (acknowledge, comeback, and engage) (Harris, 2019). Grounding techniques help athletes focus on their breathing and present thoughts, and then use movement and pressure to hone awareness before widening out their senses again. PMR allows athletes to focus on their body and controlling individual muscles, thus grounding them into present bodily awareness.

Joanne expressed difficulties with sleep, anxiety about her post-surgery pain, and was looking to increase strength in her knee pre-surgery. Given the above, PMR was integrated into the intervention. Joanne's PMR script was developed using an online resource (www.therapistaid.com/worksheets/progressive-muscle-relaxation-script), and she was taken through the script in this session. This allowed Joanne to ask any questions. For example, how tightly to tense, or how to avoid pain in her injured knee (as she was told not to tense that leg). It also allowed evaluation of the process in session. A reading of the script was then recorded and sent to Joanne for her use. Joanne decided she would use this method to help her sleep when she would feel overwhelmed with thoughts such as "*I have no control over my body*" and when her anxiety about the future operation would become high. In other words, this method helped her emotional stability and temporal perspective. Tatsumi and Takenouchi's (2014) results of structural equation monitoring indicated that the factors of emotional stability and temporal perspective (affected by present moment awareness) were mediated by psychological acceptance of the injury. This relationship, in turn, was found to positively influence dedication to athletic rehabilitation (Tatsumi & Takenouchi, 2014). As Joanne was steadily showing in-session acceptance of her injury, potential transition away from playing sport, and a positive self-image without sport, specific focus on acceptance of change was a logical next focus.

Session 5: Acceptance

How an athlete views their injury is important and can affect rehabilitation and transition. For example, seeing the injury as a setback can lengthen recovery (Madrigal & Gill, 2014). This suggests that athletes who view injury as an opportunity for growth can navigate rehabilitation more effectively. Joanne's response to her injury was a prime example of this. In line with the fundamentals of ACT, the aim was not to challenge Joanne's thoughts or encourage her to change them. To introduce the concept of acceptance, we explored the tug of war analogy. Here, Joanne was described as one end of the rope, with her brain holding the other end. Acceptance was described as letting go of the rope and, in doing so, letting go of the thoughts she was trying to change or address. Joanne found this a useful technique.

Joanne often stated that, during her first injury, she focused on her opportunity for psychological growth and often pictured her "comeback" post-surgery. However, by the time the third surgery was being organised, Joanne perceived the injury as a setback and was increasingly disheartened by negative updates, difficult physiotherapy sessions, or thoughts about a comeback. Authors have posited that regardless of competition level, validating athletes' psychological response is crucial to support athletes through effective rehabilitation and transition (Mann et al., 2007). Weiß et al. (2024) go as far as to suggest that highlighting the pain of the injury helps with injury acknowledgment and subsequently acceptance and management of the injury. For Joanne, a large portion of the pain of injury revolved around her loss of playing sports. Joanne said she felt as though she "had lost something", like she was "grieving". Indeed, it could be that Joanne was grieving the loss of the opportunity to progress to professional sport. As proposed by the Stage Model (see Tatsumi & Takenouchi, 2014), Joanne was grieving the loss of her athletic self. Studies integrating creative and artistic practices with ACT have shown promise in addressing grief (Anusuya & Gayatridevi, 2025). Therefore, Joanne wrote a eulogy to her former athletic self. The idea was to provide Joanne with an opportunity for closure on her previous athletic identity and create a sense of acceptance of her current situation. Joanne was initially hesitant and emotional at the idea of writing a eulogy. She was assured she did not need to share her work, keeping it to herself if she preferred. Joanne was provided the outline in Figure 11.2 to support this task.

Eulogy writing within ACT has also been linked to clarifying values, again linking to Barney et al.'s (2019) notion of the interrelated and multifaceted nature of ACT. Hayes et al. (2012) note how ACT values writing has often consisted of writing letters from a future self about what they hold dear, or how certain events touched their lives. Additionally, ACT exercises often include activities asking athletes to think about what they would like people to say about them at their funeral to promote committed action towards values (Harris, 2007).

Eulogy points:

- Achievements
- Things that should have been said, e.g., compliments and praise
- Acknowledge meant of the joy of playing sport with friends and family
- Things that will be missed
- Things that have changed, e.g., *loss of freedom and mobility due to injury and what that now means.*
- Apology to athletic self for not being where she thought she'd be. *For Joanne, this included impacting what it means to be a female athlete.*
- Acceptance of the loss of a part of herself

Figure 11.2 Guidance for eulogy reflective task.

Session 6–8: Preparing for Surgery Through Committed Action

Psychological skills, like goal setting, can help injured athletes in the rehabilitation process, especially in planning rehabilitation (Arvinen-Barrow et al., 2014). Weiß et al. (2024) note the importance of setting small, flexible targets related to controllable factors (such as how to spend her time). So, Joanne used goal setting to aid her planning what methods she would use post-surgery to help ease her anxiety or distract from pain (e.g., mindfulness colouring) and small tasks she would like to achieve (setting up movie nights) post-surgery (Espinozaa & Cho, 2024). In addition, family is both an emotional and tangible form of support, which can help an athlete's adherence to rehabilitation (Arvinen-Barrow & Hemmings, 2017), so Joanne was asked to consider the extent of her social support. However, Joanne was anxious of being reliant on others and in extensive pain. Therefore, in the final of the six sessions, Joanne was asked to consider how she could demonstrate her values in the buildup to her surgery and rehabilitation. To help Joanne put her values into context and provide her with a focus post-surgery, we used an ACT matrix (Azam et al., 2017; see Figure 11.3). The four quadrants represent: "what hurts", avoidance behaviours (i.e., "moving away"), "what matters" (e.g., values), and committed action (i.e., "move towards" behaviours). This

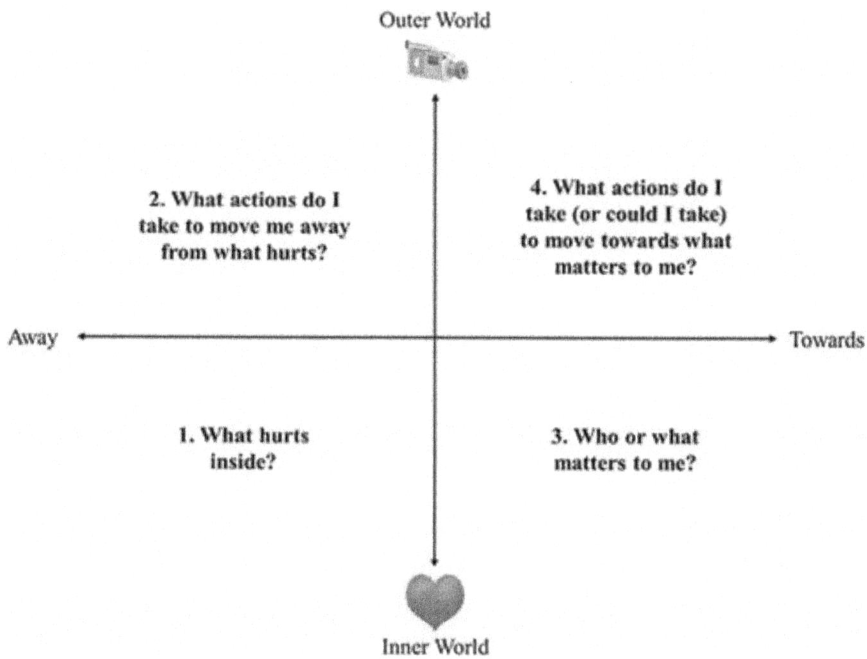

Figure 11.3 Matrix used and adapted by Joanne, taken from Azam et al. (2017).

exercise demonstrates examples of avoidance and acceptance, or psychological inflexibility and flexibility, respectively (DeGaetano et al., 2016). Aspects of the matrix were discussed in Sessions 6 and 7, and Joanne was asked to complete the matrix prior to Session 8.

During session 8, Joanne shared that she had struggled to complete the "move towards" section of the matrix as she couldn't work out how to represent her values. This prompted a discussion to remind Joanne of her values and that small actions can still equate to achieving those. For example, committing to her value of empathy would include being empathic to herself post-surgery: giving herself time to relax and concentrate on colouring books as a method of distraction and mindfulness. This reminded Joanne not to be critical of herself and accept that, during her current situation, it was okay to feel down.

Evaluation of Intervention and Its Outcomes

At the end of the eight sessions, Joanne expressed a positive experience of ACT, useful tasks, and overall improvement in herself. Assessments of Joanne's progress were based on a qualitative self-assessment. At the end of the intervention, Joanne was asked how she was feeling, how she experienced the tasks, and if she experienced any challenges. Joanne reported that she was more accepting of her circumstances and the possibility that recovery may take longer than she initially had planned. Topics she previously fixated on (e.g., being a failure for getting injured) were less frequently mentioned, positive adaptations to her self-image were discussed, and an overall level of positivity was expressed. Joanne deemed the intervention to be a success because she demonstrated psychological flexibility by adapting the skills learnt in sessions to different circumstances throughout her preparation for surgery and rehabilitation.

The present case study used qualitative measures to determine outcome success. However, the effectiveness of psychology is often determined by quantitative measures. SPPs are often evaluated by measurable improvements in performance (Chandler et al., 2016). As ACT seeks to improve psychological flexibility, practitioners seeking a quantitative measure of improvement could utilise the AAQ-II (Bond et al., 2011) to assess pre- and post-therapy differences in athletes' psychological flexibility should quantitative measures align with the practitioners' philosophical position.

Conclusion

Injury, rehabilitation, and career transition are rarely just physical; they are deeply social and psychological, shaped by how athletes make sense of loss, uncertainty, and change (Clement et al., 2015; O'Connor et al., 2005; Gledhill & Forsdyke, 2021; Kamphoff et al., 2013). Yet, despite their prevalence, the emotional and cognitive responses to these challenges remain comparatively underexplored within sport psychology (Espinozaa & Cho, 2024). The biopsychosocial (Brewer, 2009) and integrated (Kamphoff et al., 2013) models help us understand how injury ripples through an athlete's identity, motivation, and social world. Research shows that athletes often grapple with loss of identity (Lally, 2007), isolation (Williams et al., 2001), anxiety (Arvinen-Barrow et al., 2017), and low self-esteem (Brewer, 2009) – all of which can hinder rehabilitation and complicate transition out of sport (Williams et al., 2001). To mitigate these challenges, scholars have long advocated for early interventions that foster role diversification, balanced self-concept (Fuller, 2014; Lally, 2007), self-regulation (Valiev, 2024), and social support beyond sport (Arvinen-Barrow & Hemmings, 2017). Yet it is also important to deliver psychological support alongside physical rehabilitation post-sport injury to prevent the potential onset of a mental ill-health episode (Lyon-Monk et al., 2025).

This chapter highlights ACT as a particularly promising approach for addressing these issues. ACT offers a flexible, principle-driven framework for helping athletes navigate pain, uncertainty, and change (Ong et al., 2024). Its adaptability makes it valuable across professional philosophies – supporting both client-led and practitioner-led approaches (Harris, 2007, 2014; Smout, 2012). Importantly, ACT also aligns with the realities of sporting culture. In a domain where stigma towards psychological support persists (Watson et al., 2021), ACT's versatility allows practitioners to integrate mental flexibility training in ways that feel authentic and performance-relevant, rather than clinical (Arvinen-Barrow et al., 2014). In bringing theory to practice, this chapter underscores that athlete well-being cannot be an afterthought. By combining established models with applied frameworks like ACT, sport psychologists can better prepare athletes not only for the highs of performance but for the inevitable transitions that test their sense of self. In doing so, practitioners can help athletes move beyond merely recovering from injury – to rediscovering purpose, resilience, and identity beyond sport.

Note

1 In accordance with the Ethical Principles for Psychologists and Code of Conduct (American Psychological Association, 2002), confidentiality will be maintained by referring to the client using a pseudonym.

References

Anusuya, S. P., & Gayatridevi, S. (2025). Acceptance and commitment therapy and psychological well-being: A narrative review. *Cureus*, *17*(1), e77705. https://doi.org/10.7759/cureus.77705

Arvinen-Barrow, M., Hurley, D., & Ruiz, M. C. (2017). Transitioning out of professional sport: The psychosocial impact of career-ending injuries among elite Irish rugby football union players. *Journal of Clinical Sport Psychology*, *21*, 67–84.

Arvinen-Barrow, M., Massey, W. V., & Hemmings, B. (2014). Role of sport medicine professionals in addressing psychosocial aspects of sport-injury rehabilitation: Professional athletes' views. *Journal of Athletic Training*, *49*(6), 764–772.

Arvinen--Barrow-, -M--., --Pack-, -S--., & --Hemmings-, -B--. (-2017-). Social support in sport injury and rehabilitation. In *The Psychology of Sport Injury and Rehabilitation* (pp. 112–128). Routledge.

Arvinen-Barrow, M., Pack, S., & Scheadler, T. R. (2024). Social support in sport injury and rehabilitation. In *The psychology of sport injury and rehabilitation* (pp. 258–272). Routledge.

Assaz, D. A., Tyndall, I., Oshiro, C. K., & Roche, B. (2023). A process-based analysis of cognitive defusion in acceptance and commitment therapy. *Behavior Therapy*, *54*(6), 1020–1035. https://doi.org/10.1016/j.beth.2022.06.003

Azam, M. A., Weinrib, A. Z., Montbriand, J., Burns, L. C., McMillan, K., Clarke, H., & Katz, J. (2017). Acceptance and commitment therapy to manage pain and opioid use after major surgery: Preliminary outcomes from the Toronto General Hospital Transitional Pain Service. *Canadian Journal of Pain*, *1*(1), 37–49. https://doi.org/10.1080/24740527.2017.1325317

Barney, J. L., Lillis, J., Haynos, A. F., Forman, E., & Juarascio, A. S. (2019). Assessing the valuing process in acceptance and commitment therapy: Experts' review of the current status and recommendations for future measure development. *Journal of Contextual Behavioral Science*, *12*, 225–233. https://doi.org/10.1016/j.jcbs.2018.08.002

Battaglini, M. P., Pessôa Filho, D. M., Calais, S. L., Miyazaki, M. C. O. S., Neiva, C. M., Espada, M. C., de Moraes, M. G., & Verardi, C. E. L. (2022). Analysis of progressive muscle relaxation on psychophysiological variables in basketball athletes. *International Journal of Environmental Research and Public Health*, *19*(24), 17065. https://doi.org/10.3390/ijerph192417065

Battle against injury and illness. (2012, July 25). UK Sport. www.uksport.gov.uk/news/2012/07/25/battle-against-injury-and-illness

Bond, F. W., Hayes, S. C., Baer, R. A., Carpenter, K. M., Guenole, N., Orcutt, H. K., & . . . Zettle, R. D. (2011). Preliminary psychometric properties of the acceptance and action questionnaire – II: A revised measure of psychological inflexibility and experiential avoidance. *Behavior Therapy*, *42*(4), 676–688. https://doi.org/10.1016/j.beth.2011.03.007

Brewer, B. W. (2007). Psychology of sport injury rehabilitation. In G. Tenenbaum & R. Eklund (Eds.), *Handbook of sport psychology* (pp. 404–424). Hoboken, NJ: Wiley & Sons.

Brewer, B. W. (Ed.). (2009). *Handbook of sports medicine and science: Sport psychology*. John Wiley & Sons.

Brewer, B. W. (2019). Adherence issues in the prevention and rehabilitation of sport injuries.

Carapinheira, A., Mendes, P., Guedes Carvalho, P., Torregrossa, M., & Travassos, B. (2018). Career termination of Portuguese elite football players: Comparison between the last three decades. *Sports*, *6*(4), 155.

Chandler, C., Eubnk, M., Nesti, M., Tod, D., & Cable, T. (2016). Personal qualities of effective sport psychologists: Coping with organisational demands in high performance sport. *International Journal of Sport Psychology*, *47*(4), 297–317.

Clement, D., Arvinen-Barrow, M., & Fetty, T. (2015). Psychosocial responses during different phases of sport-injury rehabilitation: A qualitative study. *Journal of Athletic Training*, *50*(1), 95–104.

Cupal, D. D., & Brewer, B. W. (2001). Effects of relaxation and guided imagery on knee strength, reinjury anxiety, and pain following anterior cruciate ligament reconstruction. *Rehabilitation Psychology*, *46*(1), 28–43.

DeGaetano, J. J., Wolanin, A. T., Marks, D. R., & Eastin, S. M. (2016). The role of psychological flexibility in injury rehabilitation. *Journal of Clinical Sport Psychology*, *10*(3), 192–205. https://doi.org/10.1123/jcsp.2014-0023

Doorley, J. D., Goodman, F. R., Kelso, K. C., & Kashdan, T. B. (2020). Psychological flexibility: What we know, what we do not know, and what we think we know. *Social and Personality Psychology Compass*, *14*(12), 1–11. https://doi.org/10.1111/spc3.12566

Edouard, P., Sorg, M., Martin, S., Verhagen, E., & Ruffault A. (2024). Athletes who have already experienced an injury are more prone to adhere to an injury risk reduction approach than those who do not: an online survey of 7870 French athletics (track and field) athletes. *BMJ Open Sport & Exercise Medicine*, *10*, e001768. https://doi.org/10.1136/bmjsem-2023-001768

Espinozaa, A., & Cho, S. (2024). Factors influencing psychological responses to athletic injury and rehabilitation. *International Journal of Applied Sports Sciences*, *36*(2), 182–193.

Fuller, R. D. (2014). Transition experiences out of intercollegiate athletics: A meta-synthesis. *Qualitative Report*, *19*(46), 1–15.

Gledhill, A., & Forsdyke, D. (2021). They think it's all over: Injury-related retirement from sport. In *The psychology of sports injury* (pp. 152–160). Routledge. https://ebrary.net/187065/psychology/they_think_it_s_injury_retirement_sport

Harris, R. (2007). *Acceptance and commitment therapy (ACT) introductory workshop handout*. https://thehappinesstrap.com/upimages/2007%20Introductory%20ACT%20Workshop%20Handout%20-%20%20Russ%20Harris.pdf

Harris, R. (2010). *The happiness trap*. Exisle Publishing.

Harris, R. (2014). *The complete set of client handouts and worksheets from ACT books* [Handouts and worksheets]. In *ACT books* (pp. 383). https://thehappinesstrap.com/upimages/Complete_Worksheets_2014.pdf

Harris, R. (2019). *ACT made simple: An easy-to-read primer on acceptance and commitment therapy* (2nd ed.) New Harbinger Publications.

Hayes, S. (2004). Acceptance and commitment therapy, relational frame theory, and the third wave of behavioral and cognitive therapies. *Behavior Therapy*, *35*, 639–665.

Hayes, S. C., Barnes-Holmes, D., & Roche, B. (Eds.). (2001). *Relational frame theory: A post-Skinnerian account of human language and cognition*. Kluwer Academic.

Hayes, S. C., Pistorello, J., & Levin, M. E. (2012). Acceptance and commitment therapy as a unified model of behavior change. *The Counseling Psychologist*, *40*(7), 976–1002.

Hayes, S. C., Strosahl, K., & Wilson, K. G. (1999). *Acceptance and commitment therapy: An experiential approach to behavior change*. New York: Guilford Press.

Hayes, S. C., Strosahl, K. D., Bunting, K., Twohig, M., & Wilson, K. G. (2004). What is acceptance and commitment therapy? In S. C. Hayes & K. D. Strosahl (Eds.), *A practical guide to acceptance and commitment therapy* (pp. 3–29). Boston, MA: Springer.

Hooi, L. B., & Wah, T. E. (2018). Injured athletes and a new invention of relaxation techniques. *International Research Journal of Pharmacy and Medical Sciences (IRJPMS)*, *1*(4), 78–81.

Ivarsson, A., & Gledhill, A. (2024). Personal crisis in athletes: Injuries and retirement. In B. Strauss, S. Buenemann, C. Behlau, M. Tietjens, & K. Tamminen (Eds.), *Psychology of crises in sport*. Cham: Springer. https://doi.org/10.1007/978-3-031-69328-1_11

Jacobson, E. (1925). Progressive relaxation. *The American Journal of Psychology*, 73–87.

Kamphoff, C., Thomae, J., & Hamson-Utley, J. J. (2013). Integrating the psycho-logical and physiological aspects of sport injury rehabilitation: Rehabilitation profiling and phases of rehabilitation. In M. M. Arvinen-Barrow & N. Walker (Eds.), *The psychology of sport injury and rehabilitation* (pp. 134–155). New York, NY: Routledge.

Kerr, G., & Dacyshyn, A. (2000). The retirement experiences of elite, female gymnasts. *Journal of Applied Sport Psychology, 12*, 115–133. https://doi.org/10.1080/10413200008404218

Khokhar, S., Toseef, A., Jabbar Mahar, N., Ul Zain, F., Aiman, U., & Parveen, A. (2024). Effectiveness of progressive muscle relaxation on sleep disturbance in athletes. *The Rehabilitation Journal, 8*(02), 30–37. https://doi.org/10.52567/trehabj.v8i02.64

Kübler-Ross, E. (1969). *On death and dying*. New York: MacMillan.

Lai, C. C., Feller, J. A., & Webster, K. E. (2018). Fifteen-year audit of anterior cruciate ligament reconstructions in the Australian Football League from 1999 to 2013: Return to play and subsequent ACL injury. *The American Journal of Sports Medicine, 46*(14), 3353–3360. https://doi.org/10.1177/0363546518803932

Lally, P. (2007). Identity and athletic retirement: A prospective study. *Psychology of Sport and Exercise, 8*(1), 85–99.

Lyon-Monk, O., Arnold, R., Williams, S., Cleave, L. J., Cumming, S., Currie, A., Wass, J., & Moore, L. J. (2025). Understanding the bi-directional relationship between injury and mental ill-health in elite athletes: A six-year, retrospective cohort study. *Journal of Science and Medicine in Sport*. https://doi.org/10.1016/j.jsams.2025.10.002

Madrigal, L., & Gill, D. L. (2014). Psychological responses of division I female athletes throughout injury recovery: A case study approach. *Journal of Clinical Sport Psychology, 8*(3), 276–298. https://doi.org/10.1123/jcsp.2014-0034

Mahoney, J., & Hanrahan, S. J. (2011). A brief educational intervention using acceptance and commitment therapy: Four injured athletes' experiences. *Journal of Clinical Sport Psychology, 5*(3), 252–273.

Mainwaring, L. M., Hutchison, M., Bisschop, S. M., Comper, P., & Richards, D. W. (2010). Emotional response to sport concussion compared to ACL injury. *Brain Injury, 24*(4), 589–597. https://doi.org/10.3109/02699051003610508

Mann, B. J., Grana, W. A., Indelicato, P. A., O'Neill, D. F., & George, S. Z. (2007). A survey of sports medicine physicians regarding psychological issues in patient-athletes. *The American Journal of Sports Medicine, 35*(12), 2140–2147.

Mannes, Z. L., Waxenberg, L. B., Cottier, L. B., Perlstein, W. M., Burrell, L. E., Ferguson, E. G., Edwards, M. E., & Ennis, N. (2019). Prevalence and correlates of psychological distress among retired elite athletes. *International Review of Sport and Exercise Psychology, 12*, 265–294.

Martin, E., Walji, H.D., & Martin-Ucar, A. E. (2025). Psychological factors affecting recovery after rupture of the anterior cruciate ligament in sports: A review of definitions, impact, risks and treatments. *Journal of Surgery and Research Practice, 6*(1), 1–10.

Meyers, A. W., Whelan, J. P., & Murphy, S. M. (1996). Cognitive behavioural strategies in athletic performance enhancement. In M. Hersen, R. M. Eisler, & P. M. Miller (Eds.), *Progress in behavioural modification* (Vol. 30, pp. 137–164). Pacific Grove, CA: Brooks/Cole.

Mooney, J. (2022). *Psychological flexibility & well-being in sport*. The University of Liverpool (United Kingdom).

Moran, A. (2013). *Sport and exercise psychology: A critical introduction*. Routledge.

Northoff, G., Heinzel, A., De Greck, M., Bermpohl, F., Dobrowolny, H., & Panksepp, J. (2006). Self-referential processing in our brain – A meta-analysis of imaging studies on the self. *Neuroimage*, *31*(1), 440–457.
O'Connor, E., Heil, J., Harmer, P., & Zimmerman, I. (2005). Injury. In J. Taylor & G. Wilson (Eds.), *Applying sport psychology* (pp. 187–206). Champaign, IL: Human Kinetics.
Ong, C. W., Ciarrochi, J., Hofmann, S. G., Karekla, M., & Hayes, S. C. (2024). Through the extended evolutionary meta-model, and what ACT found there: ACT as a process-based therapy. *Journal of Contextual Behavioral Science*, *32*, 100734.
Park, S., Lavallee, D., & Tod, D. (2012). Athletes' career transition out of sport. *International Review of Sport and Exercise Psychology*, *6*, 22–53.
Podlog, L., Wadey, R., Stark, A., Lochbaum, M., Hannon, J., & Newton, M. (2013). An adolescent perspective on injury recovery and the return to sport. *Psychology of Sport and Exercise*, *14*(4), 437–446.
Raugh, I. M., Berglund, A. M., & Strauss, G. P. (2025). Implementation of mindfulness-based emotion regulation strategies: A systematic review and meta-analysis. *Affective Science*, *6*(1), 171–200.
Santi, G., & Pietrantoni, L. (2013). Psychology of sport injury rehabilitation: A review of models and interventions. *Journal of Human Sport and Exercise*, *8*(4), 1029–1044.
Smith, A. M. (1996). Psychological impact of injuries in athletes. *Sports Medicine*, *22*(6), 391–405.
Smith, A. M., Scott, S., & Wiese, D. M. (1990). The psychological effects of sports injuries: Coping. *Sports Medicine*, *9*(6), 352–369.
Smith, J., & McManus, A. (2008). A review on transitional implications for retiring elite athletes: What happens when the spotlight dims? *Open Sports Science Journal*, *1*, 45–49.
Smout, M. (2012). Acceptance and commitment therapy: Pathways for general practitioners. *Australian Family Physician*, *41*, 672–676.
Stoltenburg, A. L., & Kamphoff, C. S., & Lindstrom, K. (2012). Transitioning out of sport: The psychosocial effects of collegiate athletes' career-ending injuries. *Athletic Insight's Writings in Sport Psychology*, 113–132.
Tatsumi, T., & Takenouchi, T. (2014). Causal relationships between the psychological acceptance process of athletic injury and athletic rehabilitation behavior. *Journal of Physical Therapy Science*, *26*(8), 1247–1257.
Taylor, J., & Schneider, B. A. (1992). The sport-clinical intake protocol: A comprehensive interviewing instrument for applied sport psychology. *Professional Psychology: Research and Practice*, *23*(4), 318–325. https://doi.org/10.1037/0735-7028.23.4.318
Taylor, J., & Taylor, S. (1998). Pain education and management in the rehabilitation from sports injury. *The Sport Psychologist*, *12*(1), 68–88. https://doi.org/10.1123/tsp.12.1.68
Turner, M. J., Aspin, G., Didymus, F. F., Mack, R., Olusoga, P., Wood, A. G., & Bennett, R. (2020). One case, four approaches: The application of psychotherapeutic approaches in sport psychology. *The Sport Psychologist*, *34*(1), 71–83.
Valiev, R. A. (2024). Professional athletes' perspectives on the function of sports medicine specialists in treating psychosocial aspects of sport-injury rehabilitation. *International Journal of Integrative and Modern Medicine*, *2*(7), 215–221.
Watson, D. R., Hill, A. P., & Madigan, D. J. (2021). Perfectionism and attitudes toward sport psychology support and mental health support in athletes. *Journal of Clinical Sport Psychology*, *17*(1), 11–26.
Weiß, M., Büttner, M., & Richlan, F. (2024). The role of sport Psychology in injury prevention and rehabilitation in junior athletes. *Behavioral Sciences*, *14*(3), 254. https://doi.org/10.3390/bs14030254

Williams, J. M., Rotella, R. J., & Scherzer, B. C. (2001). Injury risk and rehabilitation: Psychological consideration. In J. M. Williams (Ed.), *Applied sport psychology: Personal growth to peak performance* (4th ed.). Mountain View, CA: Mayfield.

Wood, S., & Turner, M. (2025a). Using acceptance and commitment therapy with athletes. *Scandinavian Journal of Sport and Exercise Psychology. 7*. https://doi.org/10.7146/sjsep.v7i.150889

Wood, S., & Turner, M. J. (2025b): Integrating psychology skills training (PST) with acceptance and commitment therapy (ACT). *Journal of Sport Psychology in Action*. https://doi.org/10.1080/21520704.2025.2472341

Xu, H., Lu, Y., Huang, W., Deng, W., Lu, J., Qiu, Y., & Shen, Z. (2025). A multilevel meta-analysis of client and therapist predictors for alliance quality: Absolute and relative associations with working alliance. *Psychotherapy, 62*(4), 457–473. https://doi.org/10.1037/pst0000603

Zia, M., Sahebalzamani, M., & Rouhollahi, V. (2021). Effect of progressive muscle relaxation training in fear of re-injury in professional athletes after anterior cruciate ligament reconstruction. *Journal of Paramedical Sciences & Rehabilitation, 10*(1), 7–18. https://doi.org/10.22038/jpsr.2021.43816.2024

12 Using ACT to Navigate the Challenges of Athlete Identity

A Case Study from Applied Practice

Tom King

Learning Objectives

1. Define athletic identity and describe its role in athlete motivation and self-concept
2. Identify the risks and psychological consequences of over-identification with sport
3. Recognise the role of ACT and values-based interventions in promoting identity flexibility, psychological flexibility, and well-being in athletes

Introduction

Sport can offer athletes purpose, direction, and a sense of community (Eime et al., 2013). It can also quietly lead to overwhelming consequences of frustration, despair, and reduced athlete well-being, usually due to demands of the environment and pressure within their sport (Cresswell & Eklund, 2006). For many athletes, the line between who they are and what they do becomes blurred. Their sense of self fuses with performance until success and failure feel like a measurement on self-worth (Brewer et al., 1993; Ronkainen et al., 2016). This chapter explores the consequences of overattachment to sport, where participation in sport no longer provides athletes with a sense of self, but instead becomes their entire identity.

The case presented within this chapter focuses on Ethan (a pseudonym), an elite professional golfer whose life revolved entirely around performance. Key stakeholders provided support throughout his career, which can be a positive contribution, but over time, this can provide a singular identity associated with sport (Muratore & Share, 2022). The labels of "DP World Tour golfer" became internal truths; Ethan no longer played golf but became it. All aspects of his confidence, emotional stability, and relationships depended on the performance in a particular week.

DOI: 10.4324/9781003515203-14

Scholarly inquiry within sport psychology explains the concept of athletic identity, which refers to how strongly an individual identifies with their athletic role (Brewer et al., 1993). When an athlete's self-concept is related to sporting success, confidence, motivation, and psychological stability can be negatively influenced based on outcomes (Crocker & Knight, 2005). Closely related is the idea of identity foreclosure (Marcia, 1966), where athletes align with a single identity before exploring alternatives. In sport, foreclosure can occur when athletes enter early specialisation in a sport, are praised primarily for performance in that sport, or receive little support for identity exploration outside sport (Coakley, 1992).

In order to overcome these challenges, the current chapter considers ACT, a contemporary behavioural approach aiming to enhance psychological flexibility (Hayes et al., 1999). A rigid athletic identity becomes unhelpful when self-worth is dependent on performance, athletes struggle to manage pressure, increasing emotional vulnerability, and risk of burnout. ACT aligns well with these challenges because it targets the core processes that sustain negative athletic identity. In relation to Ethan's athletic performances, ACT could prevent being caught in negative/self-focused and sport outcome-related narratives (e.g., "I only have value when I win") and work towards an expanded concept of himself based on his own values rather than his athletic achievements (Gardner & Moore, 2012; Lundgren et al., 2018).

Understanding Athletic Identity

Athletic identity has been established as a core concept in understanding the psychological experiences of athletes. Brewer et al. (1993) define athletic identity as the degree to which an individual identifies with the athletic role and looks to sport participation as a contributing source of self-definition. In simple terms, it describes how athletes' sense of self is based on their participation and achievements in sport.

A robust athletic identity can provide both motivation and commitment and can reinforce goal-directed behaviour through adversity (Horton & Mack, 2000). High-performance sport is familiar with this type of identification due to the alignment of values, habits, and social relationships with excellence and achievement. However, sporting identification can impair those aspects of performance if the sportsperson's identity is completely reliant on their own performance, or if there is constriction of their identity to fit other roles or interests, according to Brewer et al. (1993). This constriction of identity is closely related to the concept of identity foreclosure (Marcia, 1966). Identity foreclosure occurs when an athlete has a strong connection to a particular identity, for example, a professional golfer without the exploration of other aspects of themselves. Traditionally, in sport, this happens at an early age when athletes experience success and early specialisation and receive strong external validation before developing a broader sense of who they are (Muratore & Share, 2022). The surrounding social environment and the influence of key stakeholders such as parents, peers, and coaches can reinforce the belief that athletic achievement is the core of personal value.

Those athletes who have a foreclosed identity often find difficulty in separating self-esteem from performance outcomes. Generally, when performance is successful, there is a rise in confidence and motivation; however, when performance is poor, psychological outcomes tend to drift towards frustration and self-doubt (Reinboth et al., 2004). Similarly, athletes whose self-worth depended on external performance indicators tended to experience additional emotional volatility and burnout (Lundqvist & Raglin, 2015), suggesting a pattern in performance-determined identity structure, essentially where self-esteem rises and falls with outcomes, and athletes feel psychologically vulnerable when their competence is threatened (Gustafsson et al., 2011). The association between identity and performance outcomes becomes cyclical. Suggesting that success strengthens the identification with sport, reinforcing external validations, whereas failure weakens confidence and facilitates emotional instability. Athletes with rigid athletic identities often engage in cognitive fusion, a process described in ACT as becoming fused to thoughts or labels about themselves (Gardner & Moore, 2012).

Despite these risks, a robust athletic identity isn't always unhelpful. According to Horton and Mack (2000), if identification enhances motivation and focus, this is deemed functional commitment. Whereas if identification leads to dependence and rigidity, this is deemed dysfunctional commitment. Commitment and identity investment can often lead to athlete success; the challenge lies within not only maintaining flexibility between valuing sport but also nurturing other parts of the self.

Ethan's Story

Ethan is a professional golfer, whose early life was dominated with golf and performance. From an early age, his motivation and commitment were directed towards a later career in golf. By his mid-teens, competing at the national level and a full-time competitive schedule were beginning to make his goal a reality. Key stakeholders within the environment reinforced this status, and golf became the lens through which he understood himself and the world. Early experiences with associated success led Ethan to believe that golf wasn't simply what he did, but who he was. His social experiences, daily routines, and habits were shaped around the sport. Friendships and even relationships existed primarily within golfing circles, which provided a closed sense of identity early in the life cycle. When performance was good, he felt confident and sociable; however, when performance declined, he became withdrawn and self-critical.

As his career progressed, the pressures naturally intensified. The world of professional golf can be an unforgiving environment, every shot and round publicly recorded and potentially scrutinised. Though at the early stages, progression was linear, Ethan achieved further success to progress on to the tour in which he dreamt of being on all those years ago. For a number of years, this was Ethan's life, living and breathing the sport and the identity attached to it.

However, during a challenging season both on and off the golf course, Ethan's results declined significantly. In his home life, a close family member suffered from a debilitating medical event, and his performances on the golf course became distracted and disjointed. Ethan would continuously report thoughts such as "If I don't make the cut, I'm letting everybody down" and "Everyone will think I shouldn't be at this level". These thoughts drove performance anxiety and perfectionism, and even the smallest of mistakes facilitated rumination and self-doubt. Alongside that, when on an off week, his social spaces began to feel meaningless, and he struggled to connect with those around him. A significant comment, although small in word form, "I feel lost", highlighted the need for values based work

Ethan's experiences mirror the psychological mechanisms highlighted in the literature. His identity foreclosure (Marcia, 1966) provided limited coping strategies outside of his sport. His lack of external successes left him with limited self-worth, and his previous intrinsic motivation surrounding golf had become controlled by a fear of failure (Deci & Ryan, 2000; Reinboth et al., 2004). As performances dropped, his confidence reduced, leading to emotional instability and performance anxiety (Lundqvist & Raglin, 2015; Gustafsson et al., 2011).

This case demonstrates the influences of overidentification with sport and how it can impact psychological well-being. Ethan's motivation and determination have been unquestionable, yet his ability to separate his own personal worth from performance outcomes created psychological vulnerability. This story illustrates the lived reality in professional sport of concepts discussed, including athletic identity and identity foreclosure, and how well-intentioned dedication, accompanied with their associated reinforcements, can evolve into dependency and distress.

In the next section, the chapter uses the ACT framework to explore various psychological mechanisms that maintain rigid identities. These include cognitive fusion, perfectionism, and performance-related self-worth. It then describes how values-based interventions can support purpose and stability beyond performance outcomes.

Psychological Mechanisms Behind Over-Identification

Establishing the meaning behind athlete over-identification in their sport requires exploration of the psychological mechanisms that sustain the rigidity of identity patterns. Central to this is the complex interplay between performance-based self-worth, fear of failure, and experiential avoidance, all of which create dependency on sporting success to maintain a sense of value. These mechanisms reinforce a narrow self-concept, making athletes at risk of emotional instability when performance is poor.

Performance-Based Self-Worth

Performance-based self-worth describes a mindset in which self-esteem is dependent on achievement, often developed in sport when success and approval become the primary measures of personal value (Crocker & Knight, 2005). Athletes learn at an early stage that success brings praise, attention, and respect, whilst failure offers disappointment and criticism. This conditioning links esteem directly to outcomes, creating a contingent self-worth system (Crocker & Knight, 2005).

The conditioning on sense of value creates a fragile foundation for psychological stability; athletes derive competence and confidence from performance outcomes and, as a result, experience greater fluctuations in motivation and emotional well-being (Reinboth et al., 2004). Research also demonstrates that performance-contingent self-esteem leads to a greater risk of higher levels of anxiety and burnout risk (Lundqvist & Raglin, 2015). Both lines of research enquiry are consistent with the autonomous and controlled motivation aspects of SDT (Deci & Ryan, 2000). When behaviour is autonomously motivated and driven by intrinsic motivation, it supports well-being. However, controlled motivation, driven by reward or ego validation, undermines psychological health.

Fear of Failure and Perfectionistic Tendencies

A close relative of performance-based self-worth is fear of failure, a feature common in competitive sport (Conroy et al., 2001). Fear of failure is more complex than a concern about losing, anticipation of shame, judgement, or diminished self-worth that follows a performance slump (Conroy et al., 2002). Those players struggling with rigid identities will have fear that will be generated because, instead of merely indicating a momentary problem, failure will reveal the threat to self that exists (Sagar & Stoeber, 2009). A mechanism chosen for fear of failure is perfectionism, and the belief is held that flawless execution will prevent feelings of embarrassment or shield self-esteem from the possible damage of failure (Flett & Hewitt, 2005)

However, the pursuit of perfection can quickly lead to self-criticism if the outcomes of one's performance are unsatisfactory (Hall et al., 1998). The pattern of self-criticism reinforces the rigidity of identity, with success never satisfying psychological need, and mistakes become evidence of personal inadequacy. Over time, this mindset can lead to anxiety and a fragile sense of control (Flett

& Hewitt, 2005). Fear of failure can also have influences on learning and adaptability, with attention narrowing and fewer risks taken (Sagar & Stoeber, 2009). This tends to limit growth and reinforces dependence on perfect performance as a condition for self-acceptance. In ACT terms, this is a form of experiential avoidance, where individuals try not to experience certain thoughts or emotions, in this case, painful memories (Hayes et al., 1999).

Experiential Avoidance and Emotional Suppression

Experiential avoidance is described as the effort to escape, control, or suppress unwanted thoughts, emotions, or bodily sensations. This often manifests in sport as athletes attempting to block out frustration, nerves, or self-doubt before competing. Avoidance may provide short-term relief, but paradoxically, it strengthens unwanted experiences in the long term (Hayes et al., 2006)).

Research highlights a correlation between experiential avoidance and anxiety, burnout, and reduced performance under pressure (Lundgren et al., 2018), with ACT-based studies confirming that greater psychological flexibility predicts healthier emotional regulation and consistency in performance (Gardner & Moore, 2012), whereas, in contrast, avoidance keeps athletes locked in a cycle of suppression and reactivity, creating more reliance on self-identity as a means of function.

Cognitive Fusion

Another key concept in reinforcing athlete over-identification is cognitive fusion, an ACT concept that describes becoming entangled with one's thoughts. These often appear in sport as absolute statements, such as "If I fail, I'm worthless", and when athletes fuse with such thoughts, the narrative created by the athletes is one of literal truths rather than mental events (Gardner & Moore, 2012). Athletes with rigid identities often become fused with their own story, that is, their own narrative becomes around performance and achievement. This story not only creates pride but also imposes pressure to maintain this image at all costs. Research demonstrates that cognitive fusion and rumination in athletes reduce emotional regulation and flexibility, whilst mindfulness and acceptance training increase flexibility and coping (Josefsson et al., 2017). Similarly, Mosewich et al. (2013) found that athletes who fuse with self-critical thoughts experience lower resilience and higher distress.

Identity rigidity becomes reinforced through cognitive fusion, which blurs the line between who an athlete is and their thoughts about themselves. Once athletes become fused with performance-based self-judgements, they behave defensively and tend to avoid risk, suppress emotions, and chase validation to make their story true. Defusion techniques, a core concept of ACT, help athletes to notice passing mental events rather than absolute truths.

Integration of Mechanisms

Performance-based self-worth, fear of failure, experiential avoidance, and cognitive fusion are interconnected mechanisms that collectively maintain athletic rigidity. Each mechanism limits psychological flexibility in varying ways: performance-based self-worth anchors identity in outcomes; fear of failure fuels perfectionistic tendencies and avoidance; experiential avoidance limits emotional flexibility; and cognitive fusion solidifies a narrow sense of self. Collectively,they create an internal system where self-worth, motivation, and emotion rise and fall with performance outcomes.

In the case of Ethan, these mechanisms were evident in behaviour and thought patterns. His self-worth depended on performances, fear of failure directed self-criticism, and uncomfortable emotions were avoided by social withdrawal. His identity as a golfer became fused with his beliefs around success and failure, leaving little psychological space to explore other aspects of the self. When results failed to come through, the structure collapsed, producing a loss of meaning, and created associated feelings of anxiety and frustration.

From a therapeutic perspective, understanding these mechanisms is essential for intervention. They suggest that the core issues are not simply stress around performance, but psychological inflexibility. Addressing these patterns requires approaches that provide a more flexible relationship between thoughts, feelings, and emotions, and using a values-based intervention grounded in ACT provides a platform to do so. The following segment will outline the ACT framework and its role in supporting athletes like Ethan to break from self-worth within performance, accept unpleasant internal experiences, and reconnect with values outside of sport.

ACT Framework and the Role of Values

ACT provides one possible approach to the management of rigidity, which is often observed in over-identifying athletes. Developed by Hayes et al. (1999), ACT is considered part of the third wave of behavioural therapies and represents a modern and evidence-based psychological intervention aimed at enhancing psychological flexibility and overall well-being. Instead of trying to reduce unpleasant emotions or control thoughts, ACT proposes an avenue for individuals to change their relationship with them, aiming to perform effectively, despite performance-related stressors, instead of attempting to avoid them.

The Six Core Processes of ACT

ACT integrates six interrelated processes that collectively support psychological flexibility: acceptance, cognitive defusion, contact with the present moment, self-as-context, values, and committed action (Hayes et al., 1999). In this particular case, each aspect has specific relevance to athletes who over-identify with their chosen sport. ACT does not aim to reduce anxiety or eliminate unhelpful thoughts, but to increase the athlete's capacity to perform alongside them. For athletes whose identities are closely linked with success, the shift can be transformative, meaning that they learn to see themselves as individuals who have cultivated the ability to choose to respond appropriately to challenge and adversity, rather than being defined by performance.

The Role of Values

Values work is a core concept of ACT and is especially powerful for athletes experiencing identity foreclosure. Where athletes over-identify with their sporting role, they lose connection to what previously motivated them, for example, growth or mastery. Values clarification helps to reorient focus from outcomes to processes. By identifying with personal values, athletes can develop a more stable motivational foundation that supports autonomy over control (Deci & Ryan, 2000). Research suggests that values-aligned goals foster greater psychological well-being and superior persistence (Gardner & Moore, 2012), and with athletes requiring support to create self-worth outside of performance, values work can restore a sense of personal worth, not contingent on success or failure.

Clarification of values can also support the self-as-context aspect of ACT, helping athletes to recognise their identity beyond the role of an athlete. Conceptual research suggests that relating as self-context particularly undermines rigidity associated with the conceptualised self, with values work thereby offers direction for expressions of one's overall identity independent of athletic roles (Berkout et al., 2021).

Intervention with Ethan

Ethan's work with a sport and exercise psychologist (BPS and HCPC) followed an ACT-based, values-oriented approach designed to provide additional psychological flexibility and reduce over-identification with sport and performance. The intervention unfolded over several weeks and combined experiential exercises and mindfulness-based practices with ongoing reflective dialogue.

Prerequisite Information

Due to the ongoing relationship between Ethan and the sport psychologist, mindfulness practices were already taking place in the ACT space. Specifically, mindfulness training has been well established in both clinical psychology and sport psychology, with benefits found for attentional control, emotional regulation, and resilience. General meta-analytic studies have found mindfulness-based programs to be reliable in reducing anxiety and stress and improving overall psychological well-being (Khoury et al., 2013). In a sports context, mindfulness training is related to improved attentional engagement and decreased rumination and coping (Akhtar & Baltzell, 2014). A look at mindfulness training in sports also indicates that awareness gained through mindfulness training provides athletes with greater and more consistent sport performance skills to remain engaged with their experience rather than automatically reacting to it (Gardner & Moore, 2007), although research is still ongoing as to the specific mechanisms behind its development (Lochbaum et al., 2022). For Ethan's treatment process, this background work done with mindfulness training proved advantageous. This allowed him to recognise his thoughts and feelings with increased awareness, and opportunities for more profound value-based exploration and identity flexibility could be had.

Assessment and Initial Goals

During the initial performance slump, Ethan presented with symptoms of performance anxiety, high perfectionistic tendencies, and emotional fatigue. His description of self was centred around golf, for example, phrases included "I am a golfer, this is what I do, and if I miss the cut, I feel like I've let everybody down". Due to recognised symptoms of narrowed self-identity, the Athletic Identity Measurement Scale (AIMS; Brewer et al., 1993) was administered. The full ten-item AIMS scale is scored between 10 and 70, with higher scores indicating stronger identification with the athlete's role. (Brewer et al., 1993). Ethan's initial score of 62 reflected a highly integrated athletic identity at baseline.

While the AIMS does not directly assess identity flexibility, the elevated score, combined with intake information and behavioural observations demonstrating lower flexibility markers, supported the assessment that Ethan's self-worth was strongly tied to his sporting role and performance outcomes. Therefore, the psychological assessment and supplementary interviewing confirmed high athletic identity and signs of controlled motivation, consistent with identity foreclosure and performance-based self-worth.

The goal of the work was to assist Ethan in recognising his current patterns that included avoidance of vulnerability and self-criticism, as opposed to challenging motivation. The intervention aimed to broaden his perspective and reconnect him with personal values that transcended results. Although values work was deemed central to Ethan's progress, the intervention first focused on awareness and defusion. This was aimed to increase space for values to be selected and prevent values from becoming performance rules, thus creating psychological openness to establish authentic values as opposed to outcome-based goals.

Phase 1: Awareness and Defusion

Early work focused on helping Ethan observe his thought patterns and emotional reactions. Cognitive defusion exercises took the form of noticing and labelling thoughts, creating greater distance in the language used, for example, "I'm noticing, I am having the thought, that I need to make every cut to be successful". Brief grounding practices helped Ethan reconnect with present-moment cues when thoughts fused with performance narratives. Research supports creating linguistic shifts between the thought and the self to help reduce emotional intensity (Gardner & Moore, 2012). Ethan also engaged in present-moment awareness through mindfulness exercises. These practices included simple grounding exercises and focusing on sensory experiences rather than outcomes.

Phase 1 was designed as three one-hour sessions, during which defusion and mindfulness skills were introduced and practiced (Hayes et al., 1999). Although there was a time attached to the interventions themselves, both the sport psychologist and Ethan recognised that these skills formed the foundations for developing psychological flexibility towards greater performance and well-being moving forward. Over time, Ethan reported gaining perspective on his "mind shifting from future and past to what's going on now".

Phase 2: Acceptance and Emotional Flexibility

The next phase involved increasing acceptance of difficult emotions rather than avoiding them. Ethan's attempts at suppressing anxiety and frustration came in the form of thoughts such as "I shouldn't feel nervous, I've done this my whole life". Through guided discussion and experiential exercises, Ethan and the sport psychologist explored how avoidance tendencies intensified distress and reduced focus. This acceptance work provided space for discomfort within the performance environment, reducing the internal struggle that was often unhelpful towards outcomes. In particular, an exercise adapted from the MAC (Gardner & Moore, 2007) involved visualising performance anxiety as a passing wave, as opposed to an obstacle. The psychologist encouraged Ethan to notice the waves' presence, breathe, and continue engaging in action. This exercise taught Ethan that performance anxiety could co-exist with effective action, aligned with ACT principles.

Phase 2 consisted of four one-hour sessions, situated after initial mindfulness and defusion groundwork. Due to the nature of the performance environment, acceptance appeared to require additional time and support to support directly with the sport psychologist in this case.

Phase 3: Values Clarification

Once Ethan had gained awareness of thought patterns and emotional responses, the direction of work shifted towards values exploration. Using a values sorting exercise, he identified values that were deemed important, neutral, and not important to him. Once the "important" values were established, the exercise explored his top ten core values, which included respect, skilfulness, supportiveness, acceptance, forgiveness, gratitude, fairness, patience, self-awareness, and self-care.

Through values exploration, Ethan gained clarity on qualities he wanted to express within and beyond golf. These values directed learning outcomes such as treating himself and others with respect, offering support to others, and responding to pressure with patience and self-compassion. He also developed habits of gratitude, emotional awareness, and self-care, which encouraged a more flexible and sustained approach to golf. These values were measured daily, electronically, and served as a guide to behaviour, which could extend beyond sport (see Figure 12.1). As these values became guiding principles, Ethan's performance behaviours shifted from fear-driven control to growth-oriented action.

Phase 3 involved both collaborative work with the sport psychologist and individual reflection completed by Ethan between sessions. There were two structured sessions, an hour in length, delivered by the sport psychologist, and a further two-week period of individual reflection completed by Ethan between

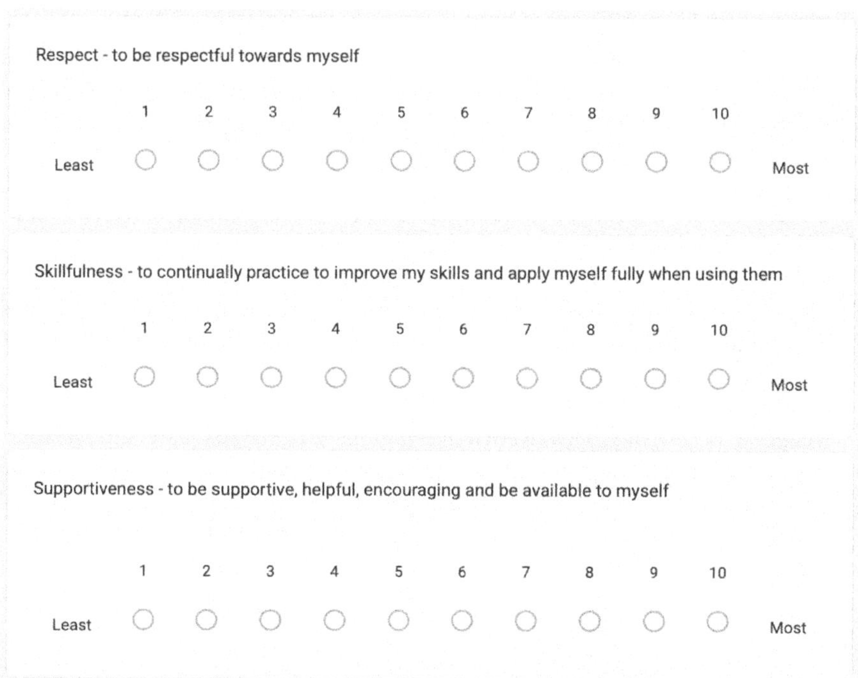

Respect - to be respectful towards myself

	1	2	3	4	5	6	7	8	9	10	
Least	○	○	○	○	○	○	○	○	○	○	Most

Skillfulness - to continually practice to improve my skills and apply myself fully when using them

	1	2	3	4	5	6	7	8	9	10	
Least	○	○	○	○	○	○	○	○	○	○	Most

Supportiveness - to be supportive, helpful, encouraging and be available to myself

	1	2	3	4	5	6	7	8	9	10	
Least	○	○	○	○	○	○	○	○	○	○	Most

Figure 12.1 Example of the digital values tracking questionnaire used to measure values-based behaviours.

meetings. This mirrors recommendations within ACT performance models where values-based work typically unfolds over one to three sessions, with continuous reflection to strengthen integration (Lundgren et al., 2018)

Phase 4: Committed Action and Integration

In the final phase of work, Ethan developed specific actions aligned with his chosen values. These included daily mindfulness practices, voice note reflections post rounds, and scheduled time for non-sport related activities. The continued measurement of values using the electronic form helped keep values alive in daily behaviour and provided the psychologist with updates on behavioural progress.

Phase 4 unfolded over a longer period than the previous phases (approximately six to eight weeks), with intervention activity already established. Research suggests that committed action typically requires several weeks of contextual application for habits to stabilise and to create a meaningful shift in behaviour (Lundgren et al., 2018)

As these behaviours progressed, Ethan reported a marked improvement in enjoyment and a reduction in performance anxiety. His results became more consistent, and his achievement progressed with regaining his full tour card. He began to describe himself as "Ethan the human, not just the golfer", something that was supported by the psychologist and the chosen interventions, but lived by Ethan.

Key Learning Points

Several key learning points became clear in Ethan's intervention:

- Awareness of cognitive fusion: Recognising that his thoughts were not truths, but mental events, provided emotional space to respond differently.
- Acceptance of discomfort: Learning that anxiety could coexist with performance allowed him to stop fighting internal experiences.
- Reconnection with values: Rediscovering his need for self-care and patience, whilst still progressing learning and development, provided enjoyment within golf as opposed to fear.
- Broadening identity: Engaging in meaningful activities outside golf reinforced a sense of balance and stability.

Outcomes

By the end of the intervention, Ethan reported a greater sense of emotional stability, reduced perfectionistic tendencies, and greater satisfaction across both personal and professional life. Quantitatively, his AIMS score decreased from 62 at baseline to 48 post-intervention, indicating a meaningful movement towards a more flexible and less performance-contingent sense of self. The work remains ongoing, with future sessions aiming to consolidate these gains and maintain identity flexibility throughout performance cycles.

From a psychological perspective, the intervention restored psychological flexibility. Ethan became more accepting of emotions, less fused with unhelpful and self-critical thoughts, more present-moment aware, and connected to values outside of the performance domain. These findings align with scholarly enquiry within ACT, demonstrating improved well-being and consistency of performance among athletes following acceptance and values-based protocols (Lundgren et al., 2018; Mosewich et al., 2013; Gardner & Moore, 2012).

Reflections on Practice

Ethan's development highlights the benefits of ACT for addressing identity-related issues within sport. The intervention did not attempt to change commitment or ambition; rather, it supported him to engage with golf in a meaningful and flexible way. Through defusion, acceptance, and values-based exercises, Ethan learned to see his identity outside of sporting performance. His case illustrates the value of psychological flexibility as a platform for sustainable performance and personal well-being.

References

Akhtar, V. L., & Baltzell, A. (2014). Mindfulness meditation training for sport (MMTS) intervention: Impact of MMTS with Division I female athletes. Journal of Happiness & Well-Being, 2(2), 160–173.

Berkout, O. V., Kolnes, M.-A., & Gross, J. J. (2021). Psychological flexibility in sport: An avenue for future research. Frontiers in Psychology, 12, 658648. https://doi.org/10.3389/fpsyg.2021.658648

Brewer, B. W., Van Raalte, J. L., & Linder, D. E. (1993). Athletic identity: Hercules' muscles or Achilles heel? International Journal of Sport Psychology, 24, 237–254.

Coakley, J. (1992). Burnout among adolescent athletes: A personal failure or social problem? Sociology of Sport Journal, 9(3), 271–285.

Conroy, D. E., Poczwardowski, A., & Henschen, K. P. (2001). Evaluative concerns and the fear of failure in sport: A cognitive – Motivational analysis. Journal of Sport and Exercise Psychology, 23(4), 317–329.

Conroy, D. E., Willow, J. P., & Metzler, J. (2002). Multidimensional fear of failure measurement: The performance failure appraisal inventory. Journal of Applied Sport Psychology, 14(2), 76–90. https://doi.org/10.1080/10413200252907752

Cresswell, S. L., & Eklund, R. C. (2006). Changes in athlete burnout and motivation over a 12-week league tournament. Medicine & Science in Sports & Exercise, 38(3), 464–468. https://doi.org/10.1249/01.mss.0000184583.01773.b2

Crocker, P. R. E., & Knight, C. J. (2005). Coping and motivation. In S. J. Bull (Ed.), Adherence issues in sport and exercise (pp. 111–134). Wiley.

Deci, E. L., & Ryan, R. M. (2000). The "what" and "why" of goal pursuits: Human needs and the self-determination of behavior. Psychological Inquiry, 11(4), 227–268.

Eime, R. M., Young, J. A., Harvey, J. T., Charity, M. J., & Payne, W. R. (2013). A systematic review of the psychological and social benefits of participation in sport. International Journal of Behavioral Nutrition and Physical Activity, 10, 135. https://doi.org/10.1186/1479-5868-10-135

Flett, G. L., & Hewitt, P. L. (2005). The perils of perfectionism in sports and exercise. Current Directions in Psychological Science, 14(1), 14–18. https://doi.org/10.1111/j.0963-7214.2005.00326.x

Gardner, F. L., & Moore, Z. E. (2007). The psychology of enhancing human performance: The mindfulness-acceptance-commitment approach. Springer.

Gardner, F. L., & Moore, Z. E. (2012). Mindfulness-and-acceptance-based interventions in sport and performance contexts. Current Opinion in Psychology, 1, 127–132. https://doi.org/10.1016/j.copsyc.2014.12.005

Gustafsson, H., Hassmén, P., & Hassmén, N. (2011). Are athletes burning out with passion? European Journal of Sport Science, 11(6), 387–395. https://doi.org/10.1080/17461391.2010.536572

Hall, H. K., Kerr, A. W., & Matthews, J. (1998). Pre-competitive anxiety in sport: The contribution of achievement goals and perfectionism. Journal of Sport and Exercise Psychology, 20(2), 194–217. https://doi.org/10.1123/jsep.20.2.194

Hayes, S. C., Luoma, J. B., Bond, F. W., Masuda, A., & Lillis, J. (2006). Acceptance and commitment therapy: Model, processes, and outcomes. Behaviour Research and Therapy, 44(1), 1–25.

Hayes, S. C., Strosahl, K. D., & Wilson, K. G. (1999). Acceptance and commitment therapy: An experiential approach to behavior change. Guilford Press.

Horton, R. S., & Mack, D. E. (2000). Athletic identity in marathon runners: Functional focus or dysfunctional commitment? Journal of Sport Behavior, 23(2), 101–119.

Josefsson, T., Ivarsson, A., Lindwall, M., Gustafsson, H., Stenling, A., Böröy, J., & Gardner, F. (2017). Mindfulness mechanisms in sports: Mediating effects of rumination and emotion regulation on sport-specific coping. International Journal of Sport and Exercise Psychology, 15(6), 521–533. https://doi.org/10.1080/1612197X.2016.1189770

Khoury, B., Lecomte, T., Fortin, G., et al. (2013). Mindfulness-based therapy: A comprehensive meta-analysis. Clinical Psychology Review, 33(6), 763–771. https://doi.org/10.1016/j.cpr.2013.05.005

Lochbaum, M., Achenbach, L., Zanatta, T., et al. (2022). A meta-analytic review of mindfulness-based interventions in sport and performance. Journal of Clinical Sport Psychology, 16(3), 241–268.

Lundgren, T., Reinebo, G., Stenling, A., & Gardner, F. L. (2018). Psychological flexibility and performance in athletes. Journal of Clinical Sport Psychology, 12(3), 264–288. https://doi.org/10.1123/jcsp.2018-0015

Lundqvist, C., & Raglin, J. S. (2015). Psychological vulnerability in elite athletes. European Journal of Sport Science, 15(2), 175–182. https://doi.org/10.1080/17461391.2014.933879

Marcia, J. E. (1966). Development and validation of ego-identity status. Journal of Personality and Social Psychology, 3(5), 551–558. https://doi.org/10.1037/h0023281

Mosewich, A. D., Crocker, P. R. E., Kowalski, K. C., & DeLongis, A. (2013). Self-compassion among women athletes. Self and Identity, 12(4), 365–379. https://doi.org/10.1080/15298868.2012.702792

Muratore, D., & Share, B. (2022). Athletic identity and transition out of sport. International Journal of Sport and Exercise Psychology, 20(4), 1046–1062. https://doi.org/10.1080/1612197X.2020.1843079

Reinboth, M., Duda, J. L., & Ntoumanis, N. (2004). Motivation in sport: The role of perceived autonomy support, competence, and relatedness. Psychology of Sport and Exercise, 5(3), 279–293. https://doi.org/10.1016/S1469-0292(03)00021-X

Ronkainen, N. J., Kavoura, A., & Ryba, T. V. (2016). Narrative and identity in athletes. Qualitative Research in Sport, Exercise and Health, 8(5), 521–540. https://doi.org/10.1080/2159676X.2016.1206608

Sagar, S. S., & Stoeber, J. (2009). Perfectionism, fear of failure, and burnout in youth athletes. Journal of Sports Sciences, 27(9), 913 922. https://doi.org/10.1080/02640410902926461

13 Delivering ACT Interventions with Neurodivergent Athletes

Samuel Wood

Learning Objectives

1. Explain how ACT processes (e.g., psychological flexibility, values, and acceptance) can support neurodivergent performers in sport contexts
2. Apply neuroaffirmative considerations to ACT interventions to create inclusive, high-performance environments

Introduction

The term neurodiversity describes differences in individual brain function and behavioural traits as part of normal variation in the population (Clouder et al., 2020). Focused on a strength-based approach to understanding individual experiences, the term emerged in response to the stigmatisation of medical diagnoses and the recognition for social models of disability (Hoare et al., 2023). As an umbrella term, neurodiversity incorporates a range of different neurotypes, including autism and attention-deficit hyperactivity disorder (ADHD). Within this chapter, we focus on working with autistic and ADHD athletes[1]. For readers less familiar with how these neurotypes might influence experiences of sport, both are outlined below.

Autism is typically characterised by differences in social communication and interaction, as well as restrictive, repetitive patterns of behaviour, interests, or activities (ICD, 2019). Autistic individuals may understand others' actions in social situations differently, meaning integration of some information can be implicated (Gillott & Standen, 2007), creating differences in the coping skills to manage stress effectively (Groden et al., 2002). Further, an insistence on sameness and a repertoire of fixed behaviours and routines can be common, leaving autistic individuals with a propensity for anxiety as well as lower self-esteem compared to neurotypical peers (Gillott & Standen, 2007). This can contribute a greater risk of long-term depression and anxiety (Hollocks et al., 2019), as well as lower quality of life (Mason et al.,

DOI: 10.4324/9781003515203-15

2019). Autistic individuals might employ maladaptive coping strategies (e.g., escape, resignation, and social withdrawal) that risk increasing life impairments, whereas adaptive coping strategies (e.g., minimisation, reaction control, and positive self-instruction) may be more effective in social contexts (Barra et al., 2021).

Autistic individuals commonly experience psychological inflexibility, reduced goal-directed actions, and vulnerability to stress and sensory stimuli (Alvares et al., 2016). Maisel et al. (2019) reported that autistic adults have elevated levels of cognitive fusion compared to neurotypical individuals, which influences an individual's behaviour repertoire (see Williams, 2010; Williams & Happé, 2010). Further, autistic individuals may experience differences in emotional processing, commonly caused by alexithymia (Kinnaird et al., 2019), and rigid and/or binary thinking (Cooper et al., 2018). This might make emotion labelling and cognitive reframing strategies that form part of second-wave cognitive behaviour therapies more challenging for autistic individuals. Yet, interestingly, this tendency for binary thinking might facilitate emotional regulation in response to uncertainty (Stark et al., 2021). Autistic traits have also been linked with aphantasia, which creates differences in executing mental imagery compared to neurotypical individuals (King et al., 2024). Understandably, this might limit the effectiveness of imagery or mental rehearsal interventions commonly used in PST interventions (Andersen, 2009).

ADHD traits include inattention and hyperactivity-impulsivity (Combs et al., 2015). According to Barkley (1997), individuals with ADHD might experience differences in cognitive inhibition, and maintaining attention to relevant cues while filtering irrelevant information. Compared to neurotypical peers, over-stimulation may lead to differences in executive functioning (e.g., cognitive, emotional, and behavioural control) and promote increased rates of perceived stress (Barra et al., 2021). Consequently, ADHD individuals may experience differences in various areas of life (e.g., educational, occupational, and interpersonal role impairments) (Mannuzza & Klein, 2000).

The prevalence of autism is 0.6% globally (Salari et al., 2022), with 1.1% of adults in the United Kingdom (U.K.) reporting a clinical diagnosis for autism (NICE, 2020). The prevalence of ADHD is around 9% globally (Song et al., 2021), with 3–4% of U.K. adults reporting a clinical diagnosis (NICE, 2024). Of interest, however, is data suggesting that the prevalence for both neurotypes is increasing. For example, in the U.K., there has been a 47% increase in individuals awaiting an autism diagnosis amongst the general population (National Autistic Society, 2024) and a 400% increase in the number of adults seeking an ADHD diagnosis since 2020 (ADHD Foundation, 2024). However, this rise may be because of increased awareness, rather than an increase in prevalence (Martin et al., 2025).

Neurodivergence in Sport

The prevalence of ADHD and autism amongst the athlete population is unknown. However, some suggest that autism and ADHD may occur at greater rates in the athlete population compared with non-athlete cohorts (Hoare et al., 2023). Indeed, some neurodivergent traits (e.g., commitment to routine, rapid response to stimuli, hyperfocus, and attention to detail) may be seen as valuable for sport, with some demands of elite sport (e.g., intense focus, structured training, and high energy expenditure) perhaps appealing to the unique abilities of neurodivergent individuals (Hoare et al., 2025; Russell et al., 2019). Despite this, autism and ADHD are typically overlooked in the broader context of elite athlete mental health (Larsen et al., 2021). Although some neurotypes may be advantageous in sport, it is important to appreciate that some traits (e.g., behavioural, cognitive, sensory, and social restrictions) might prevent individuals from engaging in sport (Pan & Frey, 2006) and may be exacerbated in elite sport settings. Importantly, within a sports context, neurodivergent athletes in most countries are exempt from para-sport, leaving them experiencing the same sporting environments (both training and competition) as their neurotypical peers. Hoare et al.'s (2023) systematic review of neurodiversity in sport highlights that neurodivergent athletes (including those with autism and ADHD) often experience unique barriers in sport settings compared to their neurotypical peers. Wood et al. (2025) highlight that some of these challenges might include a lack of belonging in sport environments, feeling overwhelmed (i.e., high self-expectation, overthinking and over-analysing situations, experiencing sensory overload from environmental stimuli, and "masking" their neurodivergence), and desiring plans to help them navigate sporting environments most effectively.

Importantly, the increased prevalence of individuals self-identifying or seeking a clinical diagnosis for ADHD and/or autism in the general population increases the likelihood of sport psychologists working with neurodivergent athletes. To maintain equality as a practitioner and uphold professional codes of conduct, upskilling sport psychologists to feel confident in working with this population will become an important area of professional development.

Supporting Neurodivergent Athletes Using ACT

The Benefits of Using ACT

Many autistic individuals report that second-wave CBTs encourage masking, leading them to perform neurotypical behaviours rather than addressing underlying distress, and promoting conformity rather than self-understanding (Stark et al., 2021). Away from sport, ACT has proven effective for autistic individuals (see Pahnke et al., 2014, 2019) – perhaps because it is conceptually grounded in principles of behaviour analysis (Hoffmann et al., 2016) – as well as proving beneficial for ADHD traits (Munawar et al., 2021). Importantly, Boulton et al. (2018) and Spain et al. (2015) suggest that there is little need to alter ACT interventions to accommodate different neurotypes. Pahnke et al. (2023) suggest that some adaptations might be helpful (e.g., concrete language, sensory-aware delivery, more explicit skills practice, and pacing), yet these are arguably addressed by employing a person-centred approach (i.e., being authentic, displaying empathy, and building rapport by remembering personal details), which will also likely help any challenges in social communication and relationship building (see Hume, 2022). In addition, sport-specific interventions (e.g., Szabo et al., 2019) show promising outcomes. Yet most sport-specific ACT work with neurodivergent individuals is case studies, small pilots, or adapted training programmes, rather than large, randomised-controlled trials (see Wood & Turner, 2024). Nonetheless, it is important to note that the growing popularity of ACT outpaces a quality evidence base for methodologically sound, third-wave studies with autistic individuals (see McNair et al., 2017; Patterson et al., 2019), especially in sport. In the following, I present how some typical strategies within an ACT intervention *might* look when working with a neurodivergent athlete, based on reflections from applied experiences.

Some Reflections from the Practice of ACT Interventions with Neurodivergent Athletes

Components of cognitive defusion appear beneficial and easily understandable for autistic individuals (Maisel et al., 2019). Acceptance and defusion might be introduced with the two friends metaphor (Harris, 2019), which essentially asks the athlete whether, when faced with a challenging/difficult time, they would prefer a harsh, critical friend or a kind, sympathetic friend. However, this task requires an element of empathy, understanding the feelings of another, which some autistic athletes may find challenging. Introducing acceptance and defusion might use abstract metaphors and concepts typical of ACT, which might be confusing for neurodivergent individuals (Byrne & O'Mahony, 2020). For example, defusion strategies that require sarcasm (e.g., having the athlete thank their brain for an unhelpful thought) might also be difficult for autistic athletes to understand. Importantly, however, these metaphors and abstract mechanisms of the ACT hexaflex can be challenging for neurotypical individuals to understand, too. Taking a person-centred approach, it is important to select different strategies if these become confusing for the athlete.

Neurodivergent athletes may tend to hyperfocus on given tasks. Introducing the concepts of values and committed action, as an alternative to focusing on sport-specific goals in training and competition, can help in these instances. When it comes to bringing the athlete's attention to the here and now, engaging the senses (e.g., what the athlete can see, hear, and feel) can be a helpful strategy. However, with some neurodivergent athletes, especially those with sensitivity issues, this can cause the athlete challenges (Wood & Turner, 2024). Here, I have found breathing exercises and mindfulness activities (e.g., puzzles) to be better grounding strategies for neurodivergent athletes.

Some General Practitioner Considerations When Supporting Neurodivergent Athletes

Focused on the domain of psychological service delivery in sport, it might be that SEPs separate neurodivergence from the specific focus of the sport-focused intervention (as discussed by Wood & Turner, 2024). Indeed, it might even be that the athlete reassures the SEP that they can "manage" the neurodivergent part of their sporting experience, insisting on a focus on the (sport-focused) presenting problem. Yet it is important not to separate the neurotype from the person (den Houting, 2019; Kapp et al., 2013). Here, showing empathy for the challenges neurodiverse athletes share will help prevent the therapeutic alliance from rupturing (Rogers, 1957).

Practitioner guidance for ADHD in athletic and rehabilitation contexts recommends structured, simplified, and externally scaffolded approaches (e.g., clear routines, brief and specific feedback, and goal-setting support) (Wolfe & Madden, 2016). For SEPs, concrete language, clear instructions, and visual schedules might help autistic and ADHD athletes (Kenworthy et al., 2014), as well as using external scaffolds (e.g., coach prompts, smartphone reminders, and teammate accountability), so the athlete receives environmental support (Phrathep et al., 2022). When implementing ACT, concrete metaphors, experiential exercises, and making clear links between values, committed action, and sport behaviours may be helpful (Pahnke et al., 2023). Further, it is important to consider differences with executive function and self-regulation, compared to neurotypical athletes. This might present as differences in planning, working memory, switching, and sustaining effort or concentration. This might be an especially important consideration for SEPs working with youth autistic athletes who may struggle with the uptake and maintenance of intervention skills, requiring SEPs to focus on scaffolding intervention processes for more effective outcomes (Kenworthy et al., 2014). Examples might include breaking goals down, creating checklists, or rehearsing routines (Li et al., 2025). Another consideration might be necessary sensory and social adaptations. This might mean SEPs delivering additional individual support in group settings, using quiet spaces to give athletes a sensory break, and considering alternative ways to practice intervention strategies (e.g., audio scripts, instead of written) (Hoare et al., 2023; Pahnke et al., 2023).

Logistically, reviewing guidance by Zolyomi et al. (2019), neurodivergent athletes might need certain accommodations if engaging in psychotherapeutic support via video call (e.g., managing sensory inputs, anxiety around "small talk", and the additional cognitive load of social interaction). In a departure from typical practice, it may be important to consider limiting small talk at the start of sessions. It might also be necessary to ensure a clear and consistent voice channel and avoid ambiguity or long, open-ended questions that can become difficult to answer if the athlete becomes distracted. Video calls allow the athlete to make reasonable adjustments to their environment (e.g., lighting and noise levels), which may be less possible if meeting in person in a neutral location. To further ease sensory and cognitive load, athletes might be asked if they would prefer audio-only channels of communication and offered shorter sessions and/or regular breaks during sessions.

Final Thoughts

ACT offers sport psychologists flexibility. For neurodivergent performers, that flexibility isn't just useful; it's essential. It can be challenging for neurodiverse athletes to disclose their needs, partly because they are struggling to understand how their neurodiversity affects them (and their performance), and partly because it can be too complex to explain any additional needs (Wood et al., 2025). This can leave the athlete finding their own solutions, carrying the responsibility of solving their challenges independently (Wood et al., 2025; Wood & Turner, 2024). Consequently, neurodivergent athletes may have developed a series of strategies to help them navigate their needs. Acknowledging the usefulness these offer the athlete, even if their effectiveness is questionable, is important.

Neurodivergence can present in a variety of ways. This limits the possibility of developing one-size-fits-all approaches to supporting neurodivergent athletes. Developing tailored support plans, which ensure continued and predictable support, aimed at preventing stress and exhaustion (see Högstedt et al., 2023). In line with the work of Reid and O'Connor (2003), support plans should be co-constructed. This prevents neurodivergent athletes feeling as though they need to "figure it out themselves", highlighting the need for balance of power, giving neurodivergent athletes autonomy to train and compete in ways that facilitate optimal performance (Wood et al., 2025). Practitioners should fine-tune routines and strategies that the athlete feels facilitate their performance, encouraging them to explore strategies beyond learned skills that may increase anxiety (e.g., masking; Cage & Troxell-Whitman, 2019).

When working with neurodivergent athletes, it can become challenging to distinguish where the presenting (sport-focused) problem remains distinct from more clinical needs of their neurodiversity. For example, the sport psychologist might be approached to help address the athlete's issues with confidence. However, the athlete's lack of confidence may come from feeling a lack of belonging or inconsistencies in performance because of challenges encountered in training and competitive environments. Although the presenting problem is a lack of

Practitioner Take-Aways for Supporting Neurodivergent Athletes

1. Lead with curiosity, not assumptions

Every neurodivergent athlete presents differently. Ask, don't guess. Let them shape the narrative of their experiences and preferences.

2. Honour existing strategies first

Before suggesting change, validate the systems athletes already built to cope and perform. Strength starts with safety and recognition.

3. Co-construct support plans

Design routines, communication styles, and coping tools *with* athletes, not for them. Collaboration protects autonomy and reduces the "figure it out alone" burden.

4. Build predictability and flexibility

Clear structure supports nervous-system safety; flexibility honours individual difference. Use both.

5. Spot masking and energy cost

Performance behaviours that "look fine" can come at a high internal price. Celebrate authenticity and reduce environments that reward masking.

6. Know your scope — and your bridge points

If concerns shift from performance skills to clinical distress, pause performance work and guide athletes toward appropriate clinical support.

7. Make ACT practical and gentle

Use values, acceptance, and self-compassion to build psychological flexibility. Keep metaphors concrete, pacing calm, and language affirming.

Figure 13.1 Practitioner takeaways for supporting neurodivergent athletes.

sport confidence, the root cause stems from their neurodiversity. This requires the practitioner to be mindful of when the athlete's needs exceed those of a sport psychologist. Gardner and Moore's (2004) Multi-level Classification System for Sport Psychology can prove helpful here, identifying when the athlete's needs shift from performance dysfunction towards performance impairment. If this happens, it is unlikely that development or refinement of sport-focused psychological skills would help (Anderson & Van Raalte, 2005), and encouraging the athlete to seek support from a clinical-based professional can prove necessary. Some key takeaways for practitioners are summarised in Figure 13.1.

Note

1 Medicine and science have typically employed person-first language (i.e., person with autism), but many individuals within the neurodiverse community prefer identity-first language (i.e., autistic person) (Vivanti, 2020).

References

Alvares, G. A., Balleine, B. W., Whittle, L., & Guastella, A. J. (2016). Reduced goal-directed action control in autism spectrum disorder. *Autism Research*, *9*(12), 1285–1293.

Andersen, M. B. (2009). The "canon" of psychological skills training for enhancing performance. In *Performance psychology in action: A casebook for working with athletes, performing artists, business leaders, and professionals in high-risk occupations* (pp. 11–34). American Psychological Association. https://doi.org/10.1037/11876-001

Anderson, M. B., & Van Raalte, J. L. (2005). Over one's head: Referral processes. In M. B. Anderson (Ed.), *Sport psychology in practice* (pp. 159–170). Human Kinetics.

Barkley, R. A. (1997). Behavioral inhibition, sustained attention, and executive functions: Constructing a unifying theory of ADHD. *Psychological Bulletin*, *121*(1), 65.

Barra, S., Grub, A., Roesler, M., Retz-Junginger, P., Philipp, F., & Retz, W. (2021). The role of stress coping strategies for life impairments in ADHD. *Journal of Neural Transmission*, *128*(7), 981–992. https://doi.org/10.1007/s00702-021-02311-5

Boulton, N. E., Williams, J., & Jones, R. S. P. (2018). Intellectual disabilities and ACT: Feasibility of a photography-based values intervention. *Advances in Mental Health and Intellectual Disabilities*, *12*(1), 11–21. https://doi.org/10.1108/AMHID-07-2017-0028

Byrne, G., & O'Mahony, T. (2020). Acceptance and commitment therapy (ACT) for adults with intellectual disabilities and/or autism spectrum conditions (ASC): A systematic review. *Journal of Contextual Behavioral Science*, *18*, 247–255. https://doi.org/10.1016/j.jcbs.2020.10.001

Cage, E., & Troxell-Whitman, Z. (2019). Understanding the reasons, contexts and costs of camouflaging for autistic adults. *Journal of Autism and Developmental Disorders*, *49*(5), 1899–1911. https://doi.org/10.1007/s10803-018-03878-x

Clouder, L., Karakus, M., Cinotti, A., Ferreyra, M. V., Fierros, G. A., & Rojo, P. (2020). Neurodiversity in higher education: A narrative synthesis. *Higher Education*, *80*(4), 757–778. https://doi.org/10.1007/s10734-020-00513-6

Combs, M. A., Canu, W. H., Broman-Fulks, J. J., Rocheleau, C. A., & Nieman, D. C. (2015). Perceived stress and ADHD symptoms in adults. *Journal of Attention Disorders*, *19*(5), 425–434. https://doi.org/10.1177/1087054712459558

Cooper, K., Loades, M. E., & Russell, A. (2018). Adapting psychological therapies for autism. *Research in Autism Spectrum Disorders*, *45*, 43–50. https://doi.org/10.1016/j.rasd.2017.11.002

den Houting, J. (2019). Neurodiversity: An insider's perspective. *Autism*, *23*(2), 271–273. https://doi.org/10.1177/1362361318820762

Foundation, A. (2024). Retrieved May 29, 2024, from https://shorturl.at/xGBp6

Gardner, F. L., & Moore, Z. E. (2004). The multi-level classification system for sport psychology (MCS-SP). *The Sport Psychologist*, *18*(1), 89–109.

Gillott, A., & Standen, P. (2007). Levels of anxiety and sources of stress in adults with autism. *Journal of Intellectual Disabilities*, *11*(4), 359–370.

Groden, J., Levasseur, P., & Baron, G. (2002). *Stress and anxiety: Assessment and coping strategies*. Inaugural World Autism Congress, Melbourne, Australia.

Harris, R. (2019). *ACT made simple: An easy-to-read primer on acceptance and commitment therapy* (2nd ed.). New Harbinger Publications.

Hoare, E., Olive, L. S., McGinty-Minister, K. L., McMurtry, C., Walton, C. C., Hall, K., Reardon, C. L., Purcell, R., & Berk, M. (2025). Neurodiversity and the mental health and well-being of elite athletes. *British Journal of Sports Medicine*, bjsports–2024–109325. https://doi.org/10.1136/bjsports-2024-109325

Hoare, E., Reyes, J., Olive, L., Willmott, C., Steer, E., Berk, M., & Hall, K. (2023). Neurodiversity in elite sport: A systematic scoping review. *BMJ Open Sport & Exercise Medicine*, *9*(2), e001575. https://doi.org/10.1136/bmjsem-2023-001575

Hoffmann, A. N., Contreras, B. P., Clay, C. J., & Twohig, M. P. (2016). Acceptance and commitment therapy for individuals with disabilities: A behavior analytic strategy for addressing private events in challenging behavior. *Behavior Analysis in Practice*, *9*, 14–24.

Högstedt, E., Igelström, K., Korhonen, L., Käcker, P., Marteinsdottir, I., & Björk, M. (2023). "It's like it is designed to keep me stressed" – Working sustainably with ADHD or autism. *Scandinavian Journal of Occupational Therapy*, *30*(8), 1280–1291. https://doi.org/10.1080/11038128.2022.2143420

Hollocks, M. J., Lerh, J. W., Magiati, I., Meiser-Stedman, R., & Brugha, T. S. (2019). Anxiety and depression in adults with autism spectrum disorder: A systematic review and meta-analysis. *Psychological Medicine*, *49*(4), 559–572. https://doi.org/10.1017/S0033291718002283

Hume, R. (2022). Show me the real you: Enhanced expression of Rogerian conditions in therapeutic relationship building with autistic adults. *Autism in Adulthood*, *4*(2), 151–163.

ICD. (2019). *Tenth revision (ICD-10)*. https://icd.who.int/browse10/2019/en

Kapp, S. K., Gillespie-Lynch, K., Sherman, L. E., & Hutman, T. (2013). Deficit, difference, or both? Autism and neurodiversity. *Developmental Psychology*, *49*(1), 59–71. https://doi.org/10.1037/a0028353

Kenworthy, L., Anthony, L. G., Naiman, D. Q., Cannon, L., Wills, M. C., Luong-Tran, C., Werner, M. A., Alexander, K. C., Strang, J., Bal, E., Sokoloff, J. L., & Wallace, G. L. (2014). Randomized controlled effectiveness trial of executive function intervention for children on the autism spectrum. *Journal of Child Psychology and Psychiatry*, *55*(4), 374–383. https://doi.org/10.1111/jcpp.12161

King, R., Buxton, H., & Tyndall, I. (2024). Aphantasia and autism: An investigation of mental imagery vividness. *Consciousness and Cognition*, *125*, 103749. https://doi.org/10.1016/j.concog.2024.103749

Kinnaird, E., Stewart, C., & Tchanturia, K. (2019). Investigating alexithymia in autism: A systematic review and meta-analysis. *European Psychiatry*, *55*, 80–89. https://doi.org/10.1016/j.eurpsy.2018.09.004

Larsen, C. H., Küttel, A., Moesch, K., Durand-Bush, N., & Henriksen, K. (2021). Setting the scene: Mental health in elite sport. In *Mental health in elite sport* (pp. 1–21). Routledge.

Li, D., Miao, C., Wang, D., & Li, C. (2025). Effect of physical activity interventions on executive functions in school-age children with ADHD: A meta-analysis of randomized controlled trials. *Journal of Affective Disorders*, *378*, 175–190. https://doi.org/10.1016/j.jad.2025.01.155

Maisel, M. E., Stephenson, K. G., Cox, J. C., & South, M. (2019). Cognitive defusion for reducing distressing thoughts in adults with autism. *Research in Autism Spectrum Disorders*, *59*, 34–45.

Mannuzza, S., & Klein, R. G. (2000). Long-term prognosis in attention-deficit/hyperactivity disorder. *Child and Adolescent Psychiatric Clinics of North America*, *9*(3), 711–726. https://doi.org/10.1016/S1056-4993(18)30114-7

Martin, A. F., Rubin, G. J., Rogers, M. B., Wessely, S., Greenberg, N., Hall, C. E., Pitt, A., Logan, P. E., Lucas, R., & Brooks, S. K. (2025). The changing prevalence of ADHD? A systematic review. *Journal of Affective Disorders*, 119427. https://doi.org/10.1016/j.jad.2025.119427

Mason, D., Mackintosh, J., McConachie, H., Rodgers, J., Finch, T., & Parr, J. R. (2019). Quality of life for older autistic people: The impact of mental health difficulties. *Research in Autism Spectrum Disorders*, *63*, 13–22. https://doi.org/10.1016/j.rasd.2019.02.007

McNair, L., Woodrow, C., & Hare, D. (2017). Dialectical behaviour therapy [DBT] with people with intellectual disabilities: A systematic review and narrative analysis. *Journal of Applied Research in Intellectual Disabilities*, *30*(5), 787–804.

Munawar, K., Choudhry, F. R., Lee, S. H., Siau, C. S., Kadri, N. B. M., & Sulong, R. M. B. (2021). Acceptance and commitment therapy for individuals having attention deficit hyperactivity disorder (ADHD): A scoping review. *Heliyon*, *7*(8).

NICE. (2020). *Autism in adults: How common is it?* Retrieved May 29, 2024, from https://shorturl.at/D0nMh

NICE. (2024). *Attention deficit hyperactivity disorder: How common is it?* https://shorturl.at/5kDOm

Pahnke, J., Hirvikoski, T., Bjureberg, J., Bölte, S., Jokinen, J., Bohman, B., & Lundgren, T. (2019). Acceptance and commitment therapy for autistic adults: An open pilot study in a psychiatric outpatient context. *Journal of Contextual Behavioral Science*, *13*, 34–41.

Pahnke, J., Jansson-Fröjmark, M., Andersson, G., Bjureberg, J., Jokinen, J., Bohman, B., & Lundgren, T. (2023). Acceptance and commitment therapy for autistic adults: A randomized controlled pilot study in a psychiatric outpatient setting. *Autism*, *27*(5), 1461–1476. https://doi.org/10.1177/13623613221140749

Pahnke, J., Lundgren, T., Hursti, T., & Hirvikoski, T. (2014). Outcomes of an acceptance and commitment therapy-based skills training group for students with high-functioning autism spectrum disorder: A quasi-experimental pilot study. *Autism*, *18*(8), 953–964.

Pan, C.-Y., & Frey, G. C. (2006). Physical activity patterns in youth with autism spectrum disorders. *Journal of Autism and Developmental Disorders*, *36*, 597–606.

Patterson, C. W., Williams, J., & Jones, R. (2019). Third-wave therapies and adults with intellectual disabilities: A systematic review. *Journal of Applied Research in Intellectual Disabilities*, *32*(6), 1295–1309.

Phrathep, D., Donohue, B., Kraus, S., Paul, M., & Mercer, J. (2022). A controlled evaluation of a sport-specific performance optimization program in an athlete diagnosed with attention deficit hyperactivity disorder and oppositional defiant disorder within the context of COVID-19. *Clinical Case Studies*, *21*(3), 209–234. https://doi.org/10.1177/15346501211048508

Reid, G., & O'Connor, J. (2003). The autism spectrum disorders. *Palaestra*, *19*(1), 20–26.

Rogers, C. R. (1957). The necessary and sufficient conditions of therapeutic personality change. *Journal of Consulting Psychology*, *21*(2), 95–103. https://doi.org/10.1037/h0045357

Russell, G., Kapp, S. K., Elliott, D., Elphick, C., Gwernan-Jones, R., & Owens, C. (2019). Mapping the autistic advantage from the accounts of adults diagnosed with autism: A qualitative study. *Autism in Adulthood*, *1*(2), 124–133. https://doi.org/10.1089/aut.2018.0035

Salari, N., Rasoulpoor, S., Rasoulpoor, S., Shohaimi, S., Jafarpour, S., Abdoli, N., Khaledi-Paveh, B., & Mohammadi, M. (2022). The global prevalence of autism spectrum disorder: A comprehensive systematic review and meta-analysis. *Italian Journal of Pediatrics*, *48*(1), 112. https://doi.org/10.1186/s13052-022-01310-w

Sibley, M. H., Pelham, W. E., Jr., Molina, B. S. G., Gnagy, E. M., Waxmonsky, J. G., Waschbusch, D. A., Derefinko, K. J., Wymbs, B. T., Garefino, A. C., Babinski, D. E., & Kuriyan, A. B. (2012). When diagnosing ADHD in young adults emphasize informant reports, DSM items, and impairment. *Journal of Consulting and Clinical Psychology, 80*(6), 1052–1061. https://doi.org/10.1037/a0029098

Society, N. A. (2024). *Autism assessment waiting times*. https://shorturl.at/vcyaW

Song, P., Zha, M., Yang, Q., Zhang, Y., Li, X., & Rudan, I. (2021). The prevalence of adult attention-deficit hyperactivity disorder: A global systematic review and meta-analysis. *Journal of Global Health, 11*.

Spain, D., Sin, J., Chalder, T., Murphy, D., & Happe, F. (2015). Cognitive behaviour therapy for adults with autism spectrum disorders and psychiatric co-morbidity: A review. *Research in Autism Spectrum Disorders, 9*, 151–162.

Stark, E., Stacey, J., Mandy, W., Kringelbach, M. L., & Happé, F. (2021). Autistic cognition: Charting routes to anxiety. *Trends in Cognitive Sciences, 25*(7), 571–581. https://doi.org/10.1016/j.tics.2021.03.014

Szabo, T. G., Willis, P. B., & Palinski, C. J. (2019). Watch me try: ACT for improving athletic performance of young adults with ASD. *Advances in Neurodevelopmental Disorders, 3*(4), 434–449. https://doi.org/10.1007/s41252-019-00129-7

Vivanti, G. (2020). Ask the editor: What is the most appropriate way to talk about individuals with a diagnosis of autism? *Journal of Autism and Developmental Disorders, 50*(2), 691–693. https://doi.org/10.1007/s10803-019-04280-x

Williams, D. (2010). Theory of own mind in autism: Evidence of a specific deficit in self-awareness? *Autism, 14*(5), 474–494.

Williams, D., & Happé, F. (2010). Representing intentions in self and other: Studies of autism and typical development. *Developmental Science, 13*(2), 307–319.

Wolfe, E. S., & Madden, K. J. (2016). Evidence-based considerations and recommendations for athletic trainers caring for patients with attention-deficit/hyperactivity disorder. *Journal of Athletic Training, 51*(10), 813–820. https://doi.org/10.4085/1062-6050-51.12.11

Wood, S., Marshall, B., Kaiseler, M., & Wood, G. (2025). Navigating neurodiversity in elite sport: Lived experiences of neurodivergent athletes. *Qualitative Research in Sport, Exercise and Health*, 1–15. https://doi.org/10.1080/2159676X.2025.2534896

Wood, S., & Turner, M. J. (2024). Using acceptance and commitment therapy to develop self-confidence in a neurodivergent athlete. *Case Studies in Sport and Exercise Psychology, 8*(1), 37–46. https://doi.org/10.1123/cssep.2023-0040

Zolyomi, A., Begel, A., Waldern, J. F., Tang, J., Barnett, M., Cutrell, E., McDuff, D., Andrist, S., & Morris, M. R. (2019). Managing stress: The needs of autistic adults in video calling. *Proceedings of the ACM on Human-Computer Interaction, 3*(CSCW), Article 134. https://doi.org/10.1145/3359236

Index

Note: *Italic* page numbers refer to figures, **bold** page numbers refer to table and page number followed by 'n' refer to notes.

For Product Safety Concerns and Information please contact our EU representative GPSR@taylorandfrancis.com
Taylor & Francis Verlag GmbH, Kaufingerstraße 24, 80331 München, Germany

www.ingramcontent.com/pod-product-compliance
Ingram Content Group UK Ltd.
Pitfield, Milton Keynes, MK11 3LW, UK
UKHW022353190926
475702UK00015B/2261

* 9 7 8 1 0 3 2 8 4 8 3 7 2 *